$25 15

MUSIC THEORY
THROUGH LITERATURE

MUSIC THEORY THROUGH LITERATURE

VOLUME I

John Baur

Memphis State University

PRENTICE-HALL, INC. *Englewood Cliffs, New Jersey 07632*

Library of Congress Cataloging in Publication Data

BAUR, JOHN, 1947–
  Music theory.

  Includes index.
  1. Music—Theory. I. Title.
MT6.B263M9 1985   781   84-3399
ISBN 0-13-607821-4

Editorial/production supervision and
  interior design: Dan Mausner
Cover design: 20/20 Services, Inc.
Manufacturing buyer: Raymond Keating
Page layout: Diane Koromhas
              Gail Cocker

© 1985 by Prentice-Hall, Inc., Englewood Cliffs, New Jersey 07632

All rights reserved. No part of this book may be
reproduced, in any form or by any means,
without permission in writing from the publisher.

Printed in the United States of America

10 9 8 7 6 5 4 3 2 1

ISBN: 0-13-607821-4   01

PRENTICE-HALL INTERNATIONAL, INC., *London*
PRENTICE-HALL OF AUSTRALIA PTY. LIMITED, *Sydney*
EDITORA PRENTICE-HALL DO BRASIL, LTDA., *Rio de Janeiro*
PRENTICE-HALL CANADA INC., *Toronto*
PRENTICE-HALL OF INDIA PRIVATE LIMITED, *New Delhi*
PRENTICE-HALL OF JAPAN, INC., *Tokyo*
PRENTICE-HALL OF SOUTHEAST ASIA PTE. LTD., *Singapore*
WHITEHALL BOOKS LIMITED, *Wellington, New Zealand*

Contents

Preface ix

Recordings xi

Introduction 1

    notation, staff, clefs, rhythm, meter, major scales, minor scales, key signatures, intervals, triads, fundamentals of acoustics, overtone series, circle of fifths, temperaments

1   Tenth to Twelfth Centuries: Gregorian Chant and Secular Monophony   28

    scalar usage, modal system, melodic control, centonization, sequence, motive, cell, phrase, rhythmic modes, cadence, major/minor implications

2   Organum   46

    melodic intervals, harmonic intervals, parallel/similar/oblique/contrary motion, phrase structure, cadence, use of borrowed chant material, rhythmic modes, ordo

3   Las Huelgas Codex, Petrus de Cruce   59

Deo confitemini/Domino
Aucun/Lonc Tans/Annuntiantes

ordo, analysis of intervals (harmonic and melodic),
triadic structure (all inversions), rhythmic disposition of parts of a motet,
chant usage, isorhythm, root movement, double-leading-tone cadence,
passing tones, neighboring tones

4   Guillaume de Machaut   76

Bone Pastor

root movement, cadence, double-leading-tone cadence, isorhythm,
panisorhythm, phrase structure of Machaut, passing tones, neighboring tones,
musica ficta, hocket, diminution, augmentation, Phrygian cadence

5   John Dunstable   91

Ave maris stella (hymn)

melodic analysis, dissonance treatment, suspensions, escape tones,
double suspensions, single-leading-tone cadence, double-leading-tone cadence,
tonal cadence (V—I), paraphrase technique

6   Guillaume Dufay   114

Agnus Dei from the Missa L'Homme Armé
Ave maris stella

dissonance usage, double-leading-tone cadence, tonal cadence, octave-
leap cadence, melodic analysis, fauxbourdon, under third,
cantus firmus technique, augmentation/diminution, retrograde motion,
paraphrase technique

7   Josquin des Prez   138

Ave Maria
Recordans de my segnora

dissonance use, sequence, rhythmic use, authentic cadence, plagal cadence,
deceptive cadence, imitation, paired imitation, canon, double canon,
secondary function, part writing in four voices (triadic doubling)

8   Giovanni Pierluigi da Palestrina   161

Kyrie from the Missa pro Defunctis

paraphrase technique, portamento resolution of a suspension,
embellished resolution of a suspension, cambiata figure, resolution of tritones,
V7 chord (with passing seventh)

9   Claudio Monteverdi   188

Pur ti miro from The Coronation of Poppea

passacaglia/chaconne, functional chordal use, figured bass, dominant seventh,
secondary function, secondary dominants, cadential $^6_4$ chord, anticipation

10   Johann Hermann Schein   199

Veni creator Spiritus (hymn)

functional use of chords, voice leading, chorale style, diatonic modulation,
pivot chords, guidelines for part-writing, guidelines for harmonization of a melody

11   Henry Purcell   216

"Dido's Lament" from Dido and Aeneas

passacaglia technique, ground bass, functional use of the minor scale,
anticipation, diminished seventh chords, half-diminished seventh chords,
secondary use of diminished seventh chords, augmented sixth chords

12   Arcangelo Corelli   238

Sonata for violin and continuo, Op. 5, No. 7

sequence (melodic and harmonic), modulatory procedure, Baroque binary form,
dissonance use (passing tones, neighboring tones, escape tones, suspensions,
anticipation), Neapolitan sixth chord, hemiola

13 Johann Sebastian Bach 246

The chorales
Prelude and Fugue in g minor, Well-Tempered Clavier Book I
Sarabande from the French Suite in b minor

continuation of chordal/modulatory/dissonance principles, reiteration of voice-leading principles, cadence use, bar form, fugue, subject, tonal answer, countersubject, stretto, Baroque binary

Index   281

Preface

When a college student completes the required theory courses, that student should be able to pick up any piece of Western music, from any period, and understand its basic traits. This is the purpose of this text: to broaden the student's musical perspective, without de-emphasizing the importance of basic skills. Being able to manipulate materials skillfully is important in any profession. In music one must also have musical insight and depth of understanding. This comes partly from theoretical study and partly from an intimate acquaintance with the music itself.

Two ideas in particular, rarely embodied in theory textbooks, prompted me to initiate and complete this long task: the use of complete musical examples, and the chronological arrangement of theoretical materials. It is vitally important for a theory textbook to utilize complete examples, since this is the only way to demonstrate the actual significance of a musical idea. A two-measure fragment may display a technique in a readily identifiable form, but only the complete piece will give the student (and teacher) the sense of how such a segment relates to the whole. I hope that the student will not only learn the theory of music, but will also take the time to experience the music itself. The most important reason for including complete examples is to enhance the learning of music—not simply to facilitate the teaching of theory.

The chronological arrangement of material has been employed before in theory texts. However, the Middle Ages has previously been discussed only cursorily, and the development of compositional techniques from century to century has never been consistently presented as the basis for a theory text. There are sound pedagogical reasons for presenting the material in this fashion. The most important is that the progression of musical and theoretical ideas from century to century becomes clear and understandable to the student. In addition, by presenting the material in this manner one can avoid any prejudicial emphasis of style or period. One need not explain why a theory course begins with the earliest notated music; in fact, beginning elsewhere ought to require justification.

The first volume is designed for the first year of a two-year theory core. The musical examples cover plainchant through J. S. Bach, with at least one example from each century. However, rather than focusing only on their historical placement, the pieces are used to provide an ascending order of skill complexity. Each chapter introduces a new skill, from melodic intervals in plainchant to harmonic intervals in organum to triads (as well as $^8_5$ constructions) in thirteenth century motets, and so on. Cadence practice, dissonance usage, melodic and harmonic practice, as well as broader compositional techniques, are introduced as they occur in the pieces quoted. In this way, the theoretical and the historical materials are gradually fused, creating a clear understanding of style for the student.

A glossary and a summary of style characteristics are included at the end of each chapter to reinforce style concepts and basic theoretical terminology.

The exercises at the end of each chapter are divided into written skills and creative application. While it is necessary to drill on clearly defined skill factors, an important part of every musician's training is the creative handling of musical material. It is hoped that the teacher will include some of the compositional exercises to encourage the student to develop his or her creative abilities.

Several people deserve a great amount of credit for their encouragement, help, and wise counsel, generously given in the course of this project. David Russell Williams has been an inexhaustable source of insight, as well as a particularly kind and helpful editor of the manuscript. Donald Freund has also provided valuable assistance, especially in the twentieth-century portion of the text.

Over the years, my students have patiently shown me the most valuable ways of presenting this material. I only hope that this text will prove as helpful to them as they have been to me.

In addition, four former professors helped to shape my musical perception in ways that will forever influence my thinking: Paul Cooper, Carol MacClintock, James Riley, and Elmer Thomas. Their musical integrity and dedication to humanity should be an inspiration to all.

Finally, I thank my wife, Elizabeth. It is impossible to measure her patience and encouragement throughout this task. I only know it would have been infinitely more difficult without her.

J.B.

Recordings

Recordings of the pieces quoted in this text are, in some cases, difficult to find. A listing of them is given below. In the case of the famous examples by Purcell and Bach, the author has not stated any preference for a particular interpretation among the numerous recordings available.

Chapter 2: *History of European Music Part One: Music of the Early Middle Ages*, volume II; Denis Stevens, musical director; Musical Heritage Society, OR 350.

Chapter 3: Petrus de Cruce, *Aucun ont trouvé; Music of the Gothic Era; The Early Music Consort of London,* David Munrow; Archiv 2723 045 (3LP).

Chapter 4: Guillaume de Machaut, *Bone Pastor; Guillaume de Machault: Messe de Nostre Dame und Motetten;* Capella antiqua München, Konrad Ruhland, director; Das Alte Werk, Telefunken SAWT 9566-B.

Chapter 5: John Dunstable, *Ave maris stella; Josquin des Prez/John Dunstable*, Purcell Consort, Grayston Burgess; Argo ZRG 681.

Chapter 6: Guillaume Dufay, *Missa L'homme armé; Missa l'homme armé*, Berkley Chamber Singers, Alden Gilchrist, conductor; Lyrichord LL150. *Se la face ay pale: Music of Guillaume Dufay, Missa Se la face ay pale;* Early Music Consort of London, David Munrow; Seraphim S60267.

Chapter 7: Josquin des Prez, *Ave Maria; Missa L'homme armé and motets;* The Prague Madrigal Singers, Miroslav Venhoda; Crossroads 22 16 0094. *Recordans de my segnora: Josquin Desprez: Chansons, Frottole and Instrumental Pieces;* The Nonesuch Consort, Joshua Rifkin, director; Nonesuch H–71261.

Chapter 8: Giovanni Pierluigi da Palestrina: No recording. There is a recording of the two examples in the exercises, from the *Missa Aeterna Christi munera: Palestrina: Missa Aeterna Christi munera, Oratio Jeremiae Prophetae, Motetti;* Archiv Stereo 2533 322.

Chapter 9: Claudio Monteverdi: *Pur ti miro; L'incoronazione di Poppea;* Alan Curtis, director; Cambridge CRS B1901.

Chapter 10: Johann Schein: No recording.

Chapter 12: Arcangelo Corelli: Sonata for violin, Op. 5 No. 7: *Arcangelo Corelli: 12 Sonate Per Violins, Op. 5;* Arthur Grumiaux, violin; Phillips 6768 178.

Introduction

NOTATION

All of notated music, except for the very earliest attempts at musical notation, has one thing in common: the designation of one or more fixed pitches. The most logical and efficient method of achieving this is through the use of a line or several lines to form a staff. Without this, musical space is extremely ambiguous. Before the tenth century, notes were indicated, but only in general relationships. Specific pitch could not be determined from the notation. This is the way it looked on the page.

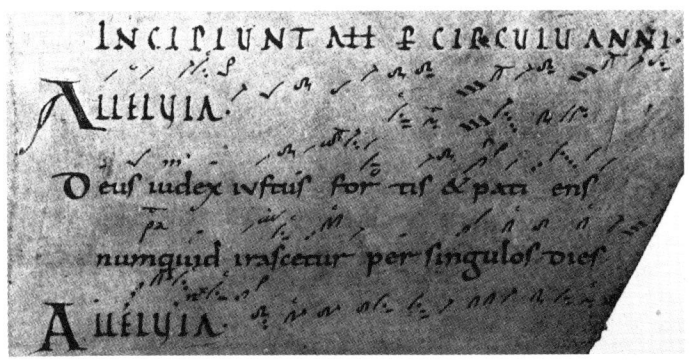

By the mid-tenth century, one pitch was designated precisely by inscribing a horizontal line representing that pitch. This gave the notation some focus. However, this was still not specific enough, and by the eleventh century composers had added a second line. The two lines usually designated the pitches *c* and *f*.

It was then a short step to add a line between these two—to indicate the note *a*—and a fourth line, on top or on bottom, to extend the singable range.

The four-line staff was common for a long period of time. However, we can see staffs of five, six, and even more lines in the eleventh century and in many subsequent centuries as well. The five-line staff was in common usage by the fifteenth century, and has remained standard until today.

The signs used to identify the pitch represented by a line are called *clefs*. The early period found two favorite notes for specific designation, *f* and *c*. The clefs looked very much like those letters.

= C clef   = F clef

The C clef can be seen in the preceding example.

The C clef gradually changed its appearance and came to be drawn as it is today.

Likewise, the F clef changed and came to be shaped

𝄢

The third note to acquire its own clef was *g*. The G clef began as

𝄞

and now is drawn

𝄞

The above three clefs have been given new names in recent centuries. The G clef is usually positioned on the five-line staff as follows:

G clef = *treble clef*

The F clef is usually positioned

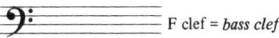
F clef = *bass clef*

The C clef, however, is moveable in modern usage, and therefore has several names, depending on its placement.

It must be pointed out that *all* clefs are theoretically moveable. However, since the early eighteenth century the above placements have been the most frequently used, and are therefore considered standard.

The one additional clef is the treble clef with an 8 below it, indicating that everything sounds an octave below the written pitch. This is traditionally used for the tenor voice in a four-voice setting.

G clef = *tenor clef*

Once the clef has been determined, all of the notes are readily identifiable: Musical space has been defined.

In each case the clef indicates a specific and not a general pitch. In other words, the *c* that is indicated by the C clef is not any of the possible *c*'s, but is always *middle c*. This note is often referred to as c^1.

All of the above indicate the same pitch even though they are in different places on the staff.

Likewise, the F and G clefs indicate specific pitches. The F clef designates the *f below* middle *c,* and the G clef gives the *g above* middle *c.*

Often the F and G clefs are used on two staves (staffs) simultaneously; these together are referred to as the *grand staff*. This happened as a result of the need for an expanded range, when keyboard music began to be written. When the two clefs are combined we find that there is a note in the middle of the two staffs, the note c^1. This is the reason for calling this note middle *c*—not because it is in the middle of the piano.

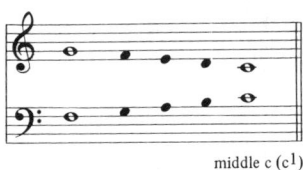

middle c (c^1)

In the twentieth century there has been an attempt to specifically label each pitch as to the octave in which it is found as well as according to letter name. Middle *c* was designated c^1 and the notes above it were said to be in the *one-line octave*.

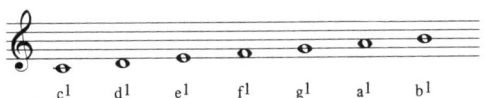

When the next c is encountered it comes c^2 and the notes above it are in the *two-line octave*.

This continues up to the highest note on the piano.

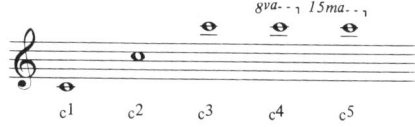

Below middle c the terms used are the *small octave, great octave, contra-octave*, and *sub-contra octave*.

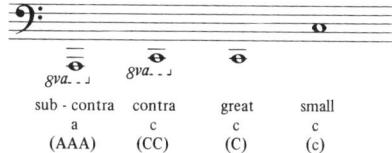

The entire staff can be written as follows:

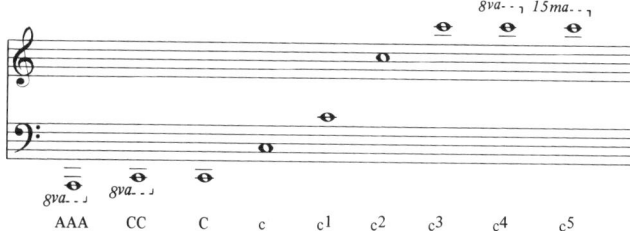

Notation of rhythm required a somewhat longer period of development than that of pitch. In addition, although pitch notation has remained fairly standard since its earliest use, rhythmic notation has changed radically from century to century. Briefly, the first attempt at rhythmic notation which occurred in the twelfth century—the system of the rhythmic modes—was fairly rudimentary, and often ambiguous. This was followed by a more specific system in the thirteenth century, a more complicated and detailed system in the fourteenth century, a simplification in the fifteenth and sixteenth centuries, and a final codification of the system in the seventeenth century. From that point onward notation has undergone changes, but not a radical reorganization, up to the present day. The changes have been subtle, and most have been intended to increase clarity and precision—the inclusion of more dynamics, accent markings, and the like.

In its basic form, the modern rhythmic system is based on simple arithmetic—the use of addition and subtraction, multiplication and division, and simple fractions. The basic divisions and subdivisions are as follows:

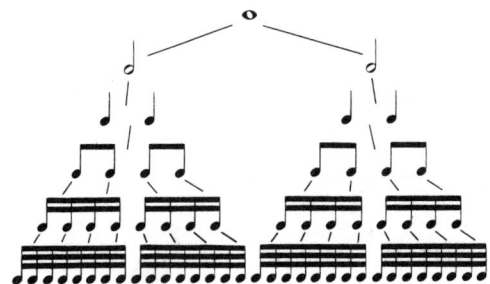

1 whole note

2 half notes

4 quarter notes

8 eighth notes

16 sixteenth notes

32 thirty-second notes

When one note value is divided into three, the other divisions remain divisible by two.

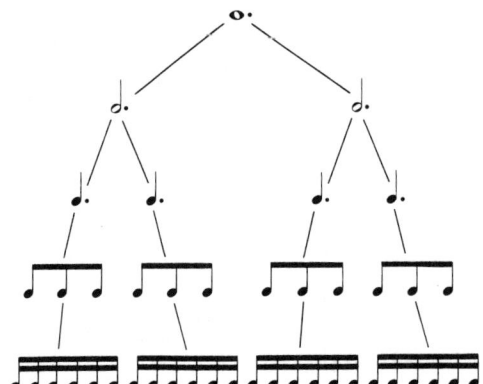

1 dotted whole note

2 dotted half notes

4 dotted quarter notes

12 eighth notes

24 sixteenth notes

This division process accounts for pulse but not pulse groupings. For this we must turn to *meter*. When a certain note value is designated the pulse, and several pulses are grouped together, the result is a metric organization. For example,

 quarter-note pulse; 4 pulses per bar

The meter is defined by the preceding values: one for the pulse and one for the number of pulses. Therefore, for the example above,

4 = the number of pulses
4 = the denominator of the kind of note receiving a pulse (quarter = $\frac{1}{4}$)
$\frac{4}{4}$ = meter. This figure is usually called a *time signature*.

Theoretically, any note can be a pulse, and there can be any number of pulses in a measure. For example,

half-note pulse $\frac{2}{2}$, $\frac{3}{2}$, $\frac{4}{2}$, *etc.*
quarter-note pulse $\frac{2}{4}$, $\frac{3}{4}$, $\frac{4}{4}$, *etc.*
eighth-note pulse $\frac{2}{8}$, $\frac{3}{8}$, $\frac{4}{8}$, *etc.*
sixteenth-note pulse $\frac{2}{16}$, $\frac{3}{16}$, $\frac{4}{16}$, *etc.*

The note value used as the pulse in some pieces is determined by the tempo of the piece.

$\frac{6}{8}$ ♪♪♪♪♪♪ in a slow tempo there are six eighth note pulses per measure

can also be

$\frac{6}{8}$ ♫♫ in a faster tempo there are two groups, each with three eighth notes; therefore, there are two pulses, each divided into three parts.

When the pulse is divided into three, as in the above $\frac{6}{8}$ or in $\frac{6}{2}$ or $\frac{6}{4}$, it is referred to as *compound meter*. If, however, the pulse is divided into two, such as $\frac{4}{4}$, $\frac{2}{4}$, or $\frac{3}{4}$, then it is referred to as *simple meter*.

simple meter
duple: $\frac{2}{4}$ $\frac{2}{2}$ $\frac{2}{8}$ $\frac{2}{16}$ *etc.*
triple: $\frac{3}{2}$ $\frac{3}{4}$ $\frac{3}{8}$ $\frac{3}{16}$ *etc.*
quadruple: $\frac{4}{2}$ $\frac{4}{4}$ $\frac{4}{8}$ $\frac{4}{16}$ *etc.*

compound meter
duple: $\frac{6}{2}$ $\frac{6}{4}$ $\frac{6}{8}$ *etc.*
triple: $\frac{9}{4}$ $\frac{9}{8}$ $\frac{9}{16}$ *etc.*
quadruple: $\frac{12}{4}$ $\frac{12}{8}$ $\frac{12}{16}$ *etc.*

Also possible are irregular groupings such as $\frac{5}{8}$, $\frac{5}{16}$, $\frac{7}{8}$, $\frac{7}{16}$, $\frac{11}{8}$, $\frac{11}{16}$, and so forth.

The score is an important document. In it, the composer must clearly communicate his ideas, and the performer must be able easily to understand the composer's intent. Therefore, it is highly desirable to be able to produce a proper score.

Clef signs are used at the beginning of each staff. Practice making treble and bass clefs as shown below.

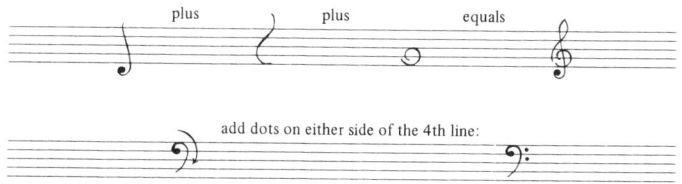

add dots on either side of the 4th line:

C clefs can be made with either a 3-like figure or K-like figure. The first is more proper—it is printed this way—but the second way may be faster to produce.

Noteheads are not truly round, but rather elliptical, and are made as follows:

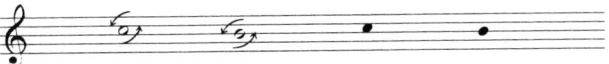

For a blackened notehead, simply make a white note and fill it in.

Stems look better if drawn with a short ruler. They properly extend from the top of the notehead to the bottom of an imaginary notehead one octave away.

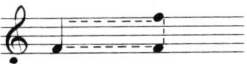

If the notehead is above or below several ledger lines, the stem should always terminate on the middle line of the staff.

If the notehead is on the middle line, the stem may properly be drawn in either direction. If the notehead is above the middle line, the stem should be drawn downward; if below the middle line, upward.

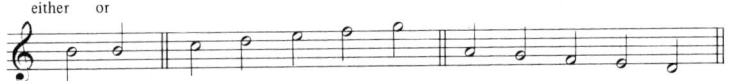

When notating two lines on one staff, the above rules do not apply. In this case, the top voice always has stems up and the bottom voice stems down. This is done in order to distinguish them even if they happen to cross.

This type of notation is often used for singers (soprano and alto, for example) and for instruments of similar range (for instance, two flutes or two oboes).

Beams which group notes together are used primarily for rhythmic clarification, which facilitates performance. It is always best to beam according to the basic meter. For example, is difficult to read because the notes are not grouped. Beaming according to a quarter-note pulse makes this series of note values far more legible.

Bar lines are now needed to further organize these note values.

The beaming principle in vocal music is often somewhat different. Especially in older scores, beams are only employed to connect notes sung to the same text syllable; where a syllable gets only one note, that note is never beamed.

Dots used to lengthen notes are placed to the right and slightly above the notehead.

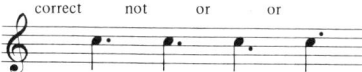

Slurs and ties are similar in appearance, but different in function. Ties are used to extend a note, whereas slurs are expressive markings, indicating a legato (smooth and fluid) performance.

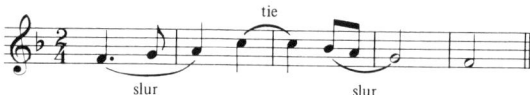

They can be used together.

Each of the above examples indicates a unique type of performance. It is important for the composer to be specific as to which type of phrasing (as indicated by the slur) he wants.

In general, all dynamic markings should be placed below the individual parts. Accents should appear close to the notehead, not the stem.

There are exceptions to these rules, however.

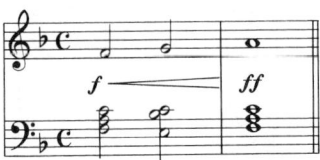

The following examples give a general idea as to the disposition, arrangement, and other notational features which you may encounter in reading scores. Note carefully the placement of noteheads, stems, beams, dynamics, slurs, ties, text, etc.

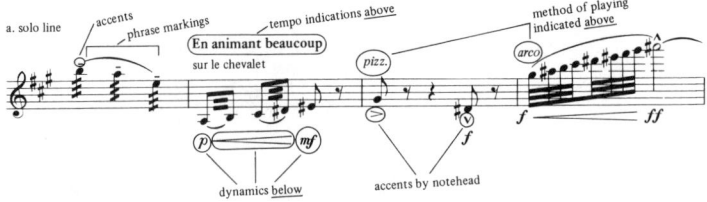

Introduction 11

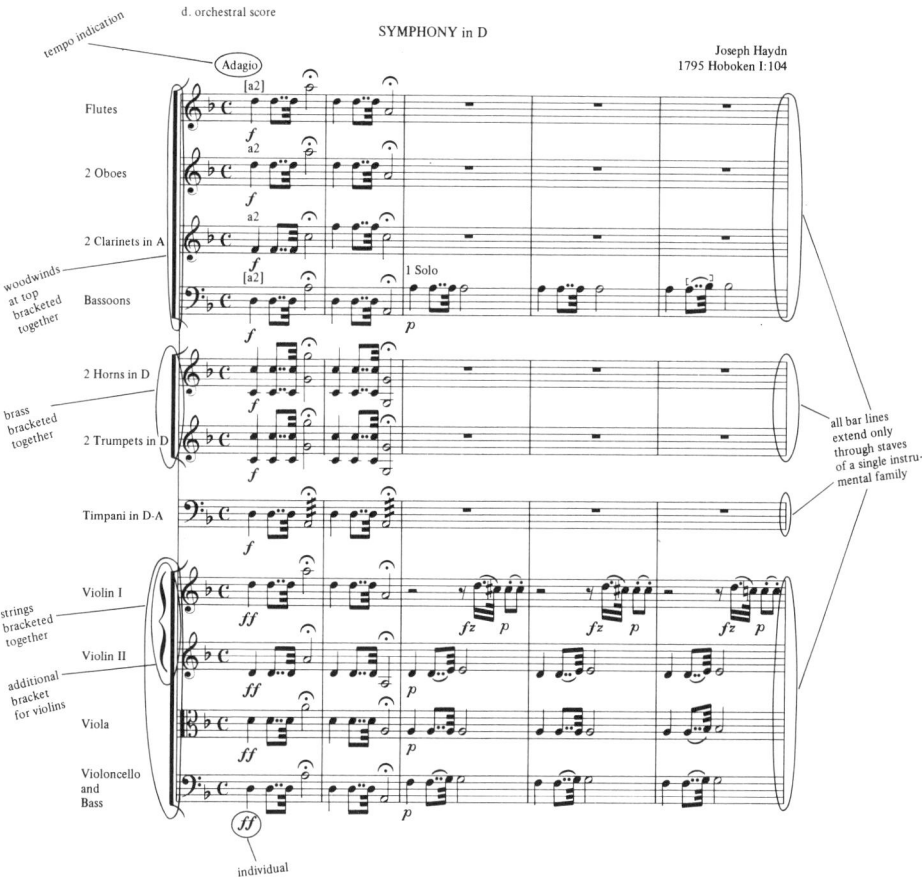

BASIC THEORY

Most musicians are familiar with scales because of their pedagogical and technical use in learning to play an instrument. The scales usually learned are those employed in the seventeenth, eighteenth, and nineteenth centuries—the major and minor scales. Indeed, a great deal of the music we hear is from those centuries; however, there is much music both from earlier periods and from our own century which does not use these scales.

In earlier periods the scalar system was that of the church modes—to be discussed further in Chapter 1. In simple terms, they were untransposed with no accidentals employed, using strictly the notes found in C major. Only their final pitches and range were different in each case.

The modes were gradually supplanted by the major and minor scale systems in the seventeenth century. This is not to say that composers suddenly discarded the modal system. Rather, it was a gradual change, which was largely completed by the middle of the seventeenth century.

The pitches of the major scale on *c* are given below.

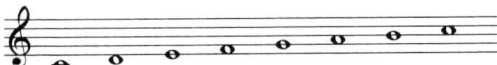

Each major scale consists of the same sequence of intervals as every other. Like most Western scales, the major scale consists of an arrangement of whole and half tones. Their arrangement constitutes the specific construction of the scale and determines the kinds of music which it will produce. The major scale consists of the following sequence of whole steps and half steps.

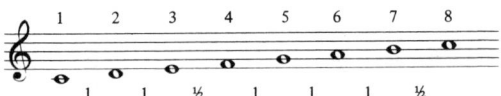

This arrangement holds true for every major scale, regardless of the starting pitch.

If no accidentals are used, there will be half steps between *e* and *f* and between *b* and *c*. In C major, *e* and *f* are the third and fourth degrees of the scale, as *b* and *c* are the seventh and eighth degrees. Therefore, if we replicate a scale with half steps between degrees 3 and 4 and between 7 and 8, maintaining the whole steps everywhere else, we will have produced another major scale.

The scale below has different tones and covers a different octave. The half steps are still between *e* and *f*, and *b* and *c*. However, in this case these notes represent the third and fourth degrees and the sixth and seventh degrees of the scale.

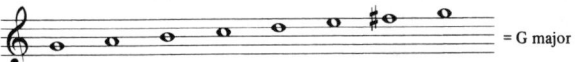

Therefore, this is not a major scale, though by alteration it can become one. The *e–f* has to be made a whole step and *f–g* has to be made a half step. An *accidental* is necessary to change the given notes to the ones we desire. By raising the *f* by means of a *sharp,* we accomplish both tasks.

 = G major

Consider another example:

Again, we have half steps between *e* and *f,* and *b* and *c,* or in this case between degrees 4 and 5, and 7 and 8. In order to have a major scale, the half step needs to be between *a* and *b* (3–4). A *flat* can be added to lower the *b* to *b♭*—thereby solving the problem.

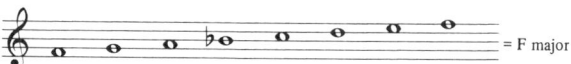

Consider a few more:

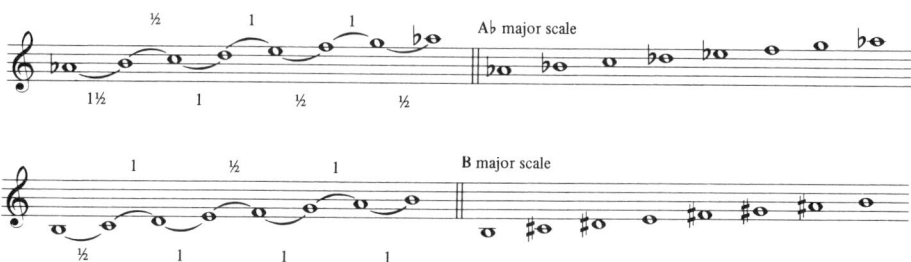

To avoid writing accidentals throughout the piece, composers began to use the *key signature.* This was simply a group of sharps or flats, placed at the beginning of a piece (and at the beginning of each staff thereafter), that were to be used throughout the piece. In most cases, especially in the eighteenth and nineteenth centuries, the signature indicates the key of the piece, that is, which major or minor scale is being used as the basis for the piece. The key signatures for the major keys are as follows:

These key signatures should be memorized.

Minor scales have a different intervallic construction from major scales and are symbolized by lowercase key names. However, they do relate to the major scales in that each minor scale uses a key signature identical to that of a major scale. This relationship between the major and minor scale is referred to as *relative;* that is, each major scale has a *relative minor scale* that uses its key signature. In every case, the keynote of the minor scale is three half steps lower than the keynote of the major scale.

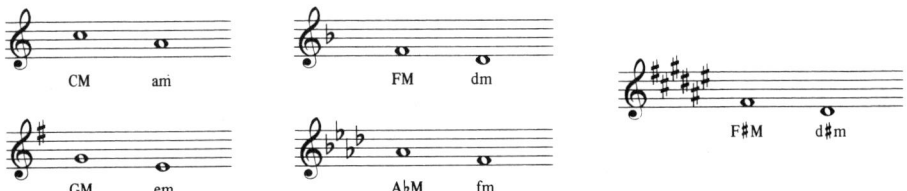

There are three possible forms of the minor scale: the *natural*, the *harmonic*, and the *melodic*. If a scale is built on the minor keynote and uses the key signature of the relative major, it is called the *natural minor scale*.

The *harmonic minor scale* is formed when the seventh degree of the natural minor scale is raised one half step. This is done to make certain desirable harmonic changes in the music, hence the name of the scale.

The *melodic minor scale* is formed if the sixth and seventh degrees are raised when moving up the scale and returned to their natural position when moving down the scale. This reflects the difference frequently seen in minor melodies between those tones used when the melodies ascend and those used when they descend.

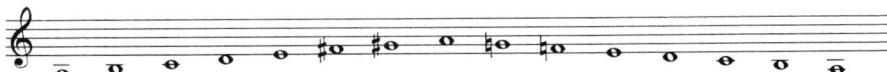

A group of intervals can be constructed above the keynote of any scale. If the notes in a major scale are used, all of the following intervals can be constructed above any given keynote.

The same intervals are constructed below, this time from the scale of E♭ major.

There are other possible intervals. If a major interval is decreased in size by a half step, it becomes *minor*. If increased in size by a half step, it becomes *augmented*.

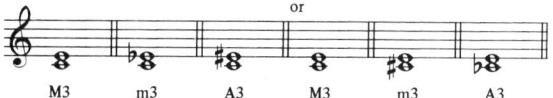

If a minor interval is decreased in size by a half step, it becomes *diminished*.

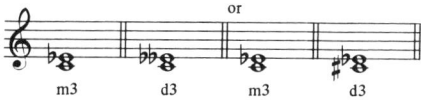

If a perfect interval is decreased in size by a half step, it becomes diminished. If increased by a half step, it becomes augmented.

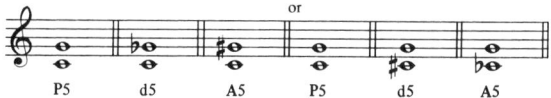

The following should be memorized:

$$A \text{---} M \text{---} m \text{---} d \qquad A \text{---} P \text{---} d$$
$$\;\;\;\;\tfrac{1}{2}\;\;\;\;\tfrac{1}{2}\;\;\;\;\tfrac{1}{2} \qquad\;\;\;\; \tfrac{1}{2}\;\;\;\;\tfrac{1}{2}$$

If two intervals are sounded together, the result is a triad. Although any three pitches result in a triad, there are four standard triads constructed from major and minor thirds: *major, minor, augmented,* and *diminished*.

A *major triad* contains two intervals, a major third and a perfect fifth.

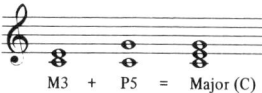

A *minor triad* contains a minor third and a perfect fifth.

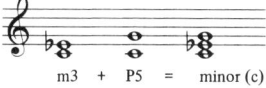

A *diminished triad* contains a minor third and a diminished fifth.

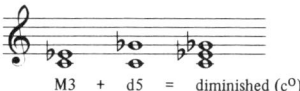

An *augmented triad* contains a major third and an augmented fifth.

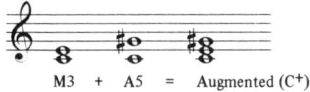

Any of these four triads can be constructed above any given pitch. The lowest note is called the *root,* the second note is the *third,* and the top note is the *fifth.*

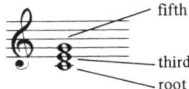

If the root is on the bottom, the triad is said to be in *root position.*

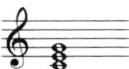

If the third is on the bottom, the triad is in *first inversion.*

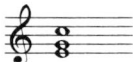

If the fifth is on the bottom, it is in *second inversion.*

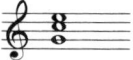

The intervals above the lowest note are different in each case.

Even though the quality of the interval may change because of the quality of triad, the basic intervals for each inversion remain the same—$\frac{5}{3}$ for root position, $\frac{6}{3}$ for first inversion, and $\frac{6}{4}$ for second inversion.

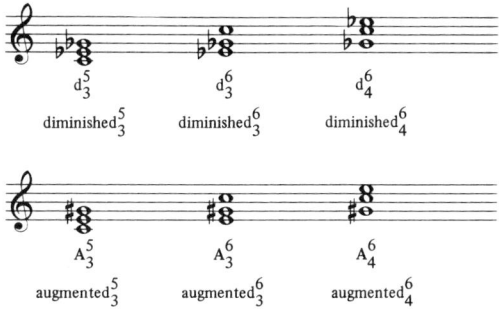

Suggested Exercises

1. Write the following key signatures.

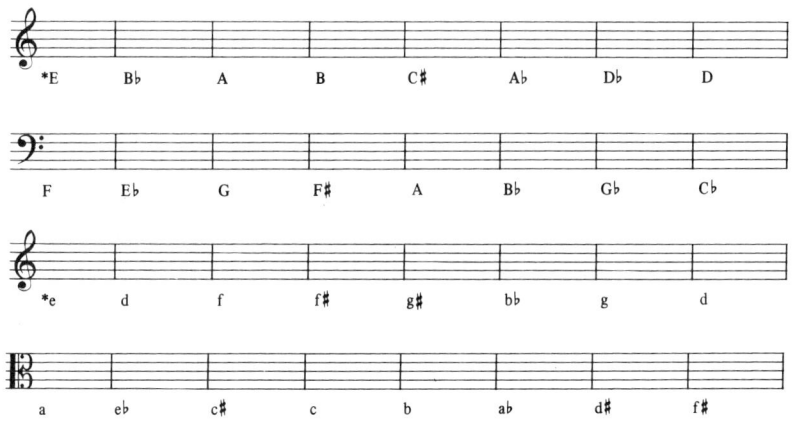

* Lowercase indicates a minor key; uppercase, major.

Write the following pitches:

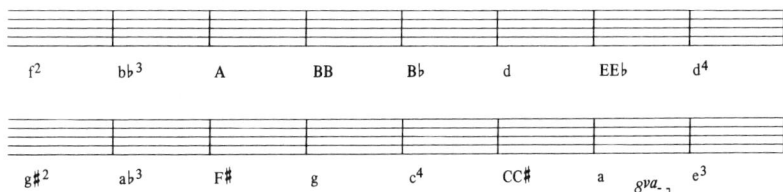

Identify the following pitches:

2. Write the following scales *without* using key signatures. Be careful to observe the clef before writing.

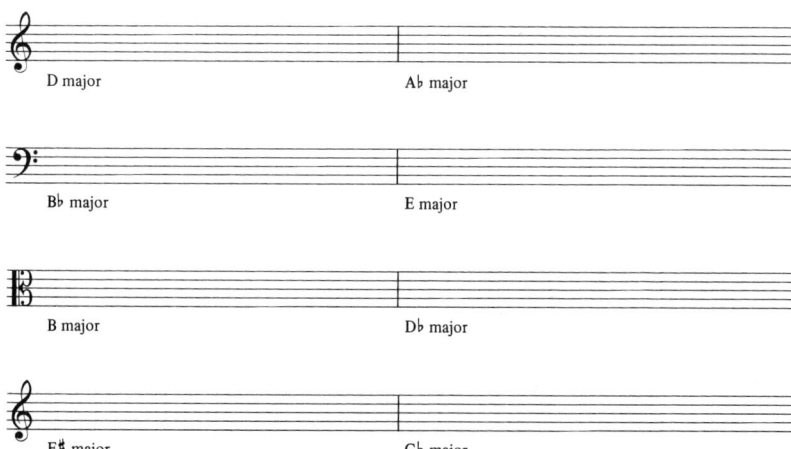

For the following minor scales, use the appropriate key signature, adding accidentals as necessary.

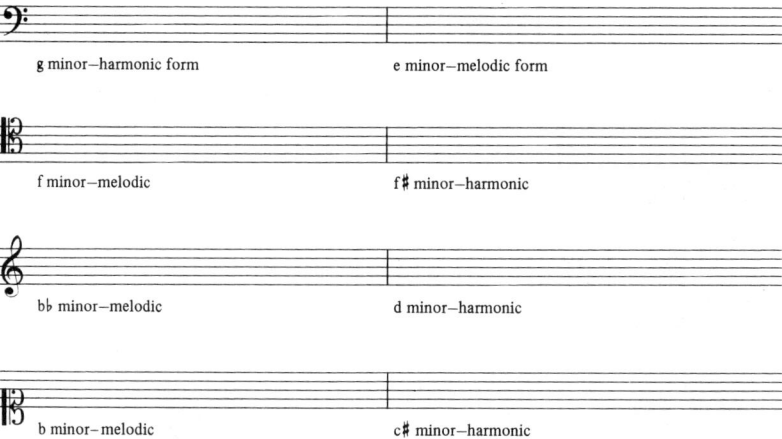

3. Write the following intervals above the given pitch. Be careful to observe the clef before writing.

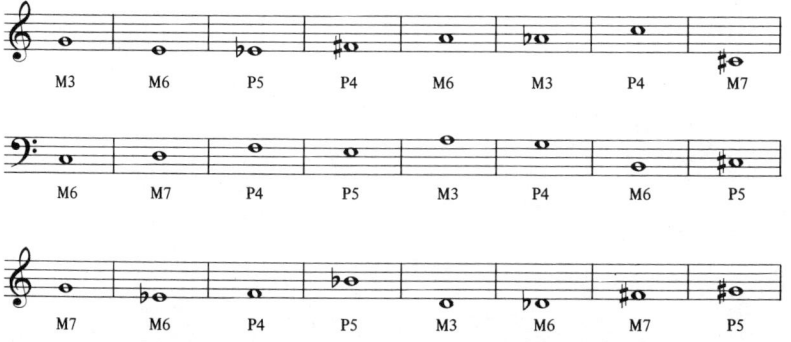

4. Write the following intervals above the given pitch.

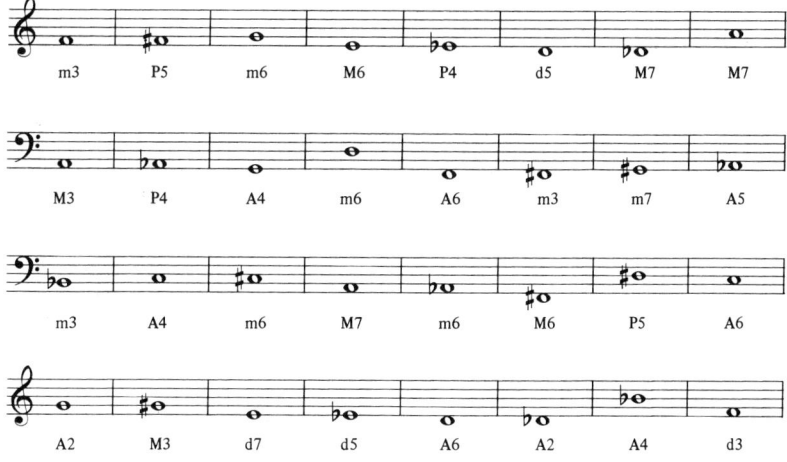

below the given pitch:

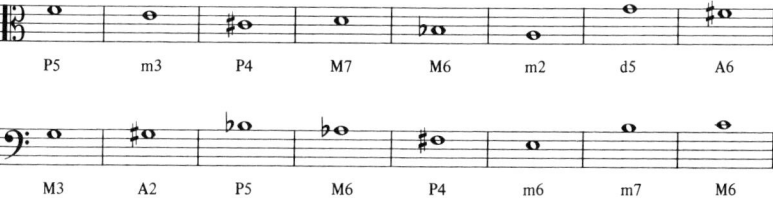

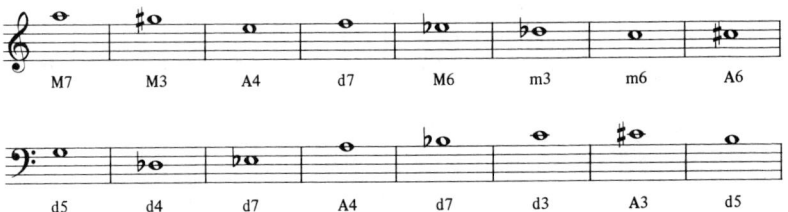

5. Write the following triads, in the indicated inversion. The lowest note is always given.

FUNDAMENTALS OF ACOUSTICS

All sound occurs as a disturbance in the air. A body excites the air in the form of a wave, sending this wave through the air and ultimately to our ears. These waves can be simple or complex, but their basic format is the same: a combination of loudness and pitch. By graphing these two components, we can "see" a sound wave.

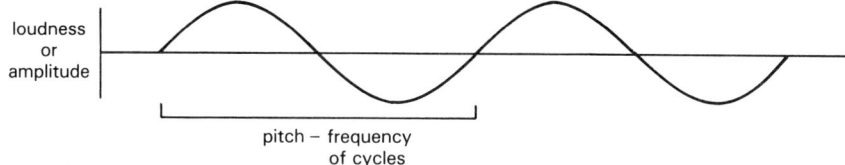

Loudness is graphed vertically, and is referred to as *amplitude*. It is measured in decibels (dB). A sound of one dB is barely audible, whereas a sound of 120 dB is approaching the threshold of pain.

The horizontal dimension of the graph reflects the pitch of a sound by showing the *frequency* with which each complete *cycle* occurs within a given period of time. One cycle is a single wave, consisting of one "peak" and one "trough." If the number of cycles is 440 per second, for example, then the pitch is a^1. The sound wave can be shown as follows:

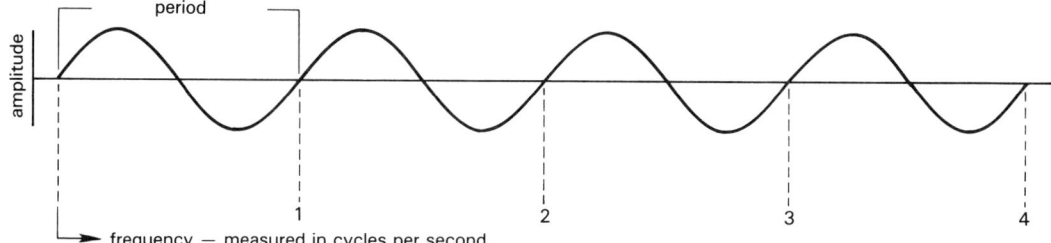

These repetitions are said to be *periodic*, a period being the time (in seconds) required for each cycle. Frequencies of below 15 cycles per second (cps) are generally not heard as pitches, and those of above approximately 20,000 cps are beyond our ear's capacity to hear at all.

There are an infinite number of different kinds of sound waves, but there are a few basic waves that form the foundation of sound. The most common is the *sine wave*. It is characterized by being extremely smooth, both in its representation and its actual sound, which is flute-like.

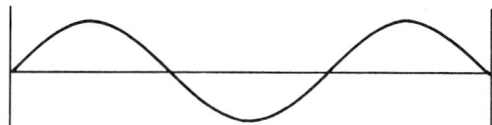

There are also nonperiodic sounds—sounds which cannot be graphed in the neat periodic structures shown above. These nonperiodic sounds are usually referred to as noise.

The psychological impact of a sound is greatly altered by the attack and decay of the sound. Some instruments, such as the piano, have innately sharp attacks, while others, such as the strings, are infinitely flexible in their attacks. The decay of a sound can be rapid and unvarying, as in the piano, or altered by continuous air pressure or bowing. Attack and decay can be visualized most clearly in the shape of the sound's *envelope,* as shown below.

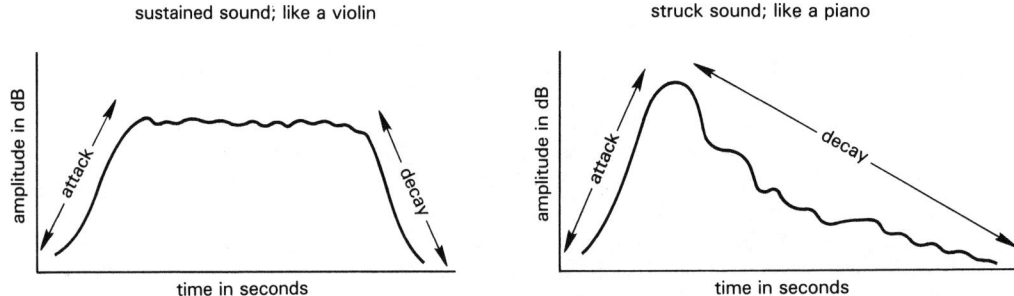

Thus far we have discussed sound waves as isolated entities, one wave at a time. In actuality, sound is considerably more complex than that. In fact, most musical sound can be seen as a large complex of sine waves all happening at once. Usually when we hear what sounds like a single note, we are hearing not only the fundamental pitch but numerous other pitches simultaneously. These "extra" pitches are called *overtones*. These overtones are "attached" to the *fundamental* pitch in varying degrees of intensity, and account for the different qualities of sound we encounter. The actual difference in the sound of a clarinet and a violin is largely the result of the different arrangement and intensity of the overtones of each. The *overtone series,* those notes which can vibrate above a given fundamental pitch, are constant intervals. When a bass C is played on a cello, piano, or bassoon, for instance, all the pitches shown below are sounded simultaneously, though most listeners will only be aware of the C.

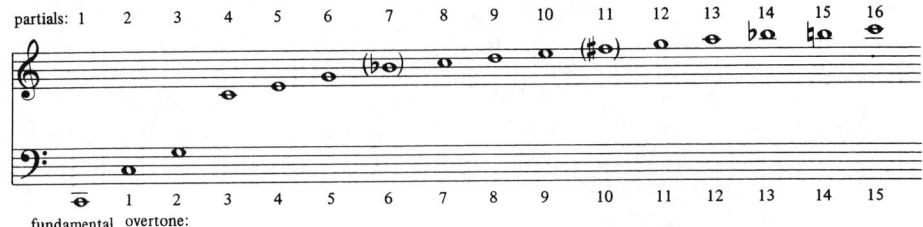

We have given only the first fifteen overtones, even though there exist many more, some of which are out of our hearing range. These other pitches will sound above any fundamental, with varying degrees of intensity. "With varying degrees of intensity" is the key phrase here. The relative strengths of the individual overtones largely determine the *timbre* of a sound. Timbre is the term used for tone color, or that which defines the unique quality of each instrument.

The numbering of the *partials* is given above the series. (Partials are identical to overtones except that they include the fundamental pitch as well; thus, the first overtone is the second partial, the second overtone is the third partial, etc.) This series of numbers provides us with the divisions of the sound-producing body. For example, if a string is long enough to produce the great C given above—such as a cello C string—then this is indicated as 1, or the full length of the string. The number 2 then indicates a ratio with the first number, 1:2. If the string is divided in a 1:2 ratio—in half—it will indeed produce an octave. This can continue all the way up:

Divide the String Into

third = octave plus fifth
fourth = two octaves
fifth = two octaves plus third
sixth = two octaves plus fifth
etc.

Pythagoras, the Greek philosopher and mathematician, did not know of the overtone series, but he did understand these ratios, which he discovered by means of experiments on a simple stringed instrument. He used the adjacent numbers to produce a scale.

1:2 = octave
2:3 = fifth
3:4 = fourth
4:5 = major third
5:6 = minor third
8:9 = major second (larger)
9:10 = major second (smaller)

Actually, Pythagoras built his scale on the basis of the first three of the above ratios. By extending the 2:3 ratio he derived the others. He found that these included all of the numbers contained in the number four—1:2:3:4. Since four was regarded as a "perfect" number in Greek times, anything relating to it was also regarded as perfect. Therefore, the octave, fifth, and fourth were called perfect intervals, and all others were regarded as imperfect (either major or minor).

Pythagoras' early work in this area produced the beginning of *temperaments*, or types of tuning for a scale. His tuning system was based on the pure fifth. A series of fifths (for example, F–C–G–D–A–E–B) could be arranged into a scale (C–D–E–F–G–A–B). He found, though, that when the series of fifths is further extended, it eventually comes back to the "same" note.

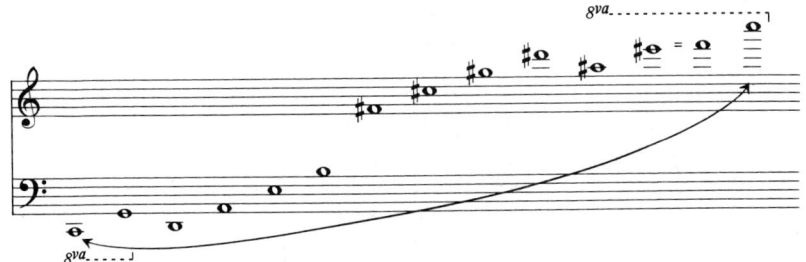

However, it should be noted that the two outer notes are out of tune—by almost a quarter step. This interval is called the *Pythagorean comma,* and attempts to deal with it have accounted for the various systems of temperament which have been proposed since Pythagoras' time.

Another way of depicting the above arrangement of fifths is in the form of a circle, the so-called *circle of fifths.* Arranged in this way, these letter-names may be regarded not only as notes, but also as harmonies and even keys. If we think of them as keys, we can notice what a logical progression they form. Starting with C and moving clockwise, each key adds a sharp to its key signature. Starting from C and moving counter-clockwise, each successive key adds a flat to its signature.

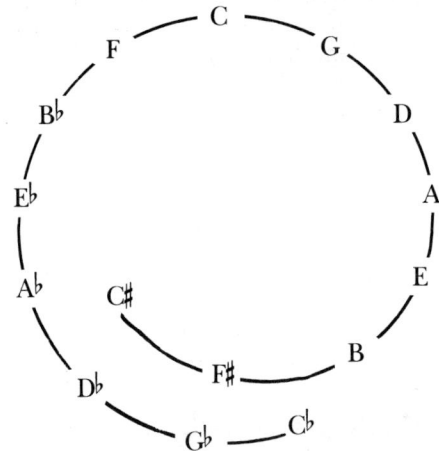

Historically, however, the result of the Pythagorean comma was the proposal of numerous systems of temperaments, or ways of tempering the scale when it began to move beyond the Pythagorean diatonic scale. The most famous ones are given below:

Pythagorean: pure fifth
Just temperament: pure fifth and pure third
Mean-tone temperament: pure third, with a smaller fifth
Equal temperament: the octave divided into 12 equal parts

The above is a *very* simplified version of a difficult and complicated process, but it outlines the basic elements.*

The study of temperaments used in history is an extremely fascinating and important one. Each country utilized different temperaments at different times and these had a decided effect on the composers.

Before Reading Chapter 1:
1. Sing the chant examples on pages 30, 31, and 33.
2. Analyze the interval structure of each of the melodies.
3. Sing the monophonic song on page 35.

---

*For further information, see Apel: *Harvard Dictionary of Music,* 2nd edition ("temperament"); Barbour: *Temperament and Tuning.*

Tenth to Twelfth Centuries: Gregorian Chant and Secular Monophony

The system of pitch construction most familiar to us is the major/minor system used in the tonal period of the seventeenth, eighteenth, and nineteenth centuries (as well as the twentieth century). There is another very important system, however, that was used, in constantly developing form, for several centuries before that: the ***modal system***, or the system of ecclesiastical modes.

The modal system was both a method of composition and a way of classifying plainchant melodies, sometimes referred to as *Gregorian chant*. It consisted of eight modes, four authentic and four plagal, each mode characterized by its final pitch (*finalis*), range (*ambitus*), and dominant (*tenor, repercussio*), as well as the pattern of tones and semitones in its scale.

The two groups of modes, authentic and plagal, shared the use of four finals. Each authentic mode was paired with a plagal mode which employed the same final. The four finals for the original eight-mode system were d, e, f, and g.

Mode I:	Dorian (authentic)	$\Big\} d$
Mode II:	Hypodorian (plagal)	

Mode III: Phrygian (authentic)
Mode IV: Hypophrygian (plagal) } e
Mode V: Lydian (authentic)
Mode VI: Hypolydian (plagal) } f
Mode VII: Mixolydian (authentic)
Mode VIII: Hypomixolydian (plagal) } g

By means of the **final** you can determine to which pair of modes the given chant melody belongs. For example, the two melodies below (fragments from the ending portions of two chants) have different finals. The first, because of its final *d*, can be assumed to be in Dorian or Hypodorian; the second, because of the *g* final, is likely to be in Mixolydian or Hypomixolydian.

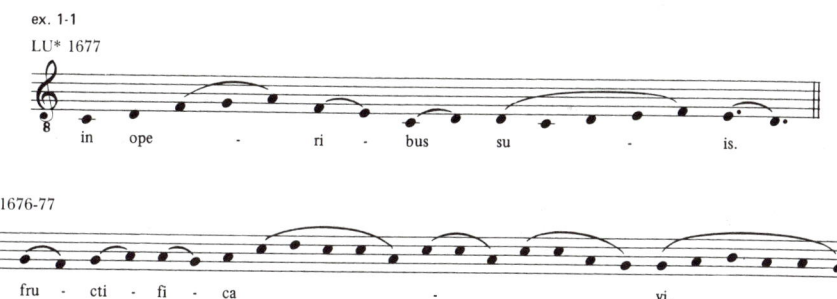

Although the finalis usually indicates the authentic/plagal pair of modes to which the chant may belong, it cannot by itself define a single specific mode. The range (or **ambitus**) of a mode, coupled with the final, will often produce such a specific classification. A plagal mode has an ambitus a perfect fourth lower than that of its authentic mode. The notes given in parentheses are sometimes used for cadential purposes and therefore should not be considered outside the mode.

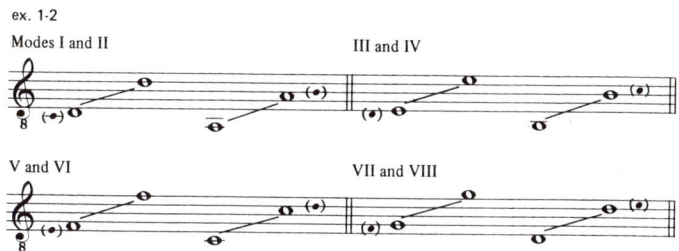

Note that the musical space occupied by each is different, thereby creating a different musical sound. Consider the following two examples. Both end on *f* but have different ranges.

*LU: abbreviation for the *Liber Usualis,* an important collection of chant.

ex. 1-3

LU 1043

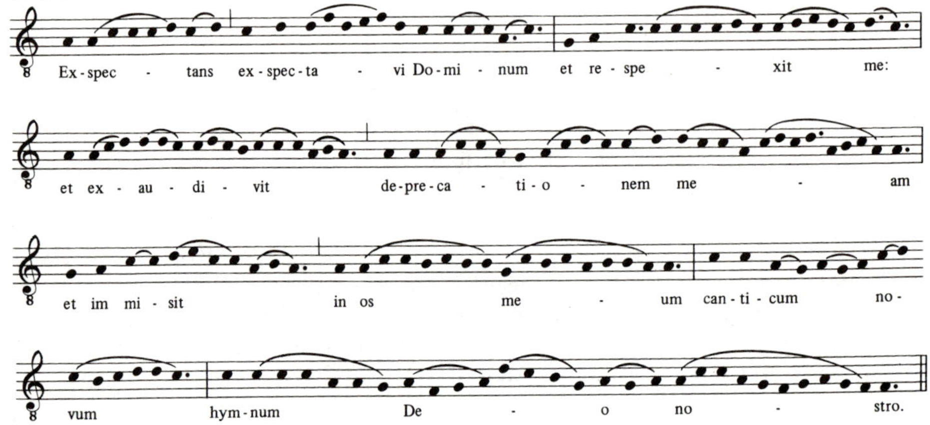

Ex-spec - tans ex-spec-ta - vi Do-mi - num et re - spe - xit me:
et ex - au - di - vit de-pre-ca - ti - o - nem me - am
et im mi - sit in os me - um can-ti-cum no-
vum hym-num De - o no - stro.

ex. 1-4

LU 1046

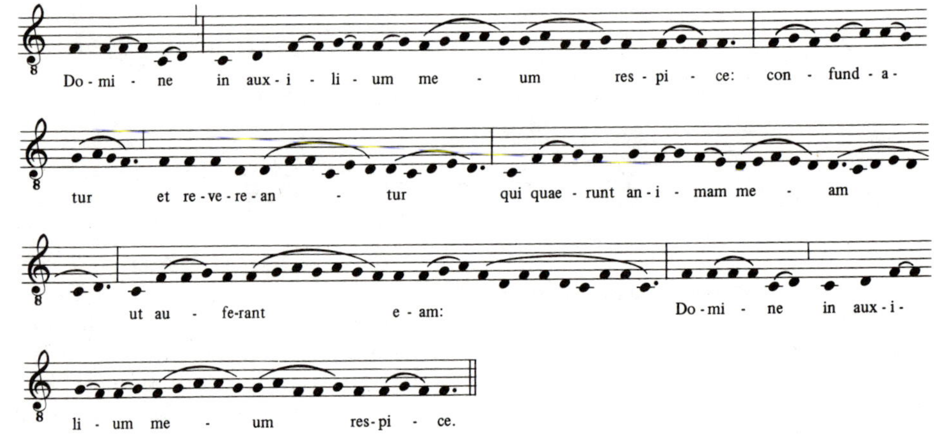

Do-mi - ne in aux-i - li - um me - um res - pi - ce: con - fund - a-
tur et re-ve-re-an - tur qui quae - runt an-i - mam me - am
ut au - fe-rant e - am: Do-mi - ne in aux-i-
li - um me - um res-pi - ce.

The result is that the first can be classified as Lydian and the second as Hypolydian.

In certain cases it is difficult to determine the mode from the finalis and the ambitus together. In such cases the ***dominant*** usually will resolve the question. Generally, the dominant of the authentic mode is a perfect fifth above the finalis. The dominant of the plagal modes is usually a third below the authentic dominant. In the event that the resultant dominant is on *b,* it is changed to *c;* thus the dominant of the Phrygian mode is not a perfect fifth above the final, but rather a minor sixth above. This is done to avoid melodic emphasis on the dissonant sound of the *f–b* tritone.

Dominant of each mode:

ex. 1-5

Mode: I II III IV V VI VII VIII

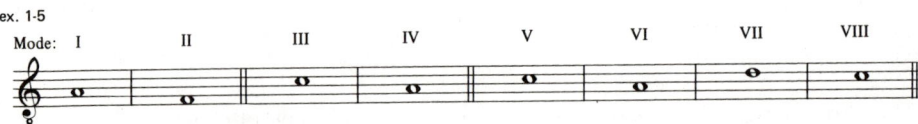

In the two following melodies we can observe the importance of the dominant in operation. Each melody is contained in the range of $c-a$ and each has the same finalis, d. Only the secondary note of emphasis in each melody can indicate the mode of each. Since a is emphasized in the first melody, its mode is Dorian; since f is emphasized in the second, its mode is Hypodorian.

Another purpose for the dominant is its use as the reciting tone of the mode. In certain chants, chiefly settings of the psalms, one note, the reciting tone, is used to sing most of the lengthy verse sections of the text. The dominant of the mode is always used as the reciting tone. At the end of the chant, the melody always descends from the reciting tone back to the final.

In addition to their final, range, and dominant, modes can also be classified by interval structure. The interval structure of each mode—that is, the placement of whole and half steps within the scale—is not only different for each, but is the factor most responsible for the characteristic sound of each.

Although music theorists did not list the eight modes as scales until the early tenth century, we may do so for analytical purposes.

ex. 1-9

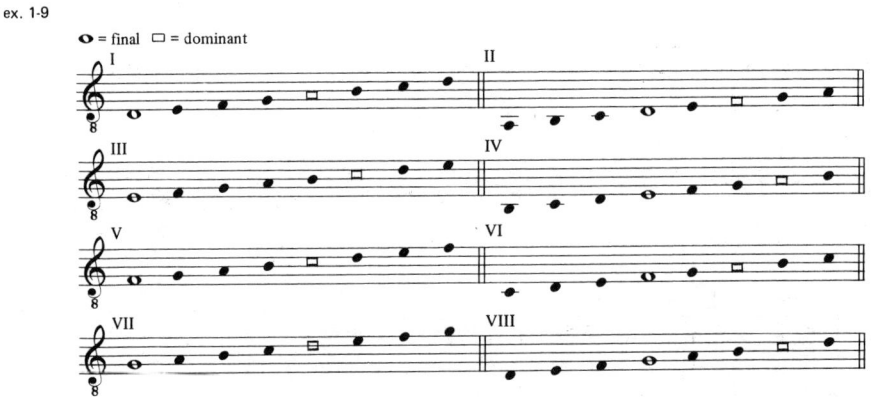

Play and sing each scale, ending on the correct final, to determine the different musical/intervallic sound of each.

If we view the authentic modes through twentieth-century eyes, we may compare them to the major-minor system.

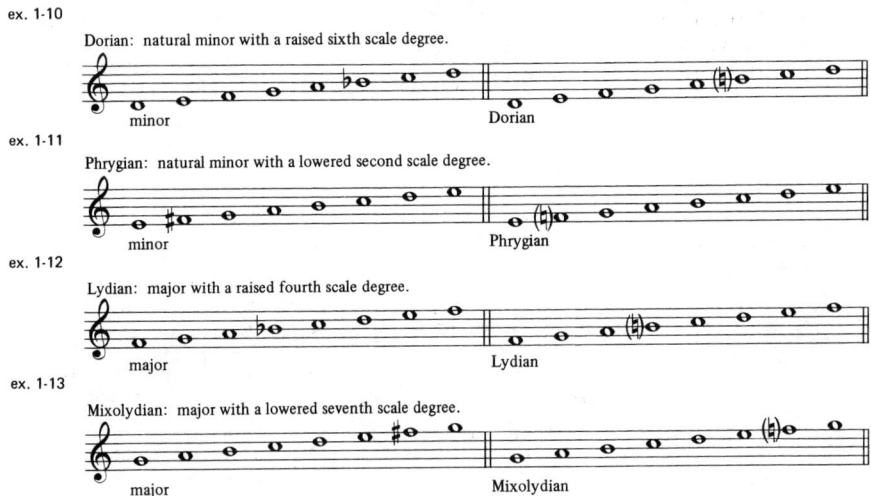

Although this was obviously not the way these modes were viewed in the Middle Ages, it may be of some use to us today.

One final subject must be mentioned in this discussion of chant melodies, the subject of **modulation.** Modulation is the process of moving from one tonal or modal level to another. Modulation opens the way to exploration of more than one mode within the same melody. It is unusual for a piece to remain on one level for a long period of time; the process of modulation, then, allows some flexibility of motion within a modal melody.

Sing through the following *Kyrie* (from Mass IX in the *Liber Usualis*). Note the melodic/intervallic motion, the ambitus (and any changes of ambitus between phrases), the finalis, and the dominant. Also look for possible use of modal modulation.

ex. 1-14

Notice the frequent use of a few notes per text syllable. This style of text setting is referred to as *neumatic* chant. By contrast, *syllabic* chant has one note per syllable and *melismatic* chant tends to have many (usually six or more) notes per syllable.

The text creates the form of the chant, by means of the three repetitions each of "Kyrie eleison," "Christe eleison," and "Kyrie eleison" again. This produces a nine-part textual form—**AAA BBB AAA.** Musically, though, it is not quite that simple. Many repetitions of short segments of melody can immediately be perceived. These short, repeated melodic phrases are termed **motives.** There are at least six motives that are arranged in a variety of ways to produce a wonderfully kaleidoscopic design.

ex. 1-15

The first and third "Kyrie" have the same motivic pattern: **a, b, c, d.** The second is a variant; **a** and **b** are replaced by a new four-note motive, which is then followed by **c** and **d.** The "Christe," as is normal both in the case of chant and in later polyphonic examples, changes radically. Not only does it shift from a tonal emphasis on D to one on A, it also used two new phrases, **e** and **f.** Again, the first and third "Christe" are identical, but the second uses a modified version of the opening "Kyrie" motives, **b, c,** and **d.**

The most striking use of the various motives is in the final "Kyrie," where all motives heretofore presented are given free rein. It begins with a new motive and then, as if to weld it to the immediately preceding "Christe," uses the motives from the "Christe." The second "Kyrie," again harkening back, uses the melody of the second "Christe." Finally, as if pulling the entire piece together into one phrase, the final phrase juxtaposes almost all the motives for a final melismatic flourish: **g, e/f** (modified), **g, e/f, b, c, d.**

The entire structure becomes both complex and musically unified as a result of the various combinations and juxtapositions. The motivic process can be compared to the growth of an organism: as it grows and develops, it gradually changes, becoming something different and yet somehow the same. The final "Kyrie" is the culmination of that development.

The mode is very clearly Dorian. The signs are quite evident: finalis of *d,* dominant solidly established as *a* (because of its use as the final note in several phrases, and because of the important motion toward and away from that note), and ambitus of c–d^1. There are two hints at modulation. One is in the second "Kyrie," where the Hypodorian mode is suggested both by the use of the low *a* and the emphasis on *f* which suggests that it is a temporary dominant. The other is in the first and third phrases of the "Christe," as well as in the following "Kyrie" phrase. This may be seen as Hypophrygian, transposed to A.

ex. 1-16

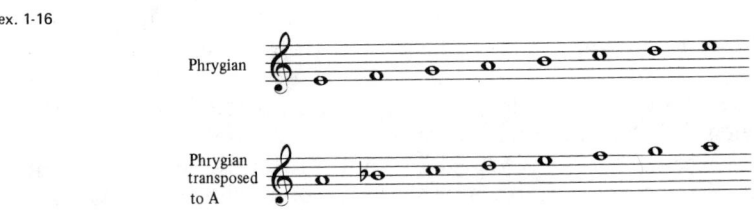

This melody, like most chant melodies, is *conjunct;* that is, it moves primarily stepwise. In addition, the curve of the line is well defined, moving toward one melodic pitch and balancing this motion by returning in the opposite direction. The first phrase is an excellent example of this, beginning with motion to the dominant and a stepwise return to the finalis. This process is then repeated to end the phrase. In general, conjunct melodic motion in chant rarely moves beyond a fifth before reversing direction. In addition, if the line leaps by a fourth or fifth (sixths are extremely rare, and sevenths are not used) it generally returns by step immediately. All of these observations point to the conjunct, smooth, and fluid lines found in plainchant.

The first **accidental** to be introduced was $b\flat$. As we have noted, the modal system was based on diatonic scales, without use of accidentals. The obvious exception to this was the use of $b\flat$. This note was used, basically, for two purposes: to avoid the melodic emphasis on the f–b tritone, and to produce a smooth, easy-to-sing line when moving a–b–a. If you would sing the *Kyrie* example again, using $b\natural$ where $b\flat$ is indicated, you will immediately understand, aurally, both points.

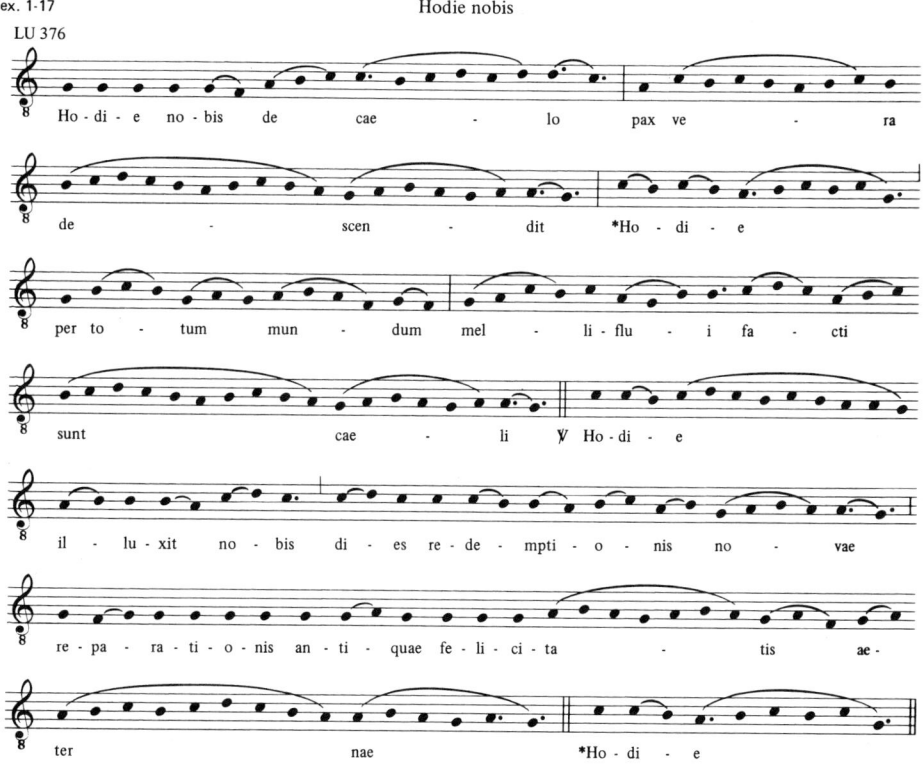

ex. 1-17   Hodie nobis
LU 376

A slightly more complicated usage of the motivic idea of organization can be found in the next example, *Hodie Nobis* (LU376). This chant employs a very important compositional principle used in many Gregorian melodies, **centonization.** The term comes from the Latin *cento* (patchwork) and indicates melodic construction by means of combining motives derived from already existing melodies. The motivic elements could be combined in almost any order (although the careful composer will always discard some combinations, based on taste and judgment) into a new melodic line. In this way the composer created something new from pre-existing material. The motives, or fragments, were different in each mode, and their shape and intervallic structure were characteristic of the mode itself. This, then, reflects the intervallic autonomy of the modes, each of which produces its own distinct sound based on its intervallic structure.

Looking at *Hodie Nobis,* you will notice how several melodic motives are introduced and varied. Four basic ideas can be readily identified, all of which are traceable to pre-existing prototypes in this mode.*

ex. 1-18

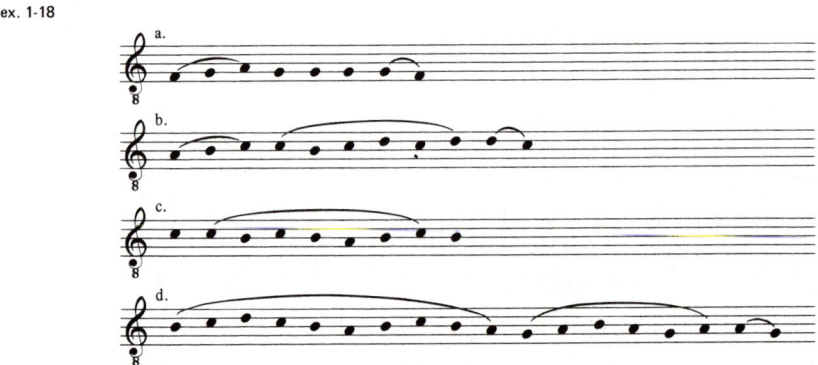

These pre-existing melodic fragments are combined, altered, and improvised upon by the composer, producing a relatively new melody. An analysis provides insight into the process.

The first phrase begins with the second part of **a,** and ends with **b.**

ex. 1-19

The second phrase consists of **c** plus **d.**

ex. 1-20

In these cases the fragments are easy to recognize. Likewise, the return of **d** for the last phrase before the Verse (V̌) is readily obvious.

*From Will Apel, *Gregorian Chant* (Bloomington, Ind.: Indiana Univ. Press, 1958) p. 338.

ex. 1-21

What happens in between is more difficult to analyze. The "Hodie" phrase is derived from **c,** the final two notes being additions. The material following cannot be directly derived from any of the previous material, so we can regard it as free invention. (However, there may be a basis for this material in pre-existing fragments.)

If we analyze fragments **c** and **d,** we find the repetition of material at different pitch levels—*melodic sequence.* This can be seen readily in **d.**

ex. 1-22

These sequential patterns define the phrase and propel it downward to the cadence. In fragment **c,** there is a smaller *cell* that is used in a slightly different way than in **d.** It produces a "turning" figure around one pitch.

ex. 1-23

The idea is similar to that used in **d,** but on a smaller scale, and therefore possibly not as recognizable.

When these two cells, or internal motives, are recognized as the basis for **c** and **d,** then the material directly after "Hodie" becomes understandable. The phrase "per totum mundum" is derived from an inverted form of **c**'s cell.

ex. 1-24

Likewise, the phrase "melliflui facti" is derived, with certain modifications, from **d.**

ex. 1-25

This last phrase is the most difficult, and the furthest removed from the original idea. Nevertheless, it shows a certain consistency of design and fluidity of thought. The composer is not just fitting pieces together; his technique is additive and developmental as well, and thus creative in an important sense.

The remainder of the melody can be analyzed in a similar way. The setting of "Hodie illuxit nobis" becomes a derivative of **c**.

ex. 1-26

"Dies redemptionis" is derived from **c** as well, with an ending from **d**.

ex. 1-27

The next phrase is an extension of the reciting-tone idea from **a**. Starting from "aeternae," **d** is used, with slight modification. The "Hodie" at the end is the same as above.

ex. 1-28

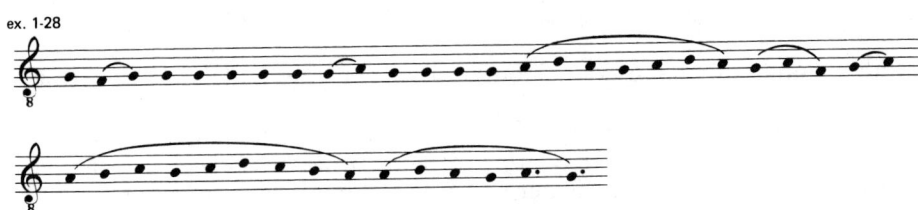

The entire structure can be diagrammed as follows:

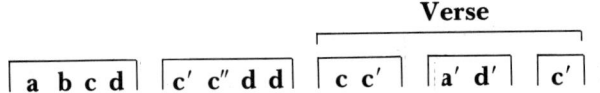

This outline shows the resulting complexity of the simple use of centonization.

In addition, it shows the importance of the concepts of repetition, contrast, and development. From a relatively simple statement of material at the beginning (**a–b–c–d**—all pre-existing material), the fragments are modified, developed, and extended to produce a complicated, yet unified and musically understandable work.

In our zeal for tracing motive design, we have not considered the use of mode. The mode is clear in this example: Mode VIII, or Hypomixolydian. The most evident signs are the final, *g;* the small range, *f–d;* and, most crucial of all, the dominant, *c,* which can be determined by the frequency with which it appears, most importantly at phrase beginnings and cadences.

We should again observe the smooth melodic contour of plainchant, which is admirably demonstrated by this example. As can readily be seen, the motion is mostly conjunct. Possibly because of the use of fragments and motives within them, as well as the employment of sequence, each phrase has a linear direction. Each moves from one point to another, not quickly or illogically, but in well-defined, well-thought-out motivic/melodic shapes.

© Ronald J. Taylor: *The Art of the Minnesinger (1968).* University of Wales Press; used by permission.

The preceding monophonic example is of an entirely different character. It employs definable meter; and clear-cut and regular phrases, and does not seem to fit easily into the modal system. A rather striking contrast to the chant examples, this is an example of **secular monophony** of the twelfth or thirteenth century.

By Walther von der Vogelweide (ca. 1170–1228), a Minnesinger in southern Germany, this piece displays remarkable tonal stability within a neat, compact **phrase structure.** It is easy to follow the phrases, which are mostly four bars long; several phrases (those for lines 3, 6, 10, and 14) are extended to six-bar lengths. Although a result of the text line, this gives the melody a more interesting quality than could have been obtained by a mere succession of four-bar phrases. The resulting arrangement of phrases is easily shown.

4 + 4 + 6 :‖ 4 + 4 + 4 + 6 + 4 + 4 + 4 + 6 + 4

If you look at the larger ideas, these multiple phrase-groupings can be combined into 8 + 6 :‖ 8 + 10 + 8 + 10 + 4, thereby making greater sense out of the overall piece. The melodic structure does not seem to contain the same kinds of repetition, sequence, and development found in the preceding plainchant examples. This is not to say that the pitches are chosen arbitrarily. To the contrary, a close look at the positioning of pitches, control of line, and variety of cadence endings leads one to marvel at the overall construction of a seemingly simple tune.

The **overall tonal pull** always seems to be toward *c*. This is suggested by the opening phrase, with its initial resolution to *c* and its ending point on *b*, the *leading tone* to *c*. The phrase before the repeat signs reaffirms this tonality with a strong cadence on *c*.

The internal phrases ceem to revolve around two notes, *e* and *g*. These notes, with *c*, make up the C-major triad (although we must remember that this is a *monophonic* piece). Cadences occur on either the tonic of the key or the dominant (if we consider *e* as part of the tonic), and the preponderance of cadences on *g* indicates a strong anticipatory drive to the tonic, *c*. This can be seen by the melody given below with important "key" notes circled.

ex. 1-30

Tenth to Twelfth Centuries: Gregorian Chant and Secular Monophony 41

It is important to note that modal music (both chant and a great many secular melodies as well) generally does not proceed as this melody does, and in particular it seldom emphasizes the dominant/tonic relationship in so strong a fashion. However, even at this early date, tonal (major or minor) melodies such as this one were being sung and played by musicians and amateurs alike. While modal music is of extraordinary importance in these early centuries, tonal music also has its roots in the modal system and gradually emerges from it. The roots are long and sometimes tenuous, but they are there nonetheless.

The regularity of rhythm in this period was a product of the system known as **rhythmic modes.** As early as the twelfth century, a fixed rhythmic system had been developed, based on the poetic meters of the ancient Greeks. There were six rhythmic modes.

1. ♩♩ ♩♩ (trochaic)
2. ♩♩ ♩♩ (iambic)
3. ♩. ♩♩ (dactylic)
4. ♩♩ ♩. (anapestic)
5. ♩. ♩. (spondaic)
6. ♩♩♩ ♩♩♩ (tribrachic)

The use of the rhythmic modes constitutes the first attempt at rhythmic notation. Basically, once a mode was defined, the remaining pitches were sung in that mode. However, there are numerous alterations and additions to this basic premise, resulting in a complex system which was used by composers of monophonic songs as well as of polyphonic compositions.

It is impossible to determine if all of the secular monophonic songs—by the trouveres, troubadours, and Minnesingers—actually employed the rhythmic modes. Probably they did not. But the system was an important step in the notation of rhythm.

STYLE CHARACTERISTICS OF CHANT

melodic use use of most diatonic intervals: major and minor seconds, major and minor thirds, perfect fourths, perfect fifths • occasional use of the minor sixth • no use of the tritone, major sixth, major or minor seventh • infrequent use of the octave • melodies usually constructed through a balance of motion, with an upward line or interval balanced by similar motion downward • use of church modes

compositional techniques free invention • centonization

Glossary

Ambitus the melodic range of a mode.
Cell a short fragment (usually two or three or four notes long) used as the basis of a larger melodic idea. It is typically shorter than a motive.
Centonization the process of writing a new chant by the use of pre-existing fragments found in other chants. These fragments are usually grouped according to their mode.
Dominant the secondary final of the mode. It is also used as the reciting tone for the mode.
Finalis the final, ending pitch of a mode.
Melismatic chant plainchant that frequently employs many (more than about 6) notes per syllable of text.
Melodic sequence the repetition of a melodic fragment at a different pitch level, in the same voice.
Modal system a method of composing plainchant as well as a method of classifying melodies according to their finalis, dominant, and ambitus. It comprises eight modes, four authentic and four plagal.
Modulation a temporary shift to another mode or to a transposed mode.
Monophonic music consisting of a single melodic line.
Motive a short, characteristic melodic idea that is used to construct a larger musical idea.
Neumatic chant plainchant that frequently employs several (ca. 3–6) notes per syllable of text.
Rhythmic modes a system of twelfth-century rhythmic notation based on the use of Greek poetic meters. There are six rhythmic modes.
Subfinal the note directly below the final of a mode. Depending on the mode, it will be a half step or whole step.
Syllabic chant plainchant that is written primarily with one note per syllable of text.

Suggested Exercises

1. With the following melodic fragments, compose a chant in each of the two indicated modes, making sure that you end properly in the mode and that the line is singable. Keep in mind the developmental possibilities in using the given fragments and that additional pitches are possible.

a. Mode 8
1

2

2. Compose a free chant, employing your own repeatable motives, in one of the modes, on the text "Kyrie eleison, Christe eleison, Kyrie eleison."
3. Using the second or third rhythmic mode, compose a song of six or more regular phrases in the style of the Minnesinger song in this chapter. Use either a mode or a C-major or A-natural-minor scale as the basis for your melody.
4. Analyze the following chant melodies, indicating repetition of motives and derived motives, as well as the mode of each example.

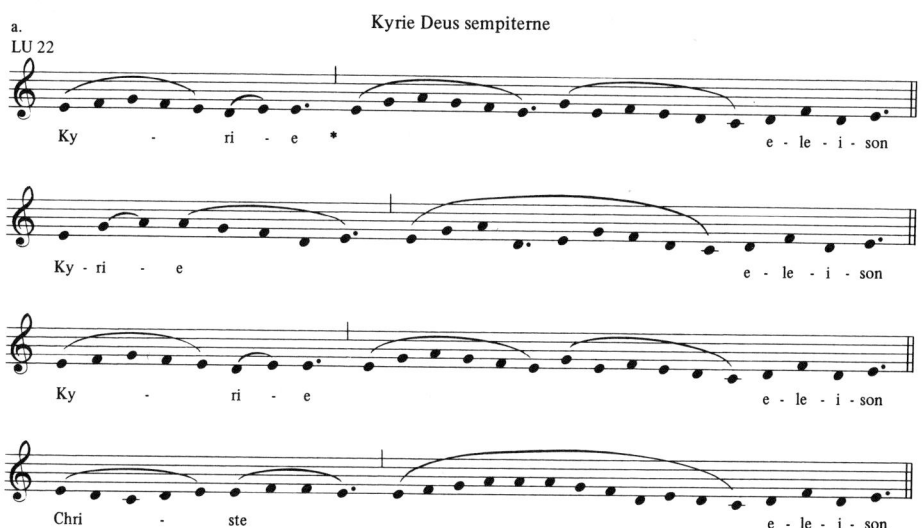

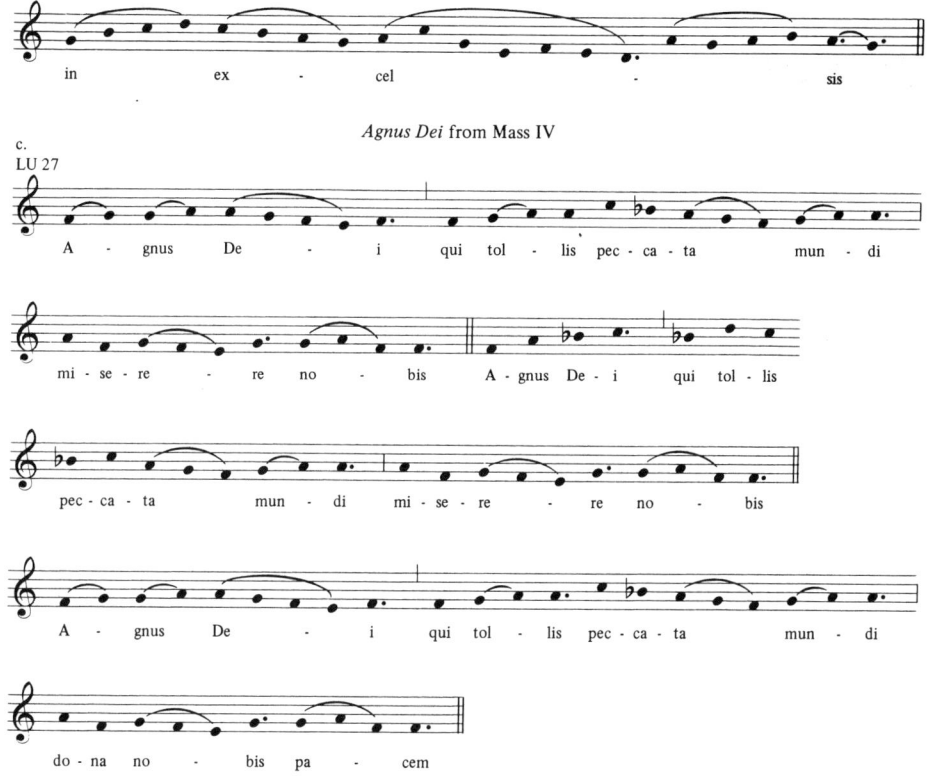

Agnus Dei from Mass IV
c. LU 27

Before Reading Chapter 2

1. Sing and play through the examples of organum found on pages 46, 47, 48, and 49.
2. Analyze the harmonic intervals found in the organum examples on pages 50 and 51.

Organum

The earliest example of music in more than one part is also an example of the simplest type: ***parallel organum.*** The music mirrors its name precisely, with totally *parallel motion* throughout. An example is given below.

ex. 2-1

Nos qui vivimus benedicamus Do - mi - num ex hoc nunc et us - quae in se - cu - lo - rum.

Reprinted by permission of the publishers from HISTORICAL ANTHOLOGY OF MUSIC, VOL. I: ORIENTAL, MEDIEVAL and RENAISSANCE MUSIC, edited by Archibald T. Davison and Willi Apel, Cambridge, Mass.: Harvard University Press, copyright 1946, 1949 by the President and Fellows of Harvard College; copyright 1974, 1977 by Alice D. Humez and Willi Apel.

This example is as simple as two-part music can be: the chant line is doubled an octave below. Another way of saying this is that the *vox principalis* (principal voice, or chant) is above the *vox organalis* (organal voice, or tenor). It can hardly be called polyphony in the true sense of the word, since the voices are in no sense independent of each other. Nevertheless, this notation of more than one voice is highly significant, since only monophonic music had been notated as far back as we can trace music notation (at least to the ancient Greeks, ca. 500 B.C.).

At the same time as the above example, there appears parallel organum at the fifth and fourth.

ex. 2-2

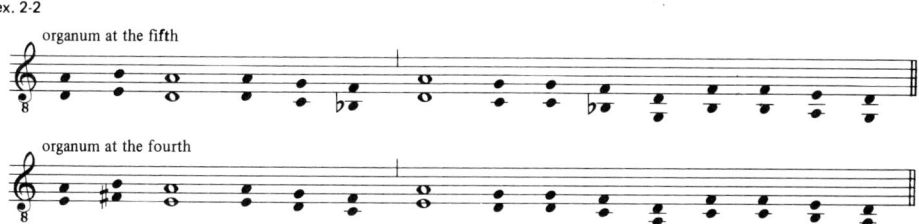

Reprinted by permission of the publishers from HISTORICAL ANTHOLOGY OF MUSIC, VOL. I: ORIENTAL, MEDIEVAL and RENAISSANCE MUSIC, edited by Archibald T. Davison and Willi Apel, Cambridge, Mass.: Harvard University Press, copyright 1946, 1949 by the President and Fellows of Harvard College; copyright 1974, 1977 by Alice D. Humez and Willi Apel.

In each case, the *vox principalis* is the top voice, with the doubling occurring below.

Another variety of this is known as **composite organum,** organum in more than two voices produced by simply doubling the organal voice up an octave and/or the principal voice down an octave.

ex. 2-3

Reprinted by permission of the publishers from HISTORICAL ANTHOLOGY OF MUSIC, VOL. I: ORIENTAL, MEDIEVAL and RENAISSANCE MUSIC, edited by Archibald T. Davison and Willi Apel, Cambridge, Mass.: Harvard University Press, copyright 1946, 1949 by the President and Fellows of Harvard College; copyright 1974, 1977 by Alice D. Humez and Willi Apel.

Because of its simplicity, none of this may seem startling on the surface, still, there are consequences of great significance that have their beginning in this music: 1) the possibility of having two voices instead of one was to prove capable of tremendous development; 2) the intervals first used—P8, P5, P4—were destined to rule supreme for four to five hundred years; and 3) the technique of using a borrowed melody—liturgical or otherwise—as the basis of a new piece was to persist through the centuries until the present.

The first logical consequence and extension of parallel organum was ***free organum.*** It is still note-against-note (that is, for each note in one part there is a note in the other), but the three intervals—P8, P5, P4—are now used freely.

ex. 2-4

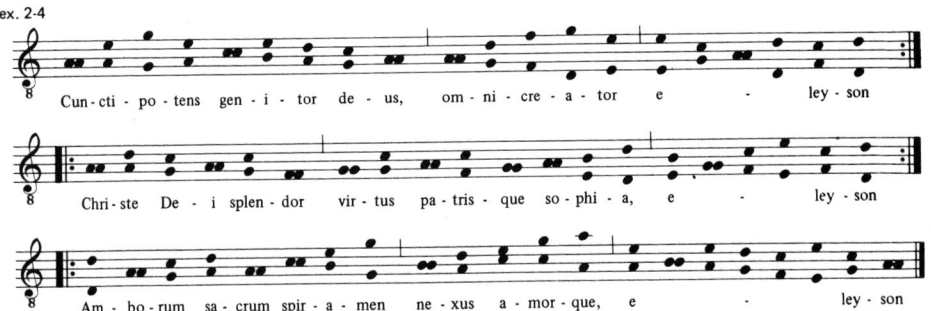

Reprinted by permission of the publishers from HISTORICAL ANTHOLOGY OF MUSIC, VOL. I: ORIENTAL, MEDIEVAL and RENAISSANCE MUSIC, edited by Archibald T. Davison and Willi Apel, Cambridge, Mass.: Harvard University Press, copyright 1946, 1949 by the President and Fellows of Harvard College; copyright 1974, 1977 by Alice D. Humez and Willi Apel.

There are also examples of free organum that employ thirds and sixths (there is one third in this example); these are a further and natural extension of the above principles.

Possibly the most important aspect of this music is the freeing of the organal voice. This produced the creative possibility of actually composing an independent second voice, albeit only a kind of embellishment of the chant line. The use of *parallel, contrary, similar,* and **oblique motion** is important in this development.

ex. 2-5

This freedom of motion provided the composer with the possibility of creating much greater harmonic interest between the two parts. Finally, the chant line has now been moved to the bottom voice—an important development because of the flexibility thereby given to the line above.

The result is the first true *polyphonic* music: music employing two or more *independent* lines simultaneously.

Free organum is still confining, though. Because of its strict note-against-note nature, there is little actual freedom for the composer. In addition, the choice of intervals is usually severely limited.

What was needed at this point was to free the organal voice from the severe constraints of the chant. This was accomplished by the development of a melismatic style in the top voice, a free-flowing melody in which there are several notes for each note of the *vox principalis*. This accomplishes several things at once. We now see freely composed melodies, a more directional melodic flow, and, more importantly, a greatly increased choice of intervals.

A great variety of harmonic intervals is used in the example of **melismatic organum** below.

ex. 2-6

Reprinted by permission of the publishers from HISTORICAL ANTHOLOGY OF MUSIC, VOL. I: ORIENTAL, MEDIEVAL and RENAISSANCE MUSIC, edited by Archibald T. Davison and Willi Apel, Cambridge, Mass.: Harvard University Press, copyright 1946, 1949 by the President and Fellows of Harvard College; copyright 1974, 1977 by Alice D. Humez and Willi Apel.

In melismatic organum all diatonic intervals will appear between the two voices. There are certain limitations, however, the most important occurring at the beginning and ending of phrases. As can be seen in the above example, the only intervals used to begin or end a phrase are the unison, P8, and P5. The P5 is rarely used to end a phrase and is never used to end an entire piece. We can see that a hierarchy of intervals is being established: the unison and P8 are the most "perfect," with the P5 only slightly less so. The P4 is still regarded by the theorists of the period as an important consonant interval. Nevertheless, composers demonstrate otherwise. We will find few examples of the prominent use of the P4 as a consonance from this time forward.

Note the flowing character of the top line. Many scale patterns are used; the line is well balanced, with upward thrusts being countered by downward motion. One prominent motive is a kind of turn figure around the upper tone of a P5.

Possibly the most important development to occur at this point was the notation of rhythm. It is possible to coordinate two singers without rhythmic notation, but the performance of three or more parts, or even the singing of two lines by an entire chorus, presents enormous difficulties in the absence of an easily intelligible notation.

We do not know precisely where or when rhythmic notation came into being, but it is certain that by the late twelfth century in Paris the system of the rhythmic modes was in full flower. The organum examples from the *School of Notre Dame* are the first to make use of the rhythmic modes.

The following example shows to what extent rhythm was used in the elaborate extension of melismatic polyphony.

Reprinted by permission of the publishers from HISTORICAL ANTHOLOGY OF MUSIC, VOL. I: ORIENTAL, MEDIEVAL and RENAISSANCE MUSIC, edited by Archibald T. Davison and Willi Apel, Cambridge, Mass.: Harvard University Press, copyright 1946, 1949 by the President and Fellows of Harvard College; copyright 1974, 1977 by Alice D. Humez and Willi Apel.

This example follows the same basic harmonic-intervallic and melodic practice as found in the example of melismatic organum. Indeed, this is really an extended melismatic example with rhythm added to the top voice.

A closer look at this example gives us an idea of its rhythmic organization and its qualities of variety and continuity. The phrases are quite short in the organal voice—usually two, sometimes three or four measures in length. They seem to use similar rhythmic units within a given section: ♩♪ ♩₇ | ♩♩ ♩♩♪ | ♩. ♩₇ | in one section, ♪ ♩ ♩ ♩ | ♪ ♩ ♩ ♩ | in another, and in the last section, ♫♫ ♩. | ♫♫ ♩. .

This rhythmic repetition reflects the system of the **rhythmic modes.** The contemporary notation employed a method of indicating repetition of patterns in a given rhythmic mode by the use of **ordo.** Ordo indicates the length of the phrase, and the number of repetitions of the modal pattern. Therefore, two or three *ordines* (plural of *ordo*) are two or three presentations of the rhythmic pattern, ending with a rest. For example:

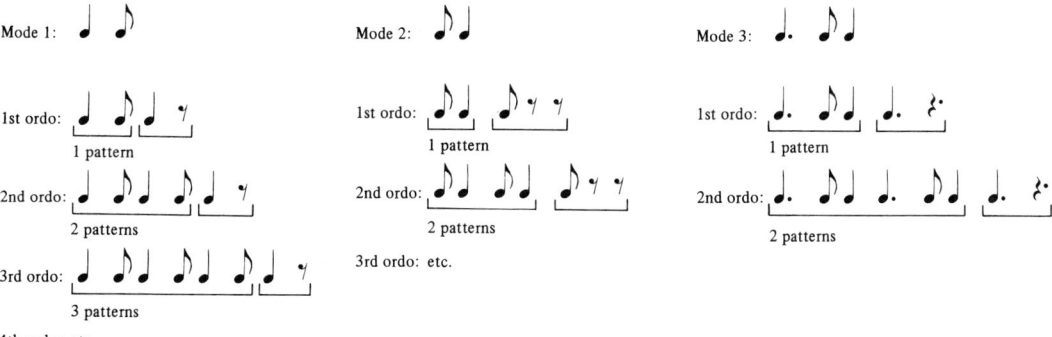

The remaining modes can be constructed in this fashion.

The purpose of these ordo patterns was practical, for it provided the notational basis for rhythm. What is given here is, of necessity, very brief and skeletal. The actual system of the repetitive ordines was not only complex, but also lacking in totally consistent usage. It did provide a very important organizational pattern for this early period, however.

One of the areas of Notre Dame organum that employed the rhythmic modes in both melodic lines was found in the portion of organum where the tenor begins to move faster, taking on a definite, and usually repetitive, rhythmic pattern. It is referred to as the *clausula*. In these sections the chant line becomes more animated and moves much more like a true contrapuntal line. In addition, we see the ordines are usually well defined as a structural underpinning for the tenor.

The significance of the clausula is not only that of a new independence, interaction and more contrapuntal nature to be found between the two parts. It is also important to note that composers recognized the significance of this important development and began to explore it fully. The result was the *motet*, the principal form or genre for the next two to three hundred years.

STYLE CHARACTERISTICS OF ORGANUM

types of organum	parallel • free • melismatic • Notre Dame
melody	borrowed chant in one voice (top voice in parallel, bottom voice in all others) • top voice in all but parallel is patterned after chant, with basically stepwise motion, few skips of over a P5, no melodic tritones
interval structure	in parallel organum: either P4, P5, or P8 • free organum: mostly P5 and P4 • cadence on unison or octave • occasional use of thirds and sixths • melismatic organum: all diatonic intervals used • P5 and octave are used for almost all cadences • Notre Dame organum: all diatonic intervals used • cadences are either P5 or octave • clausula sections use P5 or octave for each phrase ending
rhythm	only found in Notre Dame organum: use of rhythmic modes in the top voice • in clausula sections, both voices employ rhythm, the bottom voice usually being repetitious
additional features	use of borrowed chant • clausula (in Notre Dame organum) • use of rhythmic modes (in Notre Dame organum)

Glossary

Clausula a section of Notre Dame organum in which the chant line moves faster rhythmically. There is usually a repetitive rhythmic scheme in the tenor voice.

Contrary motion two-voice motion in which the voices move in opposite directions.

Composite organum parallel organum with one or more voices doubled at the octave.

Free organum two-voice organum in which the chant line is on the bottom and the top voice is freely composed, in a note-against-note style.

Melismatic organum two-voice organum (in the eleventh-twelfth century) with the chant line on the bottom and a melismatic, freely composed line above, the top part having several notes to each note of chant.

Notre Dame organum an extension of melismatic organum, with the top voice utilizing rhythmic notation based on the rhythmic modes. The ending portion of each section usually has a clausula.

Oblique motion two-voice motion in which one voice moves while the other remains on the same pitch.

Ordo (plural:ordines) one unit of a rhythmic mode.

Parallel motion two-voice motion in which both voices move by the same interval(s) in the same direction.
Parallel organum two-part organum of the tenth century consisting of a chant line and a second voice doubling the chant line at a perfect fourth, perfect fifth, or perfect octave below.
Polyphony two or more melodic lines occurring at the same time.
Similar motion two-voice motion in which both voices move in the same direction but by different intervals.
Vox organalis "organal voice"; the voice added to the chant line in organum.
Vox principalis "principal voice"; the original chant line in an organum setting.

Suggested Exercises

1. Using the given chant line, compose examples of parallel, free, and melismatic organum. Pay close attention to the singable nature of your additional voice. Analyze each harmonic interval used.

2. Using the given chant line, compose an example of Notre Dame organum. Include a section of clausula.

3. Analyze each harmonic interval of the following example of melismatic organum. Note which intervals are used at the beginning and ending of each phrase.

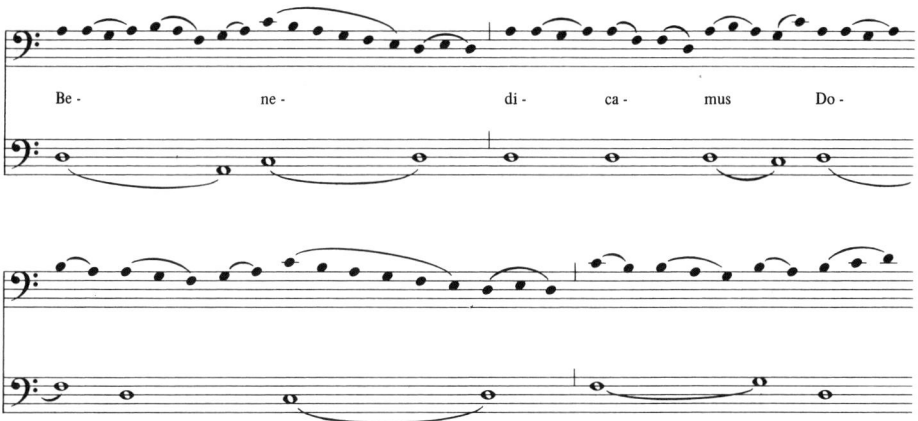

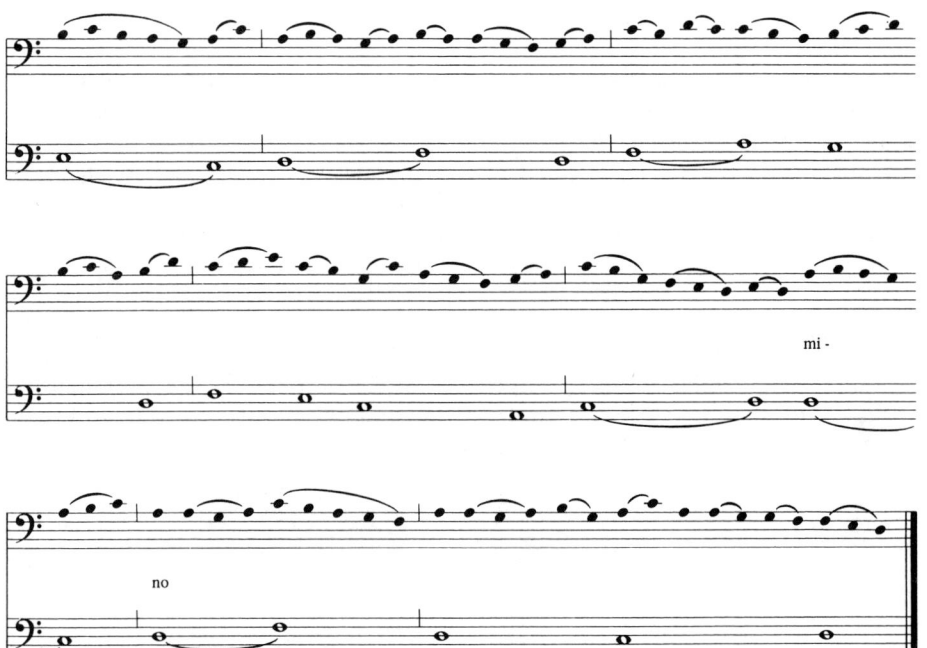

Before Reading Chapter 3

1. Sing each line of the *Deo confitemini* (page 00) and then sing or play them together.
2. Analyze the harmonic intervals throughout.
3. Bracket the phrases, paying close attention to the harmonic intervals at the cadence points.
4. Listen several times to the piece by Petrus de Cruce (page 00).
5. Sing the tenor (the bottom line). Note any repetitions of rhythm and melody. Describe these in detail.

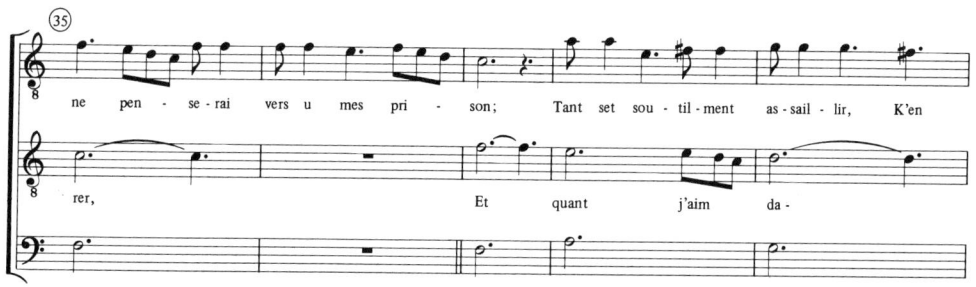

Reprinted by permission of the publishers from HISTORICAL ANTHOLOGY OF MUSIC, VOL. I: ORIENTAL, MEDIEVAL and RENAISSANCE MUSIC, edited by Archibald T. Davison and Willi Apel, Cambridge, Mass.: Harvard University Press, copyright 1946, 1949 by the President and Fellows of Harvard College; copyright 1974, 1977 by Alice D. Humez and Willi Apel.

3

Las Huelgas Codex
Petrus de Cruce

Deo confitemini/Domino
Aucun/Lonc Tans/Annuntiantes

    When a new text line is added to the top voice of a clausula the resultant piece is a ***motet*** (derived from the French *mot*, meaning word). Thirteenth-century composers produced many motets in two and three voices. Some are clausulas with a text added to the upper voice, others are newly composed. In most cases the tenor (the bottom voice) is a borrowed chant.

    The accompanying example is an anonymous two-part motet from the Las Huelgas Codex, a thirteenth-century manuscript from Spain. It is typical of the motets in the mid-thirteenth century in its rhythmic, melodic, and intervallic content. A striking quality is its persistent use of two-measure phrases, each ending with a perfect consonance. A somewhat unusual feature is the use of minor thirds to begin the first three phrases. Thus we can see that composers are beginning to extend the "rules" somewhat, even though the rest of the piece adheres to the more standard use of perfect consonances at phrase beginnings.

    The ***perfect consonances*** are, as before, the unison, octave, and perfect fifth. These are generally employed for the phrase beginnings and endings as in organum. In addition, another group of intervals was regarded as ***imperfect consonances:*** the thirds and sixths (either major or minor). Though these are considered consonant intervals, phrases should not terminate with anything except perfection. As a general rule, imperfect intervals are used only in the internal portion of the phrase and move directly to the closest perfect interval. Therefore, a third generally moves to a unison or to a perfect fifth, and a sixth moves to an octave or a perfect fifth. Theorists of the time make further, more explicit, gradations but there are numerous exceptions to them. We can follow these more general procedures for now.

The *dissonances*—seconds, sevenths, and tritones—are used in an almost haphazard way at times. The theoretical rules for their use are more negative than positive: they may not be used at the beginning or ending of a phrase, nor, generally speaking, on a strong beat. This last prohibition was not followed exclusively, but can be considered a general procedure.

For our analytical purposes the dissonances can be classified into two categories: **neighboring** and **passing tones**. Both occur on a weak part of the beat. Neighboring dissonances, or *neighboring tones*, are dissonances that are approached by step and then return to the previous note. In the first measure of the example, the e^1 is a neighboring tone.

ex. 3-1

Passing tones are also approached by step but they continue in the same direction, again by step. All of the dissonant tones in this motet can be accounted for in one or the other of these two categories. In this particular motet, the handling of dissonance is careful and well-defined. This is not always the case in the thirteenth century, as we shall see later.

The **rhythmic organization** of *Deo confitemini* is quite simple, with two-measure phrases used exclusively and clear-cut cadences in each voice. In each phrase, the *duplum* (the second voice, directly above the bottom voice, which is called the *tenor*) continues the phrase at the end of the first measure and then cadences with the tenor in the second. The only rhythmic change in the tenor is in bars 7–9, where the second measure of the phrase is extended. Everywhere else we have exact rhythmic repetition in the tenor. These rhythmic patterns grew out of the rhythmic modes, which accounts for the rhythmic simplicity of the lower part. This kind of rhythmic repetition of the tenor is sometimes referred to as *isorhythm* (iso = same). This term is used to describe many pieces of the thirteenth century; we will see the principle extended and developed in the following century and a half.

Melodically there is a certain lilt to the upper voice. The **melodic motion** is always interesting, with unexpected shifts in direction (measures 3 and 4), extension of the phrase beyond the cadence point (measures 18–19) and a careful control of high and low points. For the sake of musical interest, the ending note changes for each successive phrase: *c* for the first phrase, then, *e e d e f e a,* and finally *d*. The highest point, *a*, is achieved in measures 11–13. The composer carefully prepared this high point by means of several upward thrusts, and then carefully planned the descent down to the *d* in the final measure.

As mentioned above, the piece is constructed on borrowed material, in this case the "Domino" portion of the gradual *Haec dies* (*Graduale*, p. 203). Using the borrowed pitches and a repeated rhythmic pattern, the composer produced the entire tenor line.

ex. 3-2

Then he added the duplum. Obviously, the duplum had to fit the tenor harmonically, according to the allowable perfect and imperfect consonances. This procedure of adding lines above a fixed tenor is known as **successive counterpoint** and was the normal method of composition for approximately two hundred years.

Finally, what is the mode of this motet? Both the duplum and tenor seem to be clearly in Dorian, even though the range is an octave, *a–a*. However, when dealing with polyphonic music, the problem of modal determination is ever-present, simply as a result of differences of ranges among the voices. Later theorists solved the problem by designating the tenor as the determining voice of the mode, since this is normally the voice that uses the borrowed chant. In pieces of two or three voices, with the tenor as the lowest voice, this presents few problems. In later centuries, when a bass voice is added below the other three voices, we may want to modify our stand.

The next example is also from the thirteenth century, but from the latter part of the century. It is easy to see how much has changed in the course of the century. By the time of Petrus de Cruce (also known, in French, as Pierre de la Croix), there are several striking differences, in addition to the three-voice texture.

The first of the differences lies in the ***rhythmic organization.*** It is important to know that the division of the pulse into three parts was crucial. This was first reflected in the rhythmic modes, all of which utilize the triple division of the pulse. It was inevitable that composers would eventually extend this concept and begin to divide a pulse into two or four, or even five or more parts. This is precisely what Petrus did. The extensions are handled with expert musical flair. The striking feature of Petrus's music is his use of not only two and four, but even five, seven, and nine notes per pulse.

At first glance, one of the most prominent features of the piece is the ***stratification of rhythm.*** The bottom voice, still designated the tenor, is the slowest; the middle voice, the duplum or motetus, is slightly faster than the tenor;

and the top voice, the triplum or discantus, is much faster than the tenor and somewhat faster than the duplum. This triple-tiered idea is extremely effective musically and forms the essential musical texture in the thirteenth and fourteenth centuries.

The five-, seven-, and nine-note figures are melismatic in character and tend to employ many neighboring and passing tones. A difficult problem here, though, is how to differentiate between dissonance and consonance.

In a two-voice texture, dissonance refers to an interval between the two voices—a second, a seventh, or sometimes a fourth. You can always identify the dissonant line by its melodic approach and resolution.

ex. 3-3

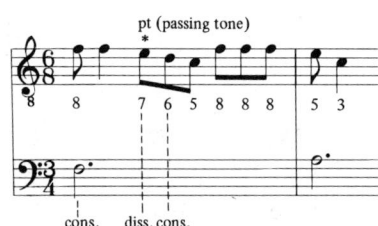

A consonance of an octave moved to a dissonance of a seventh because of the motion of the top voice. The top voice not only created the dissonance, but also resolved it; therefore that is the dissonant voice.

In a three-voice setting, the same principle exists, but there is a further complication because of the third part. Consider the situation in which each of the upper voices is consonant with the tenor, creating the simultaneous intervals of a sixth and a fifth.

ex. 3-4

Both notes are consonant with the lowest voice, but quite obviously they are dissonant with each other, being a second apart. We must somehow figure out which, if either, is dissonant.

If we follow contemporaneous ideas, the technique of successive counterpoint negates certain discussions of the problem, although later theorists do begin to deal with it. For our purposes, however, we must begin by defining what is consonant, and then both the dissonance and how it is used will be clear.

We can immediately see the octave/fifth arrangement and the triad.

ex. 3-5

The first example above shows the basic consonance in this period. We sometimes designate this chord by the figures $^8_5$, signifying an octave and a fifth above the bass. This can be used on strong beats and at cadence points. The open octave, without the fifth, is also perfectly consonant. The full triad including the third (Ex. 3-6b) is found only rarely, as is the $^6_3$, or first-inversion triad. These last two chords can be used, but not at important cadential points.

ex. 3-6

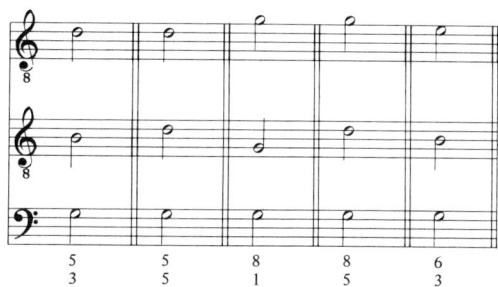

You will notice that the P4 is not found between the lower two voices, but only between the upper two. In this period, it is gradually coming to be regarded as a dissonance. Once the triad or open fifth has been well established, all notes outside of it are dissonant. Sometimes these notes are referred to as non-chord tones.

This procedure helps us in determining the dissonance in measure 1 of the motet. If the consonant sonority is F^8_5, then the e and d in the triplum are dissonant passing tones and the duplum's c has a lower neighbor, b.

ex. 3-7

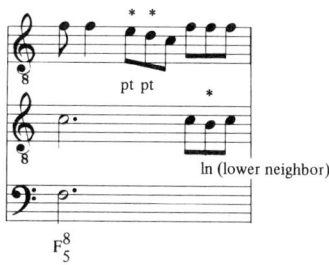

This identification of dissonance is crucial to understanding theoretical developments and helps us define the basic style features of individual composers.

Let us now consider three other important factors in this music: the root movement, or progression of triadic roots; the intervallic structure of each chord; and the linear or voice-leading motion from chord to chord.

By listening carefully to the piece, we can hear that it has a strongly **linear concept.** Each line is well controlled and well motivated. The shape of the triplum in the opening measures is a marvel of fluidity and melodic direction. It employs carefully controlled melodic and rhythmic motion down to the *c* and back up to a cadence on *g*. Although containing somewhat less motion, the lower two voices also reflect concern for direction and smoothness of line. Note the consistent stepwise motion in the following example, indicated by the beams.

ex. 3-8

A common "chord progression" is seen in measures 10–11: F_5^8 moving, via the passing tone *e* in the duplum, to G_5^8. The smoothness of linear motion in every voice is characteristic, but the dissonance, especially in its length and emphasis, is unusual and quite beautiful.

ex. 3-9

In the above example, as elsewhere, the primary vertical construction is the $_5^8$. Especially at the beginning of each measure, i.e. the beginning of a rhythmic perfection, this is the primary sound heard. Within the measure, much can happen: dissonances of all kinds, some carefully controlled (passing and neighboring tones for the most part), as well as some almost arbitrary in nature. Additional intervallic structures can be found. For example, at the end of measure 34 appears a full triad *g–b–e*. This e_3^6 moves by stepwise motion to F_5^8. Notice that the major third *g–b* "resolves" to the perfect fifth *f–c*, and that the major sixth *g–e*, "resolves" to the octave.

ex. 3-10

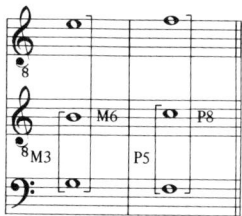

This follows the general principle stated on page 60, that imperfect consonances resolve to perfect consonances. In this case we see two imperfect consonances occurring at the same time, thereby creating a full triad.

This combined use of the M3—P5 and M6—P8 is commonly called a **double-leading-tone cadence.** Notice that the final cadence of this piece utilizes the same cadence.

ex. 3-11

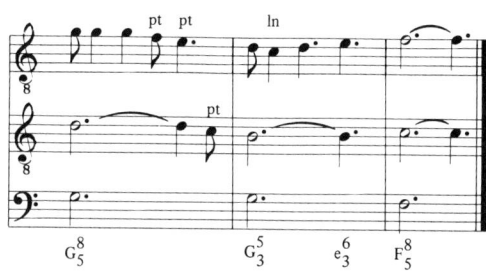

Root movement—the interval relationships between adjacent roots—can tell you a great deal about the actual sound of the piece. Root movement of a second sounds different from that of a third or fourth. In this piece you will find a predominance of root movement by seconds, occasionally with movement by a third. Root movement by fourth and fifth is not found. The vertical interval structure is another important determinant of the sound of the piece. In this case it is usually $\frac{8}{5}$, only occasionally $\frac{5}{3}$ or $\frac{6}{3}$, and no examples of $\frac{6}{4}$.

We have not yet discussed the form of the piece as a whole. As in the previous motet, there is rhythmic repetition in the tenor line. In the first 36 measures, there is a single pattern repeated every four measures:

ex. 3-12

Isorhythmic technique, on which this motet is based, combines a repeated rhythmic pattern, the *talea*, with a repeated melodic line, or *color*. In this case the simple talea is combined with a color that lasts for the entire 36 measures.

ex. 3-13

From measure 37 to the end, the color is repeated. However, all of the rests are removed from the tenor line, creating one long flow of dotted half notes. This change also produces a corresponding change in texture, with a fuller sound as a result of the constant use of three voices. In addition, there is less use of the divisions of five and seven in the triplum. The use of full triads also increases, though not dramatically.

Therefore, the overall piece is divided into two large sections, measures 1–36 and 37–63. The arrangement and length of each part probably had a special significance to Petrus. There is a basic numerological design to the piece: *three* notes per phrase in the isorhythm, 27 (3 × 3 × 3) notes in the entire color, 9 (3 × 3) repetitions of the isorhythmic phrase of four bars, a first section of 36 (3 × 3 × 2 × 2) measures and a last section of 27 (3 × 3 × 3) measures. The number 3 is thus of special importance throughout the organizational structure of the piece. Its significance could very well be related to the Christian theological notion of the Trinity, the three-in-one God.

This **numerological basis** of proportional designs for art is seen in many pieces in the Middle Ages. This concept can be traced as far back as the Greeks, and possibly even to the Egyptians; examples can be found in every succeeding century, including our own. This concept of substructure gives us a fascinating glimpse into the composer's mind, and perhaps into his philosophical perspective of the world. It is well worth our while to consider all aspects of a piece—musical, technical and structural—to try to understand as much as possible about the piece. Only in this way can we reveal the intentions and perceptions of the composer.

STYLE CHARACTERISTICS: THIRTEENTH CENTURY
based on *Deo confitemini/Domino* from the Las Huelgas Codex
and Petrus de Cruce, *Aucun/Lonc tans/Annuntiantes*

texture	two and three voices, with three predominating
harmony	within three-voice texture the prominent interval structures are: $^8_1$, $^8_5$, $^5_3$ • beginning usage of $^5_3$ and $^6_3$ (usually reserved for cadences) • interval use: primarily P5, P8, and unison at beginnings and endings of phrases • root movement: generally by second, occasionally by third, very rarely by fourth or fifth
melody	smooth, generally diatonic, with few accidentals • leaps are balanced by motion in the opposite direction • lines often "turn" around a particular note, giving it a special emphasis
rhythm	triple • some usage of five, seven, and nine divisions of the beat, but only in the triplum • syncopation is prevalent (especially ♪ ♩, from the second rhythmic mode) • stratification of the parts (top faster than bottom)
dissonance	mostly passing and neighboring tones, sometimes delayed and extended to produce pungent clashes
cadences	double-leading-tone cadence
techniques	successive counterpoint, isorhythm, borrowed melody

Glossary

Clausula   a section of Notre Dame organum in which the chant line moves faster rhythmically. There is usually a repetitive rhythmic scheme in the tenor voice. When text is added to the upper voice, the result is the early-thirteenth-century motet.

Color   the repetitive melodic pattern in isorhythmic tenors.

Dissonnance   harmonic intervals of a M2, m2, M7, m7, and tritone (d5 and A4).

Double-leading-tone cadence   M3—P5 and M6—P8. Also can be expressed as m$^6_3$—$^8_5$. A cadence in which the bottom voice moves down by whole step and the two top voices up by half step, creating an $^8_5$ construction. The top voices provide leading tones to the fifth and octave of the final construction.

Duplum   the voice above the tenor; the second voice in a motet.

Imperfect consonance   harmonic intervals of a M3, m3, M6, and m6.

Isorhythm   a compositional technique based on the strict repetition of a rhythmic pattern and a melodic pattern in the tenor line (and sometimes the upper voices) of a motet. It is found in many motets of the thirteenth, fourteenth, and early fifteenth centuries.

Motet   originally a clausula in which text had been added to the upper voice. Later, a two- or three-voice piece with multiple texts, (usually) based on a borrowed liturgical tenor.

Neighboring tone   a dissonant pitch that is approached by step and left by step in the opposite direction.

Passing tone   a dissonant pitch that is approached by step and left by step in the same direction.

Perfect consonance   harmonic intervals of a P8, P5, P4, and unison.

Root movement   the distance or interval between the roots of two successive harmonies.

Successive counterpoint   a compositional process consisting of writing each melodic line in its entirety before composing the next line above it. Used extensively in the thirteenth and fourteenth centuries.

Talea   the repetitive rhythmic pattern in isorhythmic tenors.

Tenor   the name of the lowest voice of motets and other pieces in the thirteenth, fourteenth, and early fifteenth centuries.

Triadic structure   the expression of the intervals *above* the lowest note in the construction. In the thirteenth century it is typically $^8_5$, $^5_3$, $^6_3$, or, occasionally, $^6_4$.

Triplum   the name for the voice above the duplum, the third voice.

Suggested Exercises

1. Using the given chant line and rhythmic pattern for the tenor line, write a two-part motet using isorhythmic technique. Label each harmonic interval and all neighboring tones.

ex. 3-14

2. Compose a line above the given tenor. Label all harmonic intervals and dissonances.

ex. 3-15

3. Analyze the following three-part motet from the Bamberg Codex for intervals, phrases, cadences, triads, root movement, dissonance, and overall construction. Try to hear the motet mentally, at a tempo approximately ♩. = 60.

[Haec Dies]

Las Huelgas Codex Petrus de Cruce **69**

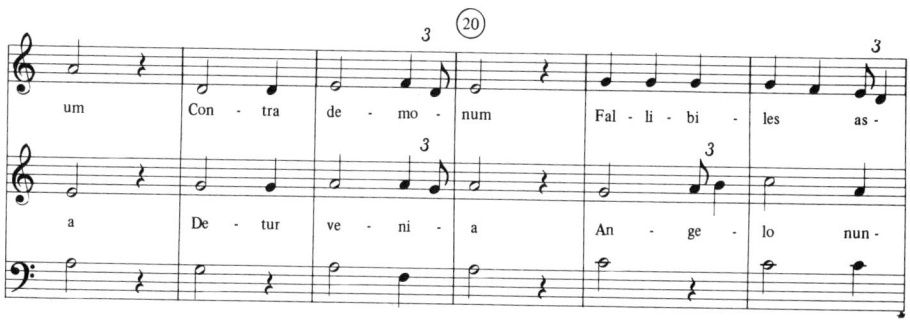

Before Reading Chapter 4

1. Listen to *Bone pastor* by Machaut (page 69) several times.
2. Analyze the pitch and rhythmic structure of the tenor (bottom) line of the motet. Note any repetitions and/or changes that occur.
3. Give an account of bass motion and interval structure in the entire piece.
4. Sing each line separately, then play and sing together.

4

Guillaume de Machaut

Bone Pastor

The beginning of the fourteenth century produced substantial changes in music. Many older concepts of sound continued, but in at least three respects the era labelled **Ars Nova** (the New Art) deserves its name: 1) a fundamental change in the use of rhythm and meter, from triple domination of meter and pulse to the inclusion of duple meter; 2) an increased use of harmonic thirds, producing greater triadic use; 3) an extensive development of the principle of isorhythm.

Although Philippe de Vitry lent the period its name through his treatise *Ars Nova*, it is Guillaume de Machaut in France (ca. 1300–1377) and Francesco Landini in Italy (1325–1397) who are considered the major composers of the era. The motet *Bone pastor* by Machaut displays the basic features of mid-fourteenth-century motet and can serve as a touchstone for the period.

There are three important differences between this motet and those of the previous century. The two upper voices are more or less equal in rhythmic character. The meter is duple, not triple. And the tenor (bottom voice), although in longer note values, is organized in a complex arrangement of rhythms, forming the structural underpinning of the piece (and probably the beginning-point for the composer as well).

Although it is often good to consider many aspects of a piece at once—linear, vertical, and structural—it is necessary in this piece first to understand the use of the ***isorhythmic principle.*** The tenor melody is borrowed from a chant, the "bone pastor" portion of the sequence *Lauda Sion*. It is repeated in the motet every 48 measures. The entire melody is given below.

ex. 4-1

The color is organized rhythmically by a specific talea. The talea used by Machaut is more complicated than the simple pattern found in the Petrus example in the last chapter. It is constructed primarily of long note values, and displays a variety of rhythmic patterns.

ex. 4-2

The initial process for the composer is to combine the talea and color into a single tenor line. From the outset, Machaut was obviously well aware that the number of notes in the color was twice that of the note units in the talea.

ex. 4-3

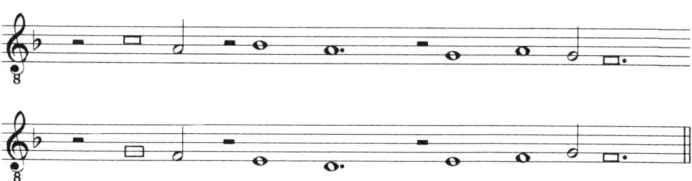

Every 24 measures there is a repetition of the talea, and every 48 measures a repetition of the color. There are, therefore, four taleae and two colores in the first 96 measures of the piece. In measure 97 a change occurs in the tenor: the original note values are replaced by shorter ones. By comparing this passage to the earlier measures, it can be seen that the new values are simply one-half the original values. They are thus, we say, in ***diminution.***

ex. 4-4

It will be noticed that in the remainder of the piece the tenor is constructed as in the beginning, with four taleae (each in diminution) and two colores. The entire structure of the isorhythmic tenor is seen below.

	96 bars				46 bars			
colores:	48		48		24		22	
taleae:	24	24	24	24	12	12	12	10

Although complicated on the surface, the premise is quite simple: a basic two-to-one proportion. Compare this to the form of the Petrus example in the previous chapter.

This rhythmic-melodic formulation serves as the basic underlying structure of the piece and is typical of many motets in this period. It should be noted, though, that there are other compositional principles and structures used in this century. Isorhythmic motets constitute one genre among many.

Attention should be turned to the rhythmic structure of the final portion of the piece, where the diminution of the talea begins (measures 97 and following). If one compares the rhythm of the triplum in measures 97–108 to that in measures 109–120, the similarity will be immediately noticed. Only measures 102 and 114 are slightly different. The same is true of the duplum as well.

ex. 4-5

The repetition begins in the upper voices at the same point as in the tenor. The name for this procedure—when *all* voices of a motet utilize isorhythmic technique—is **panisorhythm**. In the upper voices, however, there is no predetermined melodic line.

The entire second part of the piece is panisorhythmic. The first section, measures 1–96, is only partially so. A suggestion of rhythmic repetition can be seen in passages beginning at measures 25 and 49; although they do not contain rhythmic repetition, these passages certainly imply panisorhythm.

ex. 4-6

Note that the beginnings and ends of these two passages are rhythmically the same. In the middle the repetition is dropped, allowing greater development. The remainder of this first section should be analyzed for panisorhythmic tendencies.

This isorhythmic/panisorhythmic principle is an important constructional premise of the piece. It is certainly of strong importance for the composer in his ordering of compositional material. But is it heard? Can you detect this underlying, complicated structure when listening to the piece? Probably only in a very general way. It certainly helps to give the piece unity, and it seems to control the musical action to a great extent. In addition, certain of its features are certainly aurally evident, such as the change in measure 97, in which diminution has a decidedly stimulating effect on the listener. Although isorhythmic procedure is probably more an intellectual idea than an auditory one, its importance cannot be ignored. It is a primary method of organizing and presenting material in the fourteenth and fifteenth centuries.

Then what *is* heard? Taking ideas one by one, we can reconstruct the auditory effect. Certainly the melodic activity is paramount. Both the individual and collective lines create a fluid and continuous motion. Melodically, though, there is not as strong a progression forward through space as can be found in the rhythm (especially in the upper two voices). Note the opening line of the triplum:

ex. 4-7

Here we see triadic motion at the beginning followed by a continual revolving around the note *g*. This type of embellishing is a typical feature of this period, and affects not only the melody, but also the harmony and structure of the piece.

The **rhythmic motion** in the opening is important because of the compression of rhythmic values: 𝅗𝅥 becomes 𝅘𝅥 becomes 𝅘𝅥𝅮, followed by a cadence:

ex. 4-8

The solidity of the opening measure is important in launching the piece. The stability of longer notes is very important. This is then developed by the reduction of values begun in measures 3 and 4, finally brought to a cadence in measure 5.

ex. 4-9

The upper two lines almost always move in the same register, with frequent overlapping. Their rhythmic activity is complementary: When one voice moves in slower note values, the other moves faster in order to keep the flow of the piece constant. The tenor functions, much of the time, as a slowly-changing drone around which the other voices move. This is a very important feature of the isorhythmic style. The tenor, because of its register and its slower-moving nature, determines much of the harmonic activity. If the lower voice remains on one note for an extended period, the upper voices must "mark time" around a given pitch or pitches, creating a kind of harmonic stasis, until the next note of the tenor.

Machaut still utilizes the successive-counterpoint technique of previous centuries, composing the tenor first, then adding the duplum and triplum successively. There is somewhat more emphasis on the intervals of the third and sixth than in earlier composers. Most longer phrases still begin and end on perfect consonances, with the imperfect consonances used in the middle of the phrase. Full triads are used more ($\frac{5}{3}$ and $\frac{6}{3}$ mostly, with $\frac{6}{4}$ still used infrequently) but the predominant sound is still the $\frac{8}{5}$ arrangement.

Very quickly, in measure 2, Machaut reaches a full major triad, C_3^5. He hovers around this, because of the held tenor c, then moves in measure 6 to A_5^8, then to $B\flat_3^5$, g_3^6 and A_5^8 (measure 10), and finally to a cadence on G_3^5 in measure 14. This vacillation between $\frac{8}{5}$ and $\frac{5}{3}$ chords continues throughout the piece, emphasizing both the open sonorities and the "filled in" triadic sound.

Looking carefully, one cannot view the piece as a chordal, triadic conception. The impetus is most definitely linear—each line flows in a specified direction, albeit in a highly embellished fashion. Still, the upper lines are always consonant with the tenor. The conjunction of triplum/duplum/tenor in specific harmonies may not have been the primary consideration for Machaut, but he certainly knew when a triad was sounded, even if it was achieved through linear means.

The level of ***triadic use,*** especially the $\frac{5}{3}$ configuration, is much higher than in previous centuries, thereby giving the piece a decidedly new sound. In addition, there is the important use of triads in first inversion. In each case the linear motion is the most important consideration.

ex. 4-10

In each of the above examples (condensed from the piece) there is strong linear motion, since all voices move by step. There is also very consistent intervallic motion: thirds always expand to fifths, and sixths expand to octaves. However, the inner construction of each is different.

The first example demonstrates a general principle of moving a first-inversion triad outward. The outer voices move in contrary motion. There is no half-step leading tone motion. In Example 4–11, a similar motion appears, but the leading tones in both of the upper voices give the resolution a much greater impetus.

ex. 4-11

This is the common M6—P8 and M3—P5 combination found in the previous century—the ***double-leading-tone cadence.***

In Example 4–12, the upper two voices move upward by a whole step instead of a half step as before. The bottom voice moves down by *half step* (upper leading tone) instead of the whole step used in the normal double-leading-tone cadence. Since the last bass note sounds, temporarily at least, like the final of the mode, the use of the semitone above it is reminiscent of the Phrygian mode.

ex. 4-12

In simplified form,

ex. 4-13

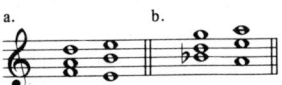

An interesting prospect would be to combine the upper and lower leading tones and resolve to the octave. Machaut indeed does this in measures 56–58.

ex. 4-14

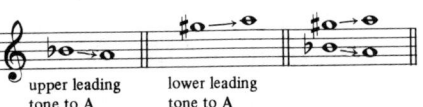

If the third voice is added, the progression is

ex. 4-15

The two leading tones create the dissonance of the augmented sixth: $b^\flat$–$g\sharp$. The resolution is "proper" in the sense that both leading tones resolve to their prospective note of resolution, *a*. This is a very early example of the so-called augmented-sixth chord, which was not widely used until the late Baroque period (after 1680). Even then the conception was from a linear impetus.

Machaut understands the use of rhythmic devices and their effect on musical progression. This motet, like most of his others, fairly bristles with rhythmic vitality.

The technique of diminution has been mentioned. Another frequent aspect of rhythmic construction appears in the way the individual line moves rhythmically from a point of repose to rapid activity and then back to repose. Melodic and harmonic features contribute to this.

ex. 4-16

Starting with a longer note, shorter notes immediately follow, producing an increasing intensity. The rhythm pushes forward through measure 58, but is retarded in measures 59 and 60. However, the upper lines create melodic (and harmonic) tension by means of the leading tones to *d* and *g* in the same two bars. The effect of the slower rhythm is thus countered by the melodic leading-tone activity. The cadence on *g* is therefore clearly heard.

ex. 4-17

On the phrase level the rhythm must be viewed as a function of the harmonic construction. All voices tend to move to and from strong points of cadence in the tenor. The harmonic motion is established from this basis and the rhythmic vitality of the piece mirrors it.

One of the most rhythmically complex areas in the piece is in the last section, beginning with the diminution of the talea. As if to mirror the shift in the talea, the upper two voices increase their own complexity with much shifting rhythmic interchange. There are many places where the line contains rapid alternation between the two voices, one resting while the other sings.

ex. 4-18

There is rather jarring syncopation in each individual line, but the cumulative effect is even stronger. The term for this process of rapid alternation of voices is **hocket.**

The effect of the melodic, harmonic, and rhythmic motion in the piece is greatly determined by the structural premise set up in the isorhythm. The ideas of Machaut are almost predetermined in the isorhythmic/panisorhythmic procedure and in his handling of it. The ideas of limited stasis and of limited harmonic activity throughout are a direct result of the isorhythm. The points of rest in the talea with their long pauses help to project this, in conjunction with its long note values.

An important concept for the composers of this era, and one that creates numerous problems for modern musicians, is *musica ficta.* Briefly, it is the use, by performers, of accidentals which are not actually written in the music. Early composers assumed that certain notes would be raised or lowered by performers, depending on their musical context; since the composer assumed that the musician would recognize where and when to place these accidentals, he did not add them to the score. The problem for modern performers is that we are so far removed from the style period that it is difficult to be sure of the proper placement of the musica ficta.

In most scholarly editions the accidentals *above* the notes are those suggested by the editor as musica ficta. The accidentals written beside the noteheads in the normal way were actually put there by the composer. The distinction to remember is that the former are suggestions by the editor, with whom you may or may not agree, but the latter are not to be questioned because the composer specifically included them in the music.

STYLE CHARACTERISTICS: MIDDLE FOURTEENTH CENTURY
based on Machaut, *Bone Pastor*

melody	smooth, with few leaps • frequently centering around a pitch in an embellishing fashion
harmony	root movement by second and third, rarely by fourth or fifth • intervallic construction: $^8_5$, $^5_3$, $^6_3$ • phrases begin and end on $^8_5$ or $^8_1$ • double-leading-tone cadence is the primary cadence • Phrygian cadence also employed • double leading tones used: upper and lower leading tones used extensively
rhythm	duple and triple division of the pulse • duple and triple meter are both used • syncopation and hocket are both primary rhythmic devices
dissonance	passing tones • neighboring tones • other types of dissonance almost capricious at times
techniques	isorhythm • panisorhythm • hocket • diminution • augmentation

Glossary

Ars nova   the New Art; designation for a musical period beginning in the early fourteenth century. The preceding period of the twelfth–thirteenth centuries was referred to as the Ars Antiqua.

Augmentation   the process of multiplying rhythmic values by two, three, four, etc.

Color   the repetitive melodic pattern in isorhythmic tenors.

Diminution   the process of dividing rhythmic values by a half, third, quarter, etc.

Double-leading-tone cadence   M3—P5 and M6—P8; Also can be expressed as m$^6_3$—$^8_5$. A cadence in which the bottom voice moves down by whole step and the two top voices up by half step, creating an $^8_5$ construction. The top voices provide leading tones to the fifth and octave of the final construction.

Hocket   the process of breaking up a melodic line between two or more voices.

Isorhythm   a compositional technique based on the strict repetition of a rhythmic pattern (talea) and melodic pattern (color) in the tenor line of a motet.

Lower leading tone   the note a semitone below the tonic.

Musica ficta   accidentals added to music in performance, but not actually notated by the composer; often used at cadences to insure a half-step leading tone, or used to avoid the tritone.

Panisorhythm   isorhythmic procedure applied to all voices of a motet simultaneously. Unlike the tenor, the upper voices do not have a repeating melody (color) but only a repeating rhythm (talea).

Phrygian cadence   a type of modal cadence in which the bottom voice moves down by half step and the upper voices move up by whole step. Found naturally in the Phrygian mode, but can be found transposed as well.

Talea   the repetitive rhythmic pattern in isorhythmic tenors.

Upper leading tone   the note a semitone above the tonic.

Suggested Exercises

1. With the given chant line, compose a two- or three-part motet using isorhythmic procedure. It should be at least 25–30 measures long, with a strong modal cadence in at least two places including the final cadence. The final two notes should only be used at the final cadence, in order to effect a modal cadence.

ex. 4-19

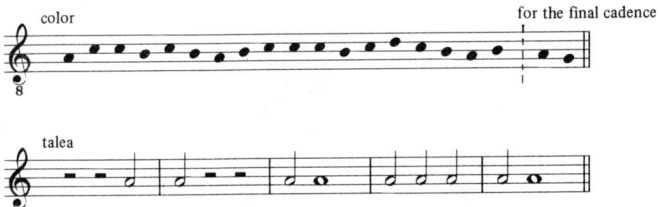

Note all interval structures, roots and any dissonance used.

2. Write double-leading-tone cadences which end on the pitches *d, c, g,* and *f*. Write Phrygian cadences which end on the pitches *a* and *e*.
3. Analyze the following motet for root movement and interval structure. Identify specifically all dissonance used.

Fins cuers doulz

Machaut

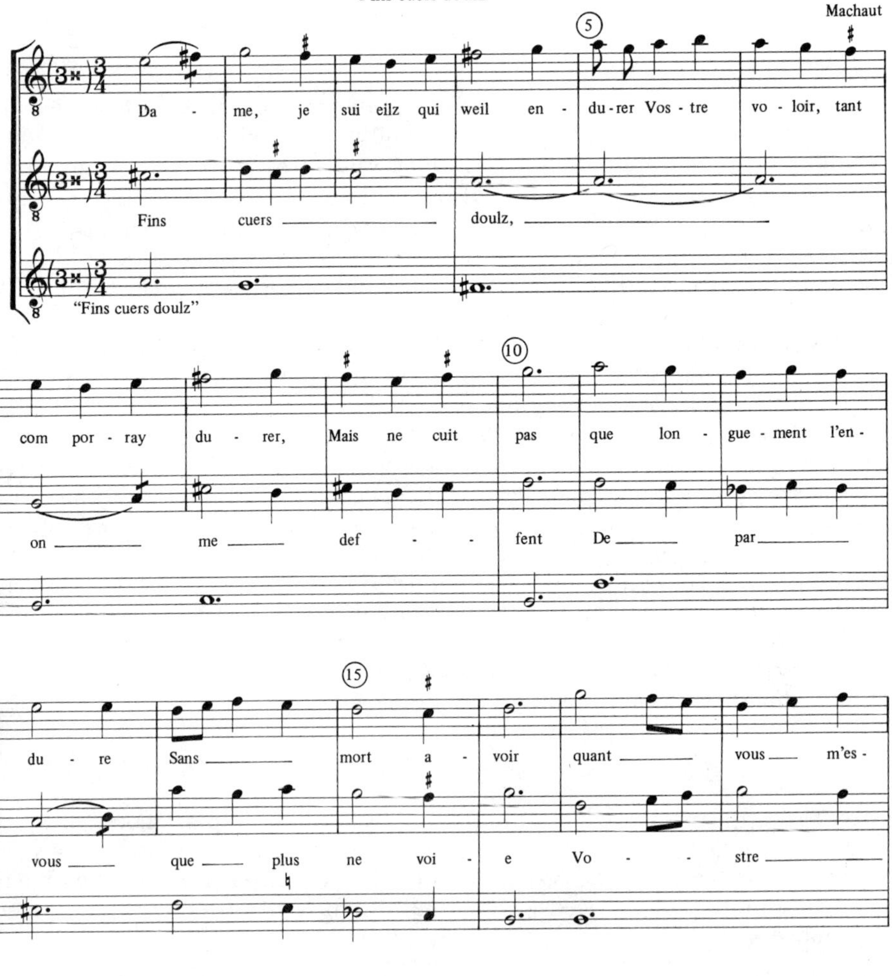

Guillaume de Machaut

© 1977, Margarita Hansen; used by permission.

Before Reading Chapter 5

1. Listen to *Ave maris stella* by Dunstable.
2. Sing the chant (shown above the polyphonic hymn) and study the intervals, cadential motion, and arrival points.
3. Sing the top line of the polyphonic hymn, and analyze it in relation to the chant.

AVE MARIS STELLA

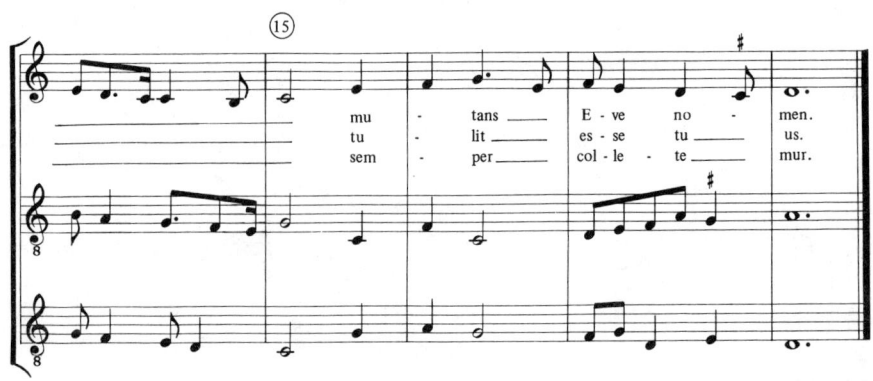

5
John Dunstable

Ave maris stella

Many changes in musical style took place in the late fourteenth and early fifteenth centuries, some of which had lasting effects. By studying and listening to the Dunstable example, it is easy to identify some of the changes: the duple division of the pulse, equality of parts both rhythmically and melodically, more use of the "sweet sound" of thirds and sixths, a discarding of the rigid isorhythmic structure in the tenor to be replaced by a fluid, faster-moving, freely composed bass.

At first glance, the piece may not appear to be based on the chant above it. With more careful examination, however, one can find in it strong traces of the *Ave maris stella* chant. The full chant is used in the top voice of the polyphonic hymn.[1] Considering the totality, this is a most important shift. The top voice has traditionally been the most melodic and, therefore, the most prominent voice.

---

[1] Although this piece and many others use the chant in a voice other than the bottom one, it should not be assumed that this was the only method at this time. Isorhythmic motets in the manner of Machaut were still being composed, but no longer were the most important genre.

With Dunstable (ca. 1385–1453) (and slightly earlier composers as well) we find that the melody is derived from chant, and indeed follows the original chant line very closely. The difference between using the borrowed chant in the top line and using it in the bottom line is significant. The sound of the piece is considerably altered now that the composer is freer to choose his own harmonic direction by composing his own bass line.

A few notes have been added to the chant, usually for embellishment of the cadence or to pass smoothly from one chant note to another, but the effect is close to the original. This procedure is called *paraphrase technique* and is used by composers in this and later periods.

Note that the **cadential levels** of the chant are followed exactly in the polyphonic version: A–D–C–D. Thus the chant helps determine the compositional direction and define the forward motion. Each cadence is carefully prepared rhythmically, melodically, and harmonically. The *musica ficta* in each case should be followed, for it adds the half-step leading tone to each cadence, thereby heightening the cadential effect.

The change in rhythm from a triple division of the beat to a duple division is one of the most obvious changes from an auditory point of view. The "squareness" of duple is quite striking after the considerable historical preeminence of triple division. It also leads the way to a more intricate and subtle use of syncopation. The syncopation in this piece is typical of the period. Measures 4 and 9 in the top voice are good examples. The delaying action of the syncopation adds extra energy to the line, and the forward thrust is greatly enhanced as a result.

The piece can be viewed as largely **homophonic.** Although the surface may present a somewhat contrapuntal nature, with interestingly independent voices, the sound of the piece is much more chordal than in previous examples we have seen. The following reduction gives a clearer idea of the background level of the harmonic progression.

ex. 5-1

ex. 5-2

As can be seen, when the embellishing tones have been eliminated the homophonic underpinning becomes clear. Dissonance of any kind—passing, neighboring, or other types (which we will cover shortly)—tends to obscure the underlying harmonic scheme. This does not mean that dissonance is undesirable, however; on the contrary, it is often the character and the life of the piece. But if we cannot differentiate between the harmony and what is dissonant to it, the clarity of the piece will be lost.

Before proceeding further, there are two more types of dissonance that must be understood. The fifteenth century was the beginning of the real codification of dissonance usage. Dissonance began to be used in certain specific ways, and exceptions to these established procedures became more and more rare. From this point in history certain types of dissonance were used in a clear fashion. Others were gradually added as possibilities, but the structure and use of dissonance was kept clear and well defined from this time onward.

Two dissonances that were emphasized in the early fifteenth century were the **escape tone** and the *suspension*. The escape tone (called *echappée* in some textbooks) is a dissonance that is approached by step and left by leap often in the opposite direction. It is rhythmically weak, as are the passing tone and neighboring tone.

ex. 5-3

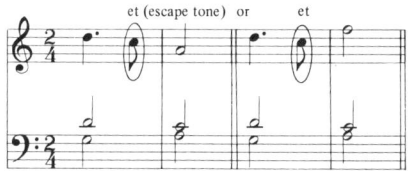

A clear example of an escape tone in the Dunstable hymn is in measure 4 of the top voice. Everything is consonant except the final c^2. It is rhythmically weak, approached by step and left by leap. Other escape tones are labelled in measures 3 and 6.

ex. 5-4

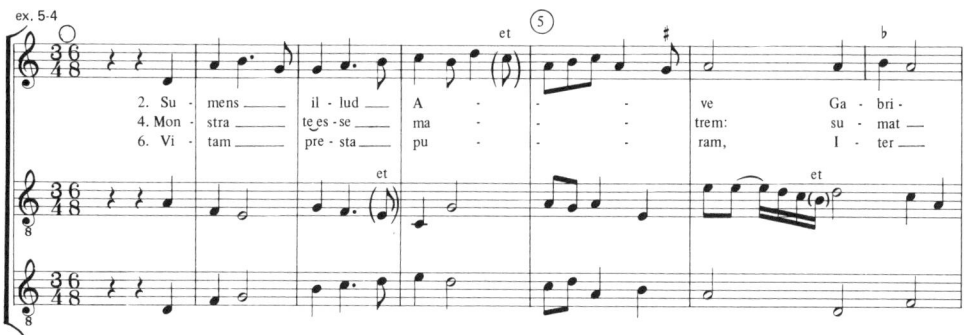

The *suspension* is one of the most important dissonances from the fifteenth century through the nineteenth century. It consists of three parts: preparation, suspension, and resolution.

	preparation	suspension	resolution
occurs on:	weak beat	strong beat	weak beat
harmonic quality:	consonant	dissonant	consonant

With only one exception, the suspension occurs in an upper voice and *always* resolves downward by step, thereby creating the following possible intervallic successions: 2–1, 4–3, 7–6, 9–8.

ex. 5-5

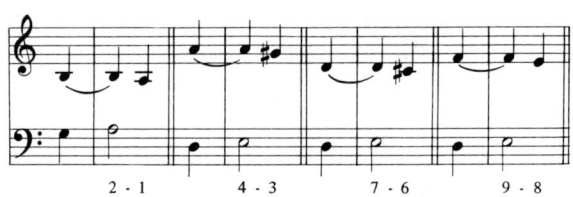

Note that the bass line moves to create the dissonance, and the other voice has its note *suspended* and then resolves. In a sense, then, it is simply a delayed consonance.

ex. 5-6

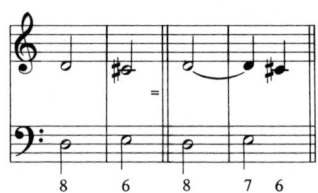

The suspension can occur in faster note values, still with the same sequence of preparation–suspension–resolution in their relative rhythmic positions.

ex. 5-7

This last example is from the Dunstable hymn, measures 17–18 (here only the top and bottom voices are given). It happens quickly but is nevertheless quite important aurally.

If two suspensions occur at the same time they are called a **double suspension.**

ex. 5-8

This can also be speeded up rhythmically, as in the Dunstable example, measures 9–10.

ex. 5-9

Suspensions of this type are found most often at cadences. They are common in the fifteenth century and continue to be used in the sixteenth century and later. (We will, however, see musical-theoretical changes that will alter their effect.) As in previous centuries, passing tones and neighboring tones are still used frequently.

Using these additional categories, all of the dissonance in this piece can be explained, allowing us to proceed to a discussion of harmonic use.

Looking only at the first six measures of the piece, we find that the **use of thirds** and full triads has increased dramatically from the fourteenth century. Almost every beat has a vertical third or third-plus-fifth. This accounts for the sweetness of sound so characteristic of this period. Dunstable was one of the first to emphasize this triadic sound, and influenced later composers greatly as a result.

Beginnings and endings of phrases, however, still maintain the open fifth-octave sound. No thirds are present in final cadences, and only on rare occasions can they be found in internal cadences (there are none in this piece, for example). Thus, although the full triad is gaining ground, it is still not used in all circumstances.

The **cadences** themselves are interesting, and point to the future. There are three important types that are prevalent in this early period: *double-leading-tone, single-leading-tone,* and *tonal* (V—I).

The double-leading-tone cadence had been used for over 200 years by the time of Dunstable. It was still the primary and most characteristic cadence in the early fifteenth century, as can be seen in measures 9–10 and in the final cadence, measures 17–18.[2]

[2] The indicated *musica ficta* should be employed, as this enhances the leading-tone effect and was probably intended by the composer.

ex. 5-10

The *single-leading-tone cadence* contains only a single leading tone, to the tonic pitch; motion to the fifth is by a whole-step progression. Instead of the M3-to-P5 and M6-to-P8 harmonic progression, we now find the m3 moving to a P5 and a M6 to a P8. Although this cadence is somewhat less frequent, especially at the final cadence, the result is striking.

ex. 5-11

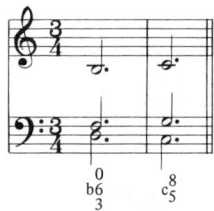

The harmonic progression, b_3^{o6} – C_5^8, is interesting. If c is considered the temporary tonic, then there is a b_6^o moving stepwise to it, or the seventh scale degree, VII_3^{o6}–tonic $_5^8$. The same motion occurs here as in the modal cadence—the linear function has changed but little. But even though the motion is still stepwise, the *sound* of the diminished triad is a powerful change.

Measures 14–15 of the Dunstable are perhaps the most complicated in the whole piece. The single-leading-tone cadence occurs on the final beat of the measure, resolving to c in the next measure. The difficulties arise in analyzing the dissonances, rather than the actual chords. Everything is consonant for four eighth notes (all parallel $_3^6$ chords). On the fifth eighth note the bass moves downward, creating 4–3 and 7–6 suspensions, both of which are resolved downward by step (properly). The final problem is the e in the duplum. This, however, is explainable as an escape tone: approached by step, left by leap. The cadence is then completed. The following will give a clearer idea of the underlying harmonic progression of the passage:

ex. 5-12

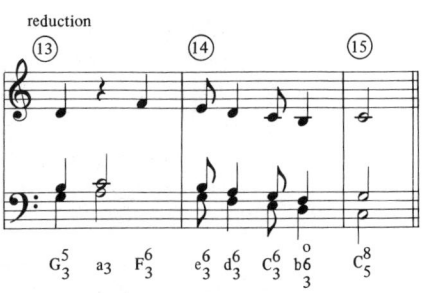

The other important cadence, especially from a historical point of view, is that which occurs in measures 5–6. The linear motion indicates a cadence on *A* (*g♯–a* and *b–a*), and a suspension (4–3 in the top voice) enhances the feeling of cadence. But, instead of a G♯-minor or diminished triad moving to the A$_5^8$, it is E major (the middle voice actually is the lowest sounding voice). This produces a root progression of *e–a*, a movement upward by a fourth. The name for this type of cadential root movement is **tonal**.

ex. 5-13

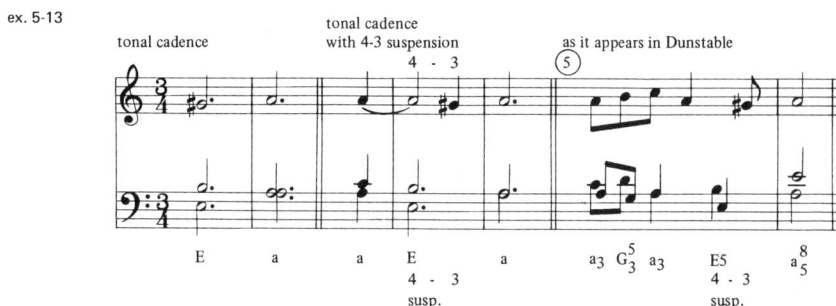

Tonal cadences become common toward the late fifteenth century, but can occasionally be found earlier. Their main importance is in the subsequent historical development of tonal music. The principle of the M6—P8 (with the g♯ leading tone) is still employed. However, the third note has radically changed the sound and function of the progression. This harmonic/cadential motion will ultimately shift the entire harmonic framework and change the fabric of harmonic writing and usage. The modal concepts gradually will be changed and replaced by tonal ones. This process, though, will take approximately 250 years to complete.

The change in the use of rhythm in this piece, as compared with the earlier fourteenth-century examples, is remarkable. The rhythm now produces a smoother flow, with rhythmic equality between the three voices. The duple division of the beat encourages this approach, as does the slower pulse. The result is a much more free-flowing, lyrical melodic line.

Along with the smoother rhythm overall, there remains the contrasting technique of **syncopation**. Syncopation refers to the shifting of the natural accent to another beat or to another part of the beat. In some cases it is rather slight, creating only a slight lilt.

ex. 5-14

In other cases it is more extended or quicker in its motion, creating greater tension and resulting in a stronger forward push to the line:

ex. 5-15

The syncopation in this example lasts an entire measure, and its complexity increases toward the end of the measure. Except for the downbeat, every note is off the beat. The tension is finally released in the cadence in the next measure.

The development of more controlled harmony and a greater emphasis on the dichotomy between consonance and dissonance are of utmost importance in this century. From the early fifteenth century onward there is an ever greater tendency toward harmonic control. That process culminates in the late sixteenth and seventeenth centuries.

A highly significant element has been introduced, if ever so slightly: the beginnings of tonal procedure. Both the single-leading-tone cadence (vii$^{o6}_{6}$—I) and the tonal cadence (V–I) imply an impetus toward a tonic pitch and the beginning of a specific relationship of triadic/chordal activity within that tonic framework. With these important harmonic developments, the early fifteenth century can be seen as the beginning of the Renaissance in music, and possibly even the true beginning of the tonal period.

STYLE CHARACTERISTICS: EARLY FIFTEENTH CENTURY
based on Dunstable's *Ave maris stella*

melody	basically smooth motion, few large leaps • strong cadences • motion toward the cadence greatly enhanced
rhythm	duple division of the pulse, predominantly, but triple meter • syncopation important—especially in the triplum
harmony	root movement by second and third still predominates • parallel $^6_3$ chords are frequently used • much more emphasis on the harmonic third • full triads are more common, but are not used at major cadences
cadences	double-leading-tone (still predominant) • single-leading-tone (used often, but not for important cadences) • tonal (used occasionally, rarely for final cadences)
dissonances	passing tones • neighboring tones • escape tones • suspensions • greater codification and more standard usage of dissonance
techniques	paraphrase • isorhythm and panisorhythm are still used for motets

Glossary

Double-leading-tone cadence   M3—P5 and M6—P8. Also can be expressed as m$^6_3$—$^8_5$. A cadence in which the bottom voice moves down by whole step and the two top voices up by half step, creating an $^8_5$ construction. The top voices provide leading tones to the fifth and octave of the final construction.

Double suspension   two suspensions occurring at the same time.

Escape tone   a dissonance which is approached by step and left by leap in the opposite direction; it is rhythmically weak.

Homophony   polyphonic texture in which the voices move rhythmically together, creating a series of chords.

Paraphrase technique   a compositional process of embellishing a chant melody melodically by adding or deleting pitches. In polyphonic music, rhythm is added as well. The line thus composed is usually used in the top voice (especially in the fifteenth century).

Single-leading-tone cadence   m3—P5 and M6—P8. Also can be expressed as $^o{}^6_3(\text{dim}^6_3)$—$^8_5$. This is a slight modification of the modal cadence. It contains a single leading tone to the octave, with a whole step up to the fifth in the middle voice, and a whole step down to the tonic in the lowest voice.

Suspension   the sustaining of one of the notes of a consonant interval while the other note moves so that the interval becomes dissonant, this dissonance then being resolved by the held note moving one step downward.

Syncopation   the temporary shifting of the normal metric accent or pulse accent.

Tonal cadence   V–I cadence, a cadence in which the root moves down a P5. The V chord must be major, since the third of the V chord functions as a leading tone to the tonic.

Suggested Exercises

1. Analyze *Quam pulcra es* by Dunstable (page 99) for the following:
   harmonic content (roots and vertical intervals)
   cadences
   dissonances
   phrase structure

2. Compose a two- or three-part piece, paraphrasing the given chant line in the top voice. Use $\frac{3}{4}$ meter. Check stylistic features, especially rhythm and intervallic use, against the Dunstable examples. Use the proper cadences, with appropriate leading tones.

3. Complete the following as indicated.

Suspensions in two voices. Write the second voice, supplying the suspension.

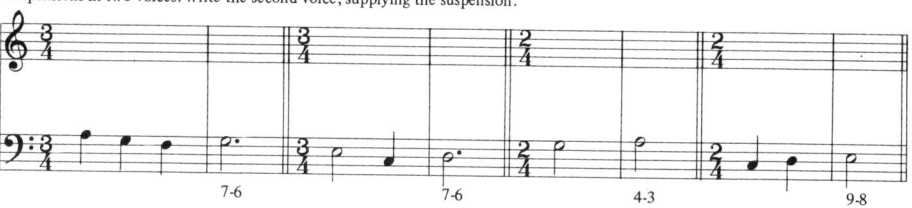

Escape tones in two voices. Write the escape tone where indicated by the asterisk.

Write the following cadences in three voices.

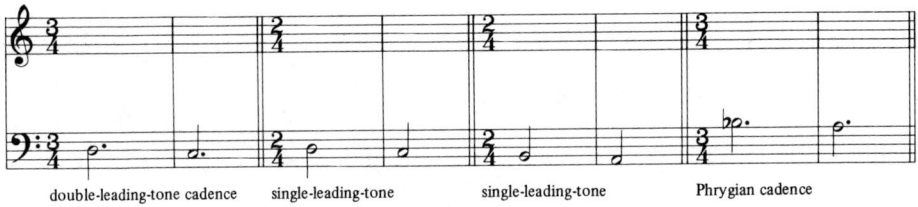

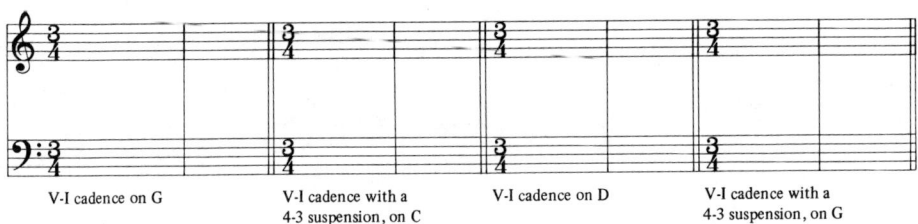

Before Reading Chapter 6

1. Listen to the *Agnus Dei* from the *Missa L'Homme Armé* by Dufay.
2. Sing and study the tenor line in the first "Agnus Dei" (pages 103–105).
3. Analyze the chord roots, interval structures, and dissonances from the beginning through measure 13, and from measure 120 to the end.
4. Sing the top line of *Ave maris stella* by Dufay (pages 112–113).
5. Analyze the phrase and cadence types.
6. Sing and play the top and bottom parts, together and separately.
7. Listen to a recording of the entire piece.

Agnus Dei from Missa L'homme Armé

Guillaume Dufay

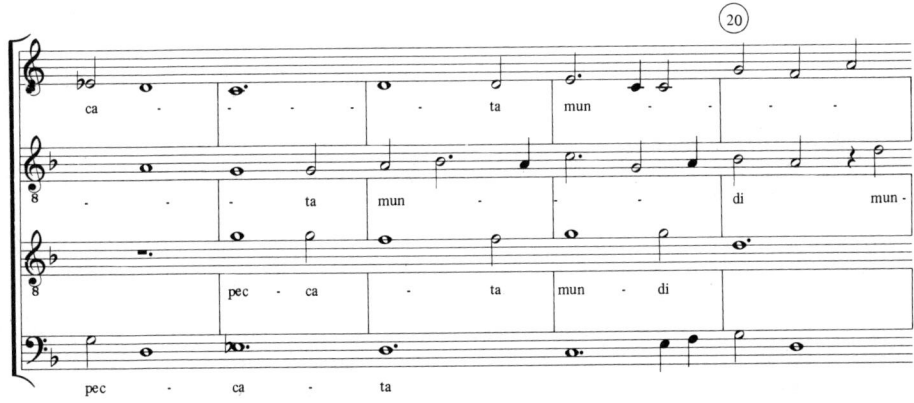

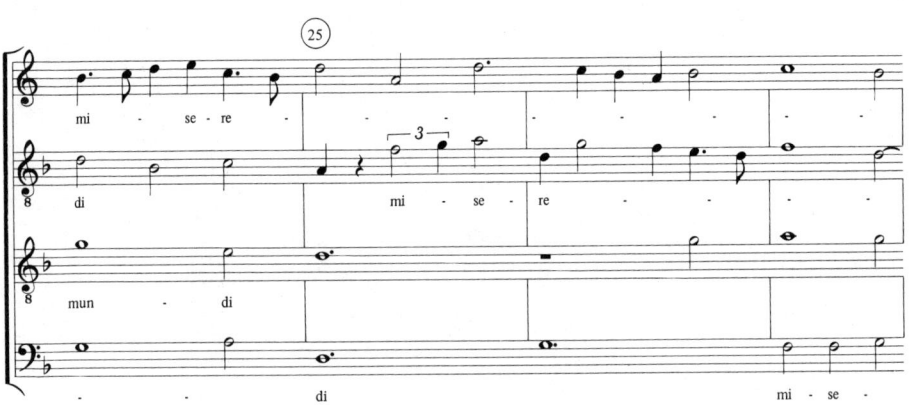

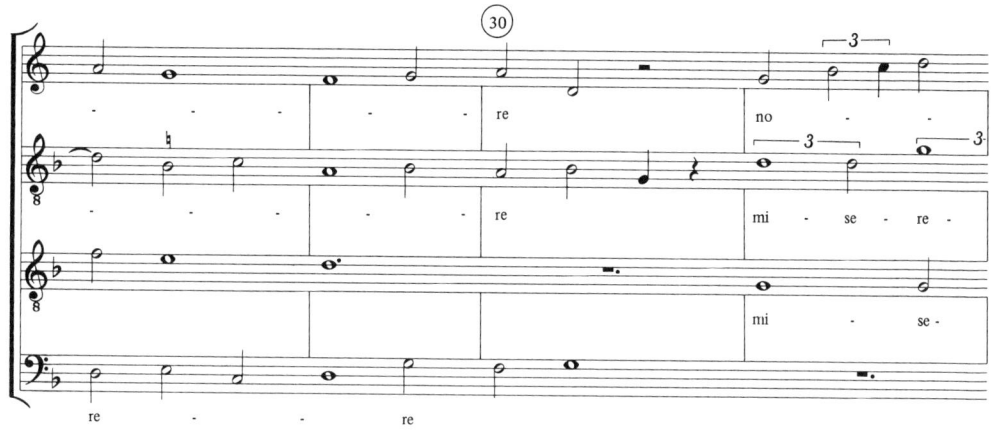
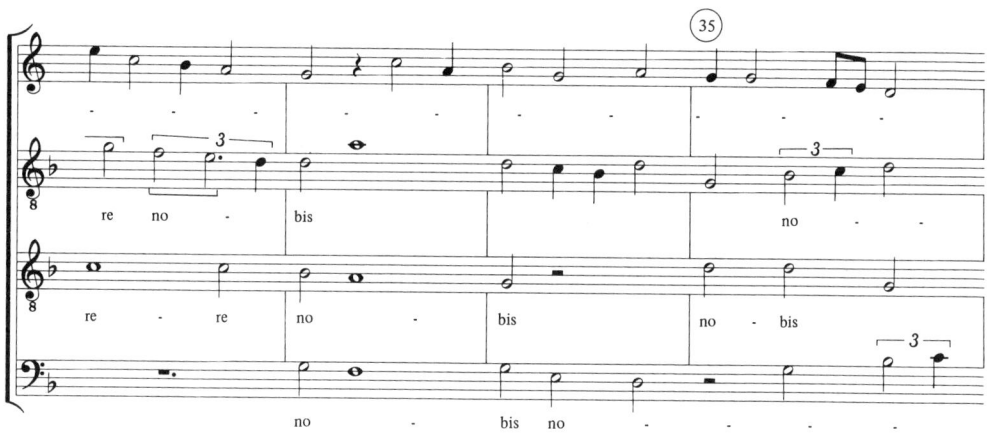

105

6

Guillaume Dufay

Agnus Dei
from the *Missa l'Homme Armé*

Ave maris stella

Although examples of four-part music existed before the mid-fifteenth century, it is not until then that pieces with more than three voices became standard. The addition of the fourth voice creates one major compositional problem: in a four-voice setting of a three-note triad, a note must be doubled. The process of doubling and of parallel and contrary motion of voices is important in understanding the composer's musical and technical process.

Guillaume Dufay was born approximately 100 years after Machaut, around the year 1400. The change in musical style and content between the two could not be greater. His early music was greatly influenced by Dunstable and earlier composers, while his later Masses took on a decidedly more personal character and direction. The major principle derived from Dunstable was the predominance of the third, a feature which was to be crucial to the development of Western music as a whole. Even in Dufay's own development we can trace a gradually more pervasive use of the third.

Dufay still observes the somewhat archaic practice of beginning and ending on a perfect consonance. In the body of the phrase, however, we find a gradual change in sound and process. (Frequently in music history we find innovations taking place "inside" a well-controlled premise.) Examine closely the next example (measures 5–13 of the *Agnus Dei I*).

ex. 6-1

The beginning and ending both use the open fifth and octave. In between there are full triads, with the harmony usually changing two or three times per measure. The dissonances are labelled, and are fairly straightforward and clear: passing tones, neighboring tones, escape tones, and suspensions. The suspensions are found at the cadence, a precedent that is carried further in later periods.

The pre-eminence of full triads radically changes the sound of the music. It is now our job to discover how this is accomplished. The basic principles of the doubling procedures, the use of inversions, and the construction of cadences must all be discussed and understood.

First of all, notice that all but three chords in the above example are in root position, and even these three are present only briefly. There are two brief triads in first inversion, in measures 7 and 8 and one in measure 9, and *no* triads in second inversion. This is a significant style feature of the period. It is usual to see a simple idea, root position triads, proceed to a relatively more complex one, first inversion triads, and gradually continue with the introduction of more complexity, second inversion.

The most common **doubling procedure** for root-position triads is to *double the root*. In every case except one (measure 9, final beat) this is true.

First-inversion triads are somewhat more flexible in terms of doubling, but a general rule could be to *double the soprano note*. This is done frequently, but is not as strong a principle as the preceding one for root position.

There are two cadences in this excerpt, a subsidiary one (measures 9–10) and a stronger one, more final in character (measures 12–13). The two cadential chords have similar doublings, and both are identical in this regard to the sonority at the end of measure 5—three roots and a fifth. This open sonority will be found for the most part at cadences, usually doubled in this way.

The strong **cadence** in measures 12–13 deserves our special attention, for it displays many of the primary characteristics of the period.

ex. 6-2

First and foremost is the root movement: D major to G (lacking a third). The root movement is by ascending fourth, a V–I motion. It is a **tonal cadence,** typical of late Dufay works, in which most of the internal cadences and many of the final cadences are tonal. Two other features of this cadence are significant as well: the use of a 4–3 suspension in the top voice (on the V chord), and the use of the **under-third.** The basic voice leading is by step, as in the past: *f♯–g* (the under third is an embellishment) and *a–g*. Notice the motion of the *d* in the bass. If this moved to *g*, there would be no fifth in the final chord. In addition, if it moved to *g* and the tenor *a* moved to the upper *d*, parallel fifths would result. The problem of parallel-fifth and parallel-octave motion between two voices came to composers' attention in the fifteenth century. It gradually became considered improper to use this motion, partly for the sake of the sound and partly because of a concern to preserve the independence of the parts. With parallel fifths or octaves, the effect is really that of doubling one line with another, not of writing two independent voices. Dufay's solution is the following:

ex. 6-3

Dufay gets around the problem by crossing voices—resolving the upper voices by step and shifting the bass up one octave. This is sometimes referred to as the **octave-leap cadence.**

The final cadence of this movement has much the same character, but the problem is solved in a different way.

ex. 6-4

This is another typical cadence of the period—V–I, with under-third motion in the soprano (as in the cadence just discussed). In this case the octave leap is not used, probably because the alto ascends to the fifth.

The most prominent **root movement** in the piece can be gleaned from a more detailed analysis of the movement. It will be seen that there are essentially three types of motion: root movement by second, occasionally by third within the body of the phrase, and by fifth (V–I) at the end of important phrases.

A V–I cadence is not accomplished simply by root movement. In addition, there must be a half-step leading tone in one voice (usually in the top) which produces a major V chord. Musica ficta is often indicated to create the leading tone of the V–I cadential progression.

Finally, notice Dufay's curious gesture at the ends of sections I and III of the *Agnus Dei*. The final measure of each utilizes the third of the triad prominently in the contra–tenor part—but it always moves back up to the fifth! It is almost as though his fervent wish is to end with a full triad, but convention stops him from doing so. Whatever his desire, this is an indication of a harmonic practice which is to take hold some 30–50 years after Dufay's death.

In a four-part setting, composers of this period tend to infuse the top line with a larger portion of the **melodic interest** and drive. Certainly this is true of the first "Agnus Dei." This "treble-dominated" style often produces a prominent melody, with shifting rhythms and marvelously controlled direction and shape, against a strong, slower-moving harmonic underpinning.

The first five measures of the superius demonstrates the strong melodic gestures of which Dufay is capable. As is usual in this period, he starts with a long note and sculpts a line which rises from tonic to dominant then falls back gradually to the tonic. There is rhythmic interest through syncopation, and a strong cadence employing the leading tone and the typical under-third motion. Note that the contra–tenor part is slower moving, providing strong support to the melody. With few exceptions, this relationship remains for the duration of the movement.

The second "Agnus Dei" is normally sung by soloists rather than the whole choir. Thus, Dufay has written parts which are more or less equal in complexity and interest and are quite difficult in certain of their rhythmic gestures.

The top voice in this section is quite complex, with much syncopation and a shifting duple-triple division of the pulse. Beginning in measure 57 the pulse is further blurred by the half-note triplets in the lowest voice.

ex. 6-5

Perhaps the most important structural device in this movement (used throughout this Mass as well as many others of the period) is **cantus firmus technique.** The principle is basically the same as other cantus-firmus pieces in other centuries, that is, a piece with a borrowed melodic line, but the execution, partly because of the four-voice setting, is somewhat different. The borrowed melody is used in its entirety in the tenor line but, unlike Machaut, there is a bass line below the tenor part. The rhythm is usually more free than in isorhythmic technique, and the line itself is more integrated into the texture.

The Mass is entitled ***L'Homme Armé*** after the fifteenth-century popular song upon which it is based. The melody lies in the tenor.

ex. 6-6

In this movement, the rhythm as well as the melody is retained, but in **augmentation.**

The addition of a bass line below the tenor creates not only a distinctive sound but a distinctive concept of construction. No longer is the borrowed melody automatically the lowest note. The addition of the bass line provides Dufay with the opportunity of creating his own harmonic sound within the piece. Ever mindful of the tenor line, the bass carves out a root progression that begins to be reflected in all of the upper parts. Always keep in mind, though, that the original impetus is linear; the bass simply provides a bit more opportunity for harmonic control.

The use of *L'homme armé* in the first "Agnus Dei" is straightforward: There is one complete presentation of the melody with no significant change in the melody line. In the second "Agnus Dei" the changes are radical. The entire melody is not used; instead, portions of the melody appear in short phrases—for example, measures 57–60 in the contra-bassus, 70–74 in the contra. In addition, the rhythm is modified at several points so as to obscure the melody, such as in measures 50 (last beat) to 56 and 62–69 in the contra.

ex. 6-7

Dufay adds the other voices in free counterpoint. The whole section is quite free and rhythmically complicated as a result. The harmonic rhythm—the rate of change of the harmony—is significantly faster than in the first "Agnus Dei."

ex. 6-8

The final "Agnus Dei," at a brief glance, does not seem to use the *L'homme armé* melody at all. However, the note by the composer, *canon: Cancer eat plenus sed redeat medius* [rule: The crab proceeds full and returns half], indicates that we should look closer. In doing so, two things emerge: The entire melody is used in the tenor from measure 113 to the end, and from measure 112 reading backwards (!) to the beginning of the piece, the entire melody can also be seen in the tenor! This reversal of direction is referred to as **retrograde** motion.[1] From measure 113 to the end, the melody is in diminution when compared to the beginning. This explains the above rule: The crab (retrograde) proceeds full (in full note values) and returns half (is presented forward in diminution). When the other voices are added they produce the most complex of the three large sections of the *Agnus Dei*. The ending has some of the fastest harmonic rhythm of the entire piece.

[1]Retrograde motion was referred to as "crab" motion in this period, the reference being to the walking pattern of that shellfish.

ex. 6-9

It is suggested that you study this piece further and in much greater detail. The root movement and dissonance treatment, along with the rhythms, cadences, and cantus firmus technique, produce a sound unlike that of any other period of music. The combination of all these factors form the basis of a period of musical growth which lasts for at least 150 years. In certain harmonic respects the procedures developed here lead directly to tonal music and beyond.

An unusual compositional idea to emerge in the fifteenth century is that of **fauxbourdon.** This technique is apparently derived from a kind of English organum called English discant. Presumably, English discant arrived in France from England via Dunstable in the early part of the century.

Traditionally, fauxbourdon has been considered to be motion by parallel $^6_3$ chords, though in actual fact this is a bit too simplistic. The first use of the technique of fauxbourdon was by Dufay. Dufay's pieces in fauxbourdon were constructed on two principles: the top voice was derived from a chant line (using paraphrase technique), and the middle voice was "improvised" a perfect fourth below the top voice. Therefore the composer only wrote the top and bottom parts and assumed that the middle part would be filled in.

Given the above facts, it is not hard to imagine the sound of such a piece. Since the composer assumes the perfect fourth between the top and middle voices, there are only two consonant notes for any lower voice: the octave or sixth below the top voice.

ex. 6-10

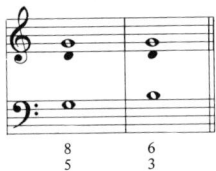

All other pitches will be dissonant with one or the other of the upper voices.

The composer now can write a two-part piece by creating a top voice of paraphrased chant and a bottom voice in mostly parallel motion with the top. With these principles in mind, we may now analyze the Dufay example (page 112).

The chant is easily discovered in the top voice, which has a phrase structure very similar to the chant, although the Dufay version is much more embellished. The bass line is usually an octave or sixth below the top; on occasion, however, it produces a dissonance, either in passing motion (as in measure 9) or by escape tone (as in measure 11).

The *cadences* are, as you might assume, always double-leading-tone or slightly modified.

ex. 6-11

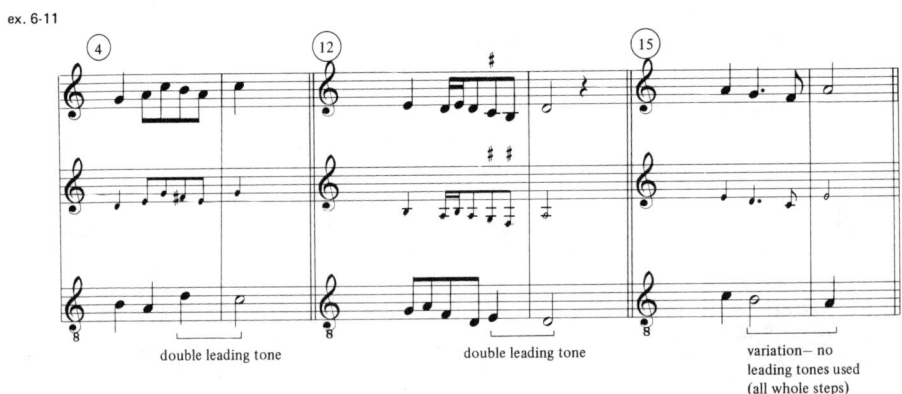

Among the dissonances which Dufay employs here is the escape tone. His typical escape tone is the under-third used at the cadence.

ex. 6-12

In this case, as is normal in fauxbourdon, there is a ***double under-third***. The same is true for suspensions in fauxbourdon, which will always be double suspensions because of the doubling effect of the middle voice.

STYLE CHARACTERISTICS OF THE MID TO LATE FIFTEENTH CENTURY
based on Dufay, *Agnus Dei* from the *L'Homme Armé* Mass, and *Ave maris stella*

melody	generally smooth • few skips larger than a third or fourth (occasionally a fifth)
harmony	mainly bass motion by second and third, but an increased use of descending fifth motion, especially at the cadence • full triads are used more frequently than before • root position and first inversion are prominent • second inversion is still infrequently used • cadences: V–I (tonal) and double-leading-tone (used less frequently than before)
dissonance	passing tones and neighboring tones • escape tones (especially under-thirds at cadences) • suspensions (especially 4–3 suspensions at cadences)
rhythm	triple meter • duple division of the pulse • basically smooth, but with areas of great syncopation
techniques	paraphrase • cantus firmus • fauxbourdon • isorhythm

Glossary

Augmentation   the process of multiplying rhythmic values by two, three, four, etc.

Cantus firmus technique   a compositional technique in which a borrowed melody (liturgical or secular) is quoted in the tenor voice.

Double under-third   two voices employing the under-third at the same time; usually occurs in a modal rather than a tonal cadence, and is mandatory in a piece using fauxbourdon technique (if the top voice uses the under-third).

Fauxbourdon   a fifteenth-century compositional technique which employs a top line, usually of paraphrased chant, and a bottom voice moving mostly in parallel sixths with the top voice, below, with an unwritten middle voice which exactly doubles the top voice a perfect fourth lower.

Harmonic rhythm   the speed and rhythmic pattern of harmonic change.

Octave leap cadence   V–I cadence in which the bottom voice moves up an octave to create the fifth of the next chord, while an inner voice (usually the tenor) moves down a step to the tonic, the bass of the final chord.

Retrograde   performance of a melody (or any musical entity) backwards.

Suspension   a dissonance that is prepared by the same note which is consonant in the preceding construction; the lowest voice moves to a strong beat making this pitch dissonant; the suspended note resolves downward by step on the weak beat.

Under-third   melodic motion at the cadence in which the leading tone moves down a second and then skips up a third to the tonic.

Suggested Exercises

1. Analyze *Se la face ay pale* by Dufay for the following:
   cadence—identify specifically
   root movement—root plus interval structure
   dissonance—label specifically

2. Complete the following as indicated.

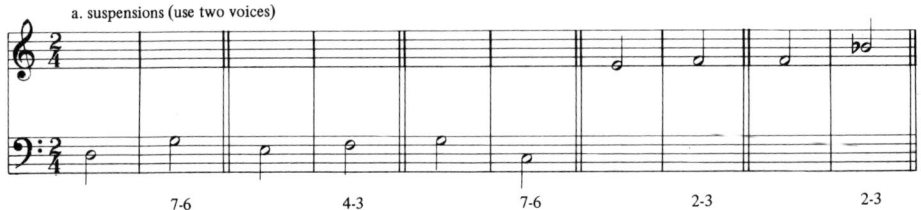

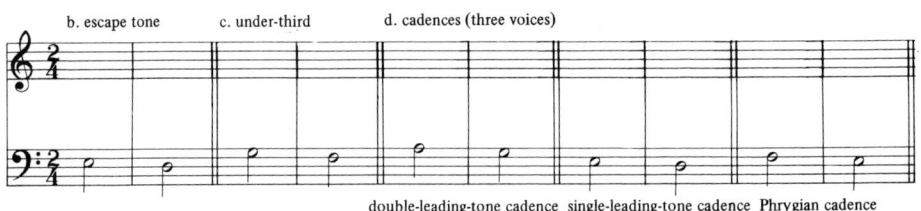

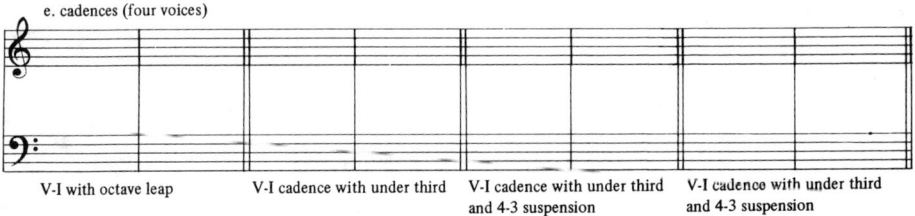

3. Compose a three-part fauxbourdon hymn on the given fragment of chant. Be careful to outline the cadences before beginning.

4. Complete the following in four parts, employing smooth voice motion and avoiding parallel fifths and octaves between any two parts.

Before Reading Chapter 7

Ave Maria by Josquin des Prez (pages 127–136)

1. Listen to the motet.
2. Sing and study the soprano line in measures 1 to 88.
3. Analyze the root movement in measures 94 to 108.
4. Note the types of cadence and dissonance throughout the piece.

Recordans de my segnora by Josquin des Prez (pages 136–137)

1. Sing and study the bass and alto lines throughout the piece. Then sing and compare the tenor and soprano lines.
2. Find and analyze the major cadences.
3. Find and identify the major sections of the piece.
4. Analyze the root movement in measures 1 to 10.
5. Why is the final note in the bass in brackets?

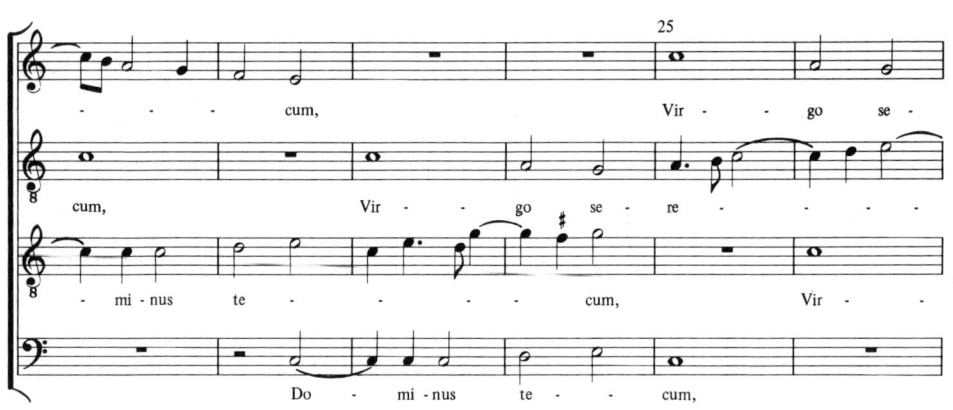

35
ve cu - jus con - cep - - ti - o,
ve cu - jus con - cep - - ti - o, con - cep - - - ti -
A - ve cu - jus con - cep - - ti -
A - ve cu - jus con - cep - - ti -
40
So - lem - ni ple - na gau - di - o, Coe -
o, So - lem - ni ple - - - na
o, So - lem - ni ple - na gau - di - o, Coe - le -
o, So - lem - ni ple - na gau - di - o, Coe -
45
le - sti - a, ter - re - stri - a, No - va re -
gau - di - o, Coe - le - sti - a, ter - re - stri - a, No -
- sti - a, ter - re - stri - a, No - va re - plet -
le - sti - a, ter - re - stri - a, No - va re -

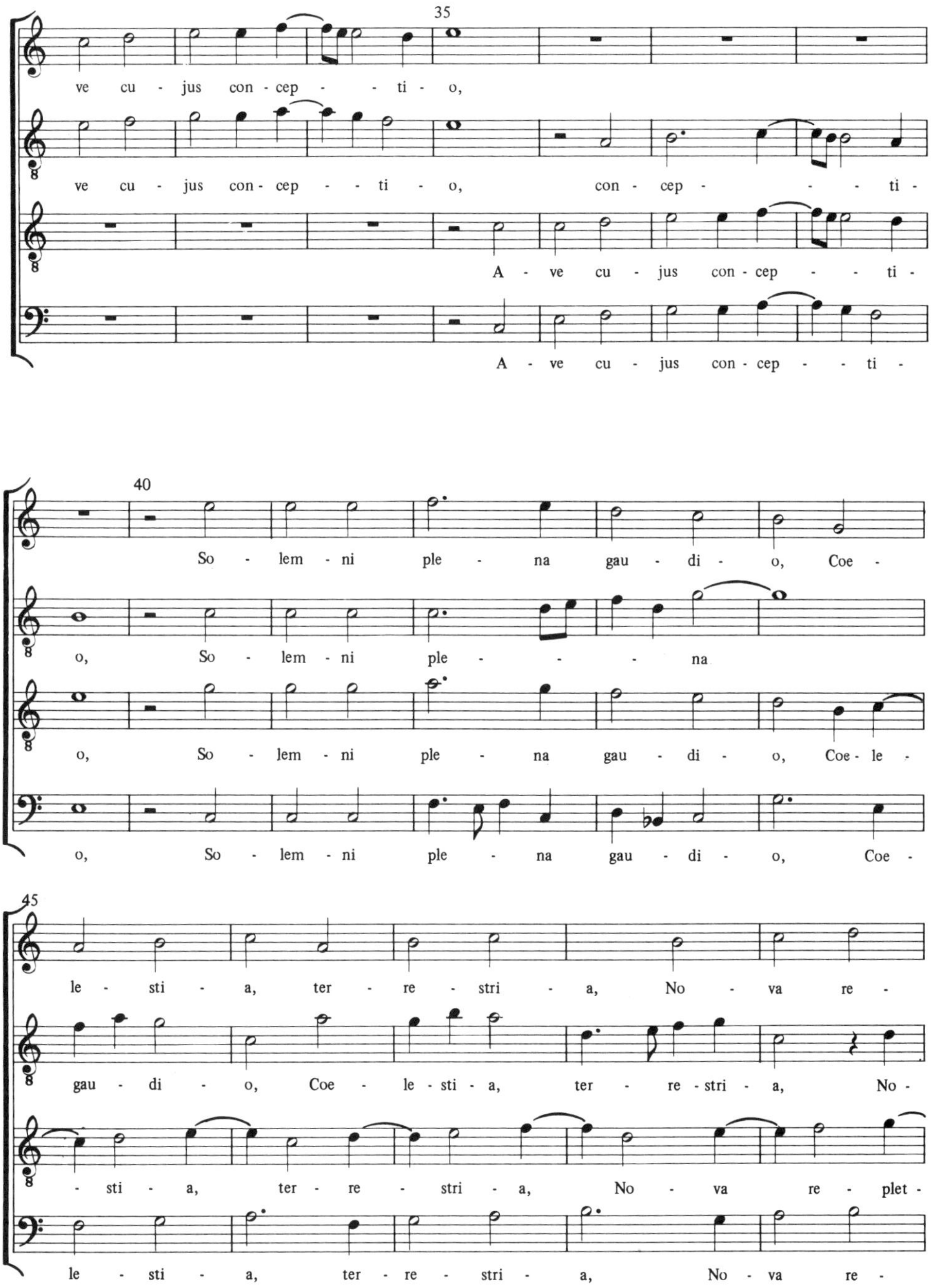

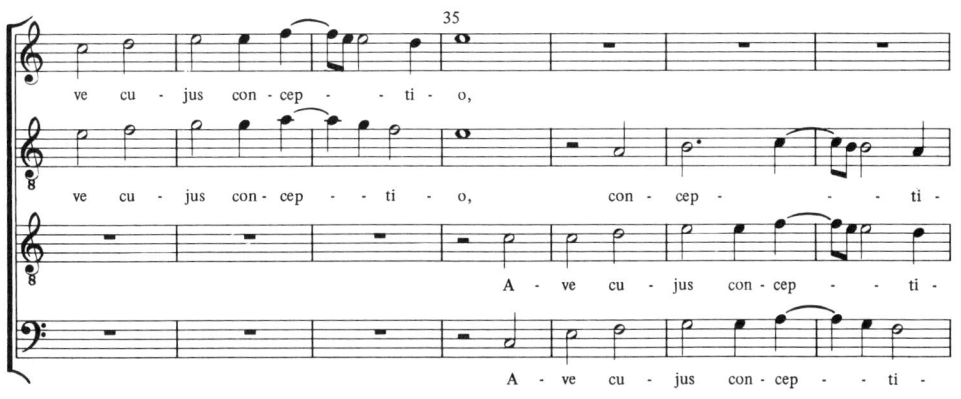

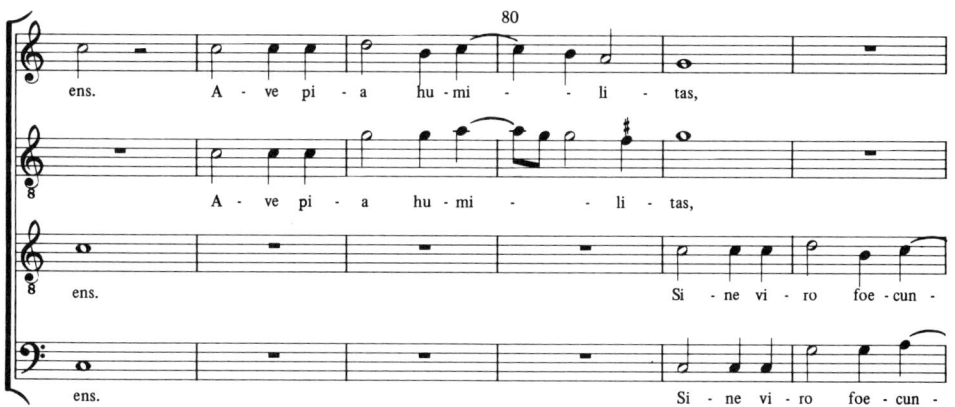

131

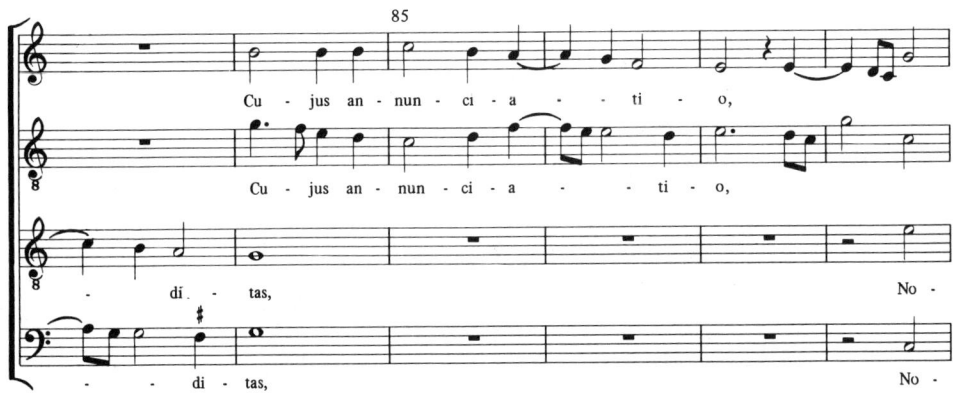

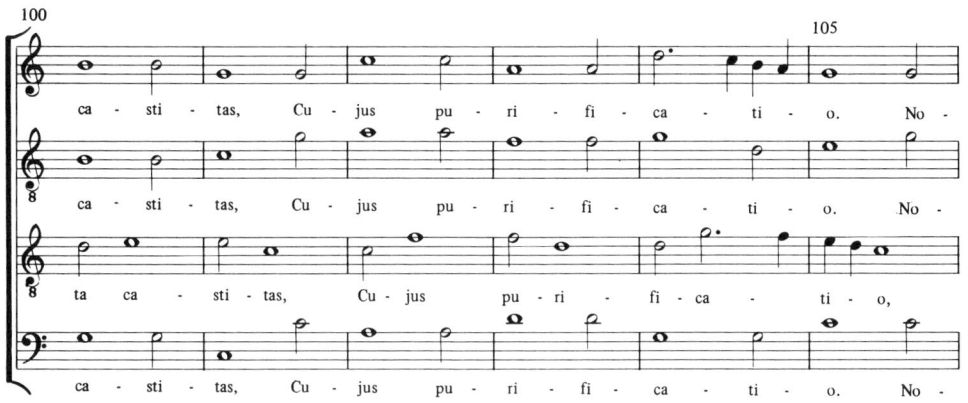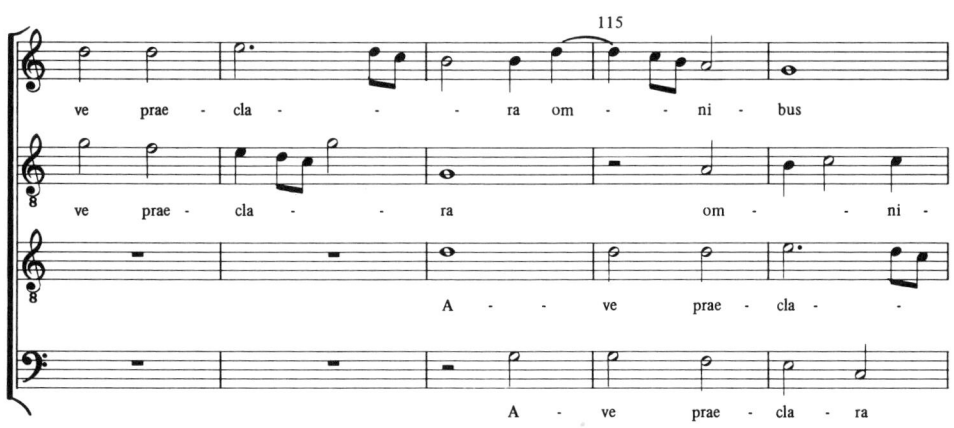

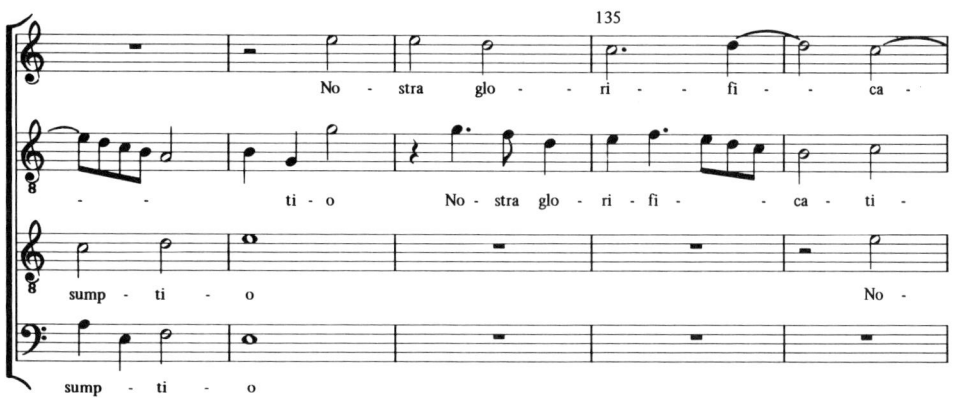

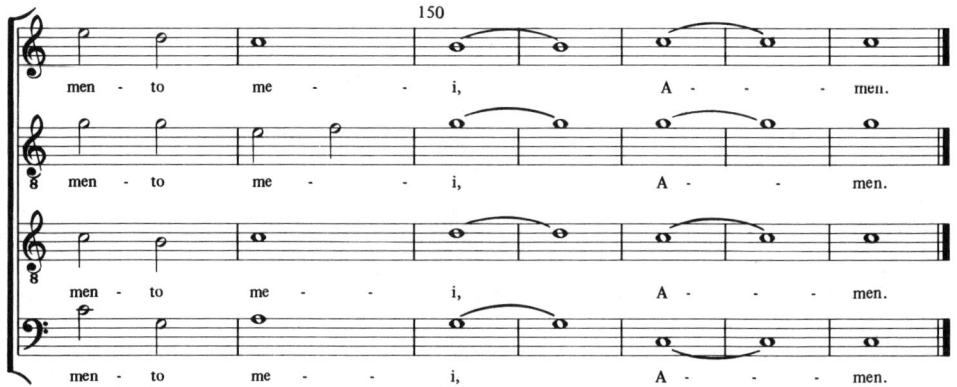

Translation:

> *Hail Mary, full of grace. The Lord is with Thee, Virgin serene, Hail to Thee, whose conception, full of solemn rejoicing, was to fill all in heaven and earth with new gladness. Hail to Thee, whose birth was to be our solemnity, as the rising morning star which comes before the sun. Hail virtuous humility and sinless fruitfulness, whose annunciation was to be our salvation. Hail true virginity and immaculate chastity, whose purification was to be our cleansing. Hail to Thee, excellent in all the angelic virtues, whose assumption was to be our glorification. O Mother of God, be mindful of me. Amen.*

Recordans de my segnora[1]

Josquin des Prez

7

Josquin des Prez

Ave Maria
Recordans de my segnora

Josquin des Prez (ca. 1440–1521) was one of the most remarkable composers of all time. Respected by musicians, religious authorities, and laymen alike, he set the standard for the style of the sixteenth century almost single-handedly. To understand the style of Josquin is to understand the basic tenets of two or three generations of European music. He is at the crossroads of the modal period and the tonal period, and in some ways summed up the former and helped move toward the latter.

In the accompanying example, the famous motet *Ave Maria*, the important structural basis is no longer a cantus firmus, or a borrowed element of any kind. Pervasive **imitation** controls the flow of melodic/harmonic motion and the presentation of ideas. A short melodic fragment, clearly constructed and immediately "imitated" in each of the other voices, is used for each phrase of text. The processes of *through-imitation* and *points of imitation* were the mainstays of sixteenth-century polyphonic writing regardless of whether or not a borrowed cantus firmus was used.

Josquin's sensitive control of line, texture, and structure led him to vary his use of imitation. Sometimes it appears in all four voices, sometimes in pairs of voices; sometimes the imitation is at the same pitch, sometimes at different pitch levels. Homophonic sections often alternate with imitative ones. The result is an extremely variegated design that is at once cohesive and free.

A quick comparison of the **linear construction** of Josquin with that of Dufay and earlier composers shows a remarkable change. Rhythmically, the line has been smoothed out to avoid the rough syncopations of the past. In addition, the direction of the line is exceedingly well conceived; there is always a direct push to and from a well-defined goal, either within the phrase or toward the cadence.

ex. 7-1

This highly structural/directional melodic motion will ultimately have a great effect on the harmonic thrust as well.

In some cases a new device known as *sequence* is used to effect a greater sense of forward direction. **Melodic sequence** is the repetition of a melodic line at a different pitch level, in the same voice.

ex. 7-2

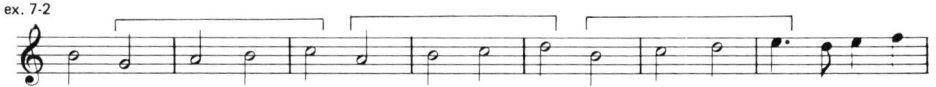

Examples such as the above are further described as **tonal sequence** because the repetition of the line stays within the diatonic scale. (Tonal sequence need not always refer exclusively to tonal music, as it is possible to observe this in modal music as well.) Another type of sequence, not found in Josquin quite as often, is **real sequence,** in which every interval is exactly the same in the repetition, usually necessitating some kind of chromatic alteration.

ex. 7-3

From a rhythmic standpoint, each line usually begins with a longer note, or group of notes, and gradually moves to smaller note values, a process that constantly increases the tension and forward momentum and ultimately results in a cadential resolution. This may not be a new concept (we have seen it in both Machaut and Dufay) but it is more clearly structured in Josquin than in earlier composers.

ex. 7-4

In addition, the phrases have a tendency to become even longer as the piece progresses (note the soprano in measures 1, 8, 14, and 25).

Various "rules" can be derived from Josquin's rhythmic usage, rules which remain generally applicable for the entirety of the sixteenth century. They should be considered as basic guides and not as absolute standards, however.

1. Any note value can be used in pairs.
2. Syncopations are allowed in certain cases:

This last case is described by the next rule.

3. A note may never be tied to one of greater value, but may always be tied to one of equal or lesser value.

Notice the reason: by singing each example it will be observed that the tie creates tension, and that this tension must be released. The explosion of release is satisfying with shorter notes, but if tied to a larger note the unreleased tension inhibits the flow of the line.

4. Finally, eighth notes must always be used in pairs, except when one follows a dotted quarter. The eighth may never precede the dotted quarter on the strong beat.

Smoothness of line is determined by the direction and control of the melodic aspect as well as the rhythmic. Josquin understood the effects of each and was especially subtle in his inner construction of each. Much of the life and sparkle of the piece can be attributed to the rhythmic and linear control, so carefully maintained throughout the piece.

Harmonically there are several items that become fascinating when viewed in a historical perspective. ***Triadic use*** is ever more prominent and the harmonic sound now emphasizes the third and sixth more than the fifth and octave. There is hardly an $\frac{8}{5}$ construction in the whole piece; even when only two voices are sounding, they almost always produce intervals of the third and sixth. The exception to this, as we might expect, occurs at major cadence points (measures 94, 109, and especially the end) where there is a return to the open-fifth-with-octave sonority that has been carried forward from Medieval times. The idea of purity and perfection of sound represented by this archaic principle is still part of the concept of music, at least at important cadences.

The body of the phrase, however, uses much the same **root movement** as in previous periods: mostly motion by second and third. The difference in sound is attributed to the voice-leading and linear changes, emphasis on limitation, rhythmic changes, and the prominent use of complete triads. The prohibition of parallel fifths and octaves between parts, begun in the past century, becomes solidified into dogma in this period. Only in extremely rare circumstances do we find parallel motion between any two parts. This prohibition was to remain in effect for at least 300 years after the time of Josquin.

The primary impetus of this style is linear. However, this does not prevent the use of triads. The harmonic content is important, but it is derived and controlled by the **melodic motion** of the individual lines—voice leading. The voice-leading principles seen in this motet are generally applicable to the general style of the period. As we have seen, no parallel fifths or octaves are used. The individual lines are smooth, with skips of rarely more than a third or fourth. Leading tones resolve to their tonics by moving up a half step. Finally, the lines are usually balanced, with motion up and down each complementing the other.

Two other aspects of voice leading and chordal arrangement seem to be important features of this style. First, roots and thirds are doubled within the triad, while fifths are only rarely doubled; second, a **linear 6–5–6 motion** above the bass is an important determinant of certain root movements. The first point has to do with strength of sound. The strength of a triad is generally enhanced by doubling the root when the chord is in root position. In some cases the root and third are both doubled. However, rarely is the fifth doubled, and only at the most significant cadences is the third omitted from the chord. If the triad is in first inversion the root is still often doubled, but the third and fifth are also doubled on occasion, depending on the specific voice leading. We may follow the same basic principle established earlier for first-inversion triads, that of doubling the soprano pitch.

The linear 6–5 motion is also significant. Root movement by third is immediately created by its use, a result of a smooth, linear motion. The fluidity of line accounts for the smooth harmonic sound as well.

The cadences in Josquin are a logical extension of previous developments. An actual double-leading-tone cadence will not be seen except in a few very early pieces. The tonal V–I cadence is predominant. However, several other **cadences** have developed, both tonal and modal.

In the *Ave Maria* the V–I or authentic cadence is certainly the most prominent, especially at important points (measures 52–53, 108–109, final cadence), but two others are used frequently within the piece: the vii$^{\circ}_6$–I cadence (the single-leading-tone), and the Phrygian cadence (measures 38–39). They both display the same basic linear motion as the double-leading-tone, as we have seen before.

ex. 7-5

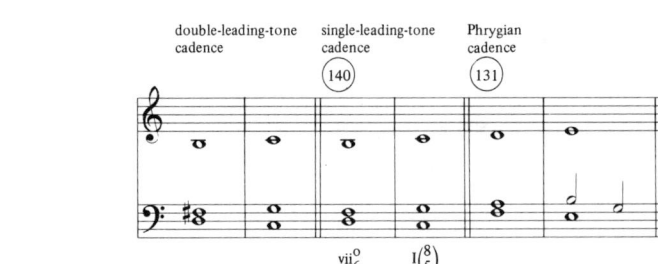

In the first case, the single leading tone and the resultant diminished-triad sound are the most important characteristic traits. This is the same as the previous single-leading-tone cadence. The second example, although with the same basic motion, is characterized by the half-step motion in the bass voice, with whole steps elsewhere typical of the Phrygian mode. It should be noted that in each case the resolution is to an open $^8_5$ construction. However, the cadence in measure 132 immediately adds the third to the chord. In this period there is a strong inclination to add the third to the triad, both within the phrase and at the phrase ending.

One additional tonal cadence is used as well, the ***deceptive cadence.*** As the name implies, this occurs when an authentic cadence is expected and a deceptive shift results. The deceptive motion occurs when the V chord resolves to a chord with a root a second above V—that is, to the vi chord, instead of the tonic triad.

ex. 7-6

The purpose for this could very well be one of extension. The V–I cadence produces a strong sense of finality; if fluid forward motion is desired, a V–vi cadence is helpful in extending the piece and avoiding finality. In addition, it is a most effective way of building tension, thereby enhancing the final V–I cadence.

An important tonal cadence not used in this particular piece (but implied near the final cadence) is the ***plagal cadence.*** In the plagal cadence, the root movement is by *fourth down;* if inverted, the motion is by *fifth up.*

ex. 7-7

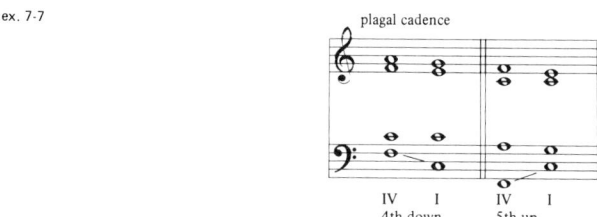

The composers of this period do not employ any radical ***dissonance.*** In fact, it is safe to say that the sixteenth century used dissonance somewhat less than in than in earlier periods. In addition, it was handled in a very carefully controlled manner. Passing tones and neighboring tones were still used; greater emphasis was given suspensions, especially at the cadence. Escape tones were used on occasion, but less often than in the fifteenth century.

One type of suspension that comes into greater use is the so-called **bass suspension.** It follows the normal process of suspensions, but instead of a voice being suspended *above* the bass, the bass itself is the suspended note. The only intervallic configuration for this type of suspension is 2–3.

ex. 7-8

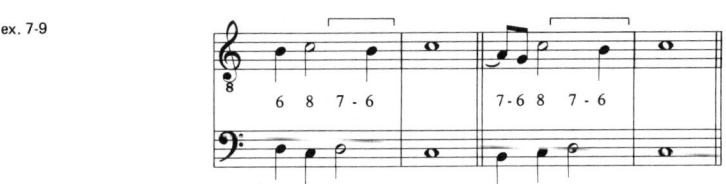

In reality the 2–3 suspension is the inversion of the 7–6 suspension. The two voices are simply exchanges, and each moves in its original manner.

ex. 7-9

This suspension is used especially in two-voice settings; we can see several examples in the present motet.

By employing a V–I cadence in the proper way the composer can establish his tonal area and solidify it. There are two methods of carrying this idea forward. The first is to have different tonal levels within a given piece. This can be accomplished by having a V–I cadence to pitch levels both on the main tonic of the piece and others. The second is to employ the principle of root movement of down by fifth to a more lengthy sequence of chords than the final two. Both of these ideas are used in their embryonic stage by Josquin.

The first concept is the beginning of a system of **secondary tonics,** or the tonal emphasis of pitch levels other than the primary one of the piece. If we consider the *Ave Maria* to have a general tonic of *C*, then most of the cadences should revolve around that tone, as they do. There are some exceptions, however. In measure 83 there is a 2–3 suspension and the use of an *f♯* to cadence on *G*, not *C*. This shift to *G* is established by the *f♯* leading tone and is strong enough to fix it temporarily in our ears as a tonic. It does not destroy *C* as the primary tonic of the piece, but the *f♯* itself is strong enough to effect an audible, if temporary, shift of tonic.

ex. 7-10

The other type of fifth-related chord does not involve accidentals, new leading tones or a shift away from a primary level. It is just the opposite: a defined chordal structure that solidifies and directs the sound to a specific tonic pitch. Although not the predominant chordal structure of this piece or this century, there are several specific instances in which it occurs.

ex. 7-11

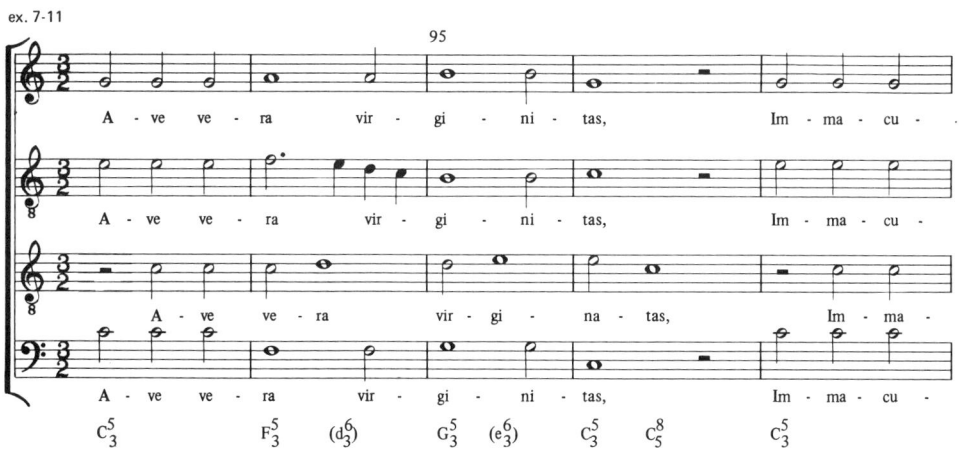

This chordal motion is important and should be studied with care. In measure 102ff the chordal motion is especially important: a (F_6)—d—G—C and a (F_6)—b^0—e—a—F—G—C.

The effect of downward fifth motion is overwhelming. Its impetus produces strong motion toward the tonic of *c*. This principle is one of extending the fifth motion of a V–I cadence *back* from the cadence, through root movement of a fifth downward, to produce a stronger motion toward the final, tonic pitch. In this way, we can see at least the beginnings of a tonal thought process as early as the beginning of the sixteenth century.

Another important musical aspect is that of form. There is a strong sense of sectional design in the piece, determined primarily by the textual divisions and the new *points of imitation*[1] begun at each. Each phrase of imitation becomes progressively longer and more complicated.

---

[1] A point of imitation is a section with overlapping imitative entries at each point of a new text.

ex. 7-12

The ultimate complexity occurs in the final phrase of imitation of the first major section of the piece, beginning at measure 50.

From measure 55, Josquin moves to a pairing of voices and a thinning of the texture. The middle point of imitation (measures 65–75) involves all four voices, but it is preceded and followed by a two-voice texture.

A homophonic section follows in measure 94. On the surface it is simple and chordal. This is deceptive, though, because the passage contains a strict **canon** between the soprano and the tenor. A canon occurs when two or more voices are in *exact* imitation throughout, often at a different pitch level. Note the soprano and tenor voices below.

ex. 7-13

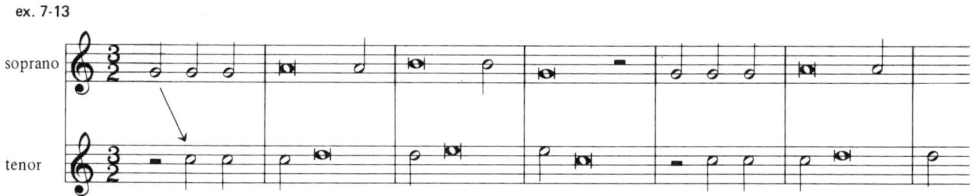

The astonishing quality of Josquin's canonic works lies in his ability to handle canon with such ease and expertise, and to disguise the technical nature of the devices used. In this section of the piece, it is disguised by the strongly homophonic nature of the setting.

The easiest way to compose a canon, for the beginning student at any rate, is to write one voice up to the point of entry of the second voice, and then immediately transpose it and write in the second part. Then the first voice can be continued so as to coincide properly with the transposed measure.

ex. 7-14

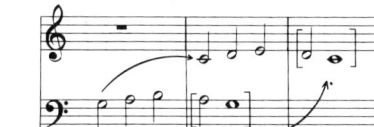

This procedure, sometimes referred to as "leap-frog" technique, can be continued through the entire canonic section.

Throughout the piece the imitative sections flow easily and logically from one to the other. Deceptive cadences are employed when appropriate for extension, while phrases are closed with V–I cadences. The lines are superbly controlled; the harmony, voice leading, and doubling are carefully considered. The shape and balance of musical ideas is finely tuned. Josquin has the rare ability to hold numerous techniques and musical ideas in perfect control all at the same time. We can still learn a great deal from this remarkable genius.

The second example by Josquin (page 136) is neither a sacred piece nor a vocal piece. Conceived for instruments, it is a lively, fast-moving composition that sweeps the listener away. On the surface it is simple and straightforward, with a compelling melodic flair. Upon closer examination it becomes much more complex.

Technically, it is a **double canon**—that is, two different canons unfolding at the same time. The lower two voices are exactly the same, but a perfect fourth apart and beginning at the time interval of a half note. The upper two parts are related in the same way. Each of the voices begins with the same one-measure motive, creating the sound of four-part imitation and obscuring the more complicated framework of canon.

ex. 7-15

The difference between canon and imitation is actually one of length. Imitation usually occurs for a few measures, while canon is a procedure of strict imitation that lasts for an extended period of time, either for an entire section or for the whole piece.

A detailed study of the piece would yield great insight into music of the period—its rhythm, melody, voice leading, and contrapuntal technique. However, we will examine only two musical aspects, harmony and phrasing.

In several features of its harmonic activity, *Recordans* very much resembles the *Ave Maria:* emphasis on linear motion to determine chordal direction and goals, tonal cadences, secondary tonics with dominants that function on those levels, and root movement within the phrase that emphasizes the fifth. The lines are firmly cast, with clear and compelling impetus. The harmonic interplay and direction is also clear and, considering the ultimate complexity of the linear aspect, quite remarkable.

The lines and chords center around *a, d,* and *c* as important tonal centers. The canonic entries begin on *a* and *d,* and the final cadence confirms *d* as the central tonic. The opening phrase, though, moves almost immediately toward a secondary level of *c* (in measures 4–5). The root movement of d–G–C in measures 6–7 suggests an extension of the *c* tonal area, but Josquin shifts, via musica ficta, to *a* in measure 9. He finally reaches *d* once again in measure 10 at the end of the phrase. These secondary levels are important in creating variety and interest within the piece. They also reflect the use of the canon, by employing the same line on two different levels at the same time.

ex. 7-16

The g♯ functions as a leading tone to *a*. This is immediately contradicted by the stronger cadence on *d* by the use of the c♯ leading tone. In addition, the g♯ is part of the g♯–b–d diminished triad (used as vii° of *a*) and the c♯ is part of the a–c♯–e dominant triad of *d*. The secondary level of *a* is an important one nonetheless.

ex. 7-17

The phrase structure is generally simple. Each line can be easily divided into its phrases, which are mostly of four measures each. The phrasing becomes much more complex when all voices are taken together, however, since there is a constant shift and pull between voices because of the offset rhythm of the canons. This only resolves itself at major cadence points, such as in measures 5, 9–10, 15, 19, 31, and 35–36.

Notice the relationship of the opening motive to those of the middle section (starting in measure 20) and ending section (a literal repeat of the beginning, starting in measure 28). The shift in rhythm is quite subtle but significant; the piece is much more interesting as a result of this rhythmic displacement.

A good exercise would be to sing each voice of the piece and then to play and sing two or three lines at a time, finally performing the entire piece. In addition, a detailed analysis of triads and dissonance use would provide further insight into the style.

STYLE CHARACTERISTICS: EARLY SIXTEENTH CENTURY
based on Josquin's *Ave Maria* **and** *Recordans de my signora*

melody	smooth, with rarely a skip of more than a fourth or fifth • balanced, with curving line • directional, moving from one point to another
harmony	root movement by a second or third is prominent • fifth movement is prominent at the cadence with increasing fifth motion back from the cadence • increased harmonic rhythm, with harmonies changing every half note, sometimes even every quarter • cadences are mostly tonally oriented: authentic (V–I), vii$^{\circ}_{6 \atop 3}$—I, deceptive (V–vi), plagal (IV–I), Phrygian
dissonance	passing tones and neighboring tones • escape tones are used sparingly • suspensions are prominent, espccially at the cadence
rhythm	controlled, smooth, developmental (moving from larger to smaller values) • syncopation is used primarily for suspensions • phrases are variable in length with a great deal of overlapping
texture	polyphonic, with homophonic sections • four-voice setting is typical • five voices also possible • pairing of voices—the use of two voices followed by the same phrase in the other two—is common
techniques	imitation • canon • sequence • double canon • paired imitation

Glossary

Authentic cadence   a cadence with root movement of a P5 down. (V–I) It must be a *major* V chord moving to an $^8_1$ or $^8_5$ construction or, rarely, $^5_3$. The third of the V chord functions as a leading tone to the tonic.

Canon   the exact, note-for-note repetition of an entire melodic line in another voice, starting at a different time. The successive voices follow each other at a short interval, usually one to five measures.

Chordal doubling   the process used to double one note of a triad in a four-voice setting.

Double canon   two completely different canons which proceed together in a single polyphonic setting.

Imitation   the repetition of a short melodic idea at the same or different pitch level, in a different voice. This usually occurs at a short interval, generally one to five measures.

Phrygian cadence   a type of modal cadence (M3—P5 and M6—P8) in which the bottom voice moves down by half step and the upper voices move up by whole step. Found naturally in the Phrygian mode.

Plagal cadence   a cadence with the root movement of a perfect fourth down. (IV–I)

Point of imitation   a series of imitative entries. Usually a new one begins at each new phrase of text.

Sequence   the immediate repetition of a melodic idea at a different pitch level, in the same voice.

Tonal sequence   sequence which employs only the tones of the diatonic scale.

Real sequence   sequence which employs exact, interval-for-interval repetition, and thus usually requires tones from outside the diatonic scale.

Suggested Exercises

1. Make a complete melodic/motivic analysis of the *Ave Maria* motet. Copy all important melodic phrases (especially the phrases used in each of the points of imitation) and compare them in terms of rhythm, melodic shape, direction, contour, and use of intervals.
2. Find and identify all the suspensions in the motet.
3. Using the given chordal outline, write a four-voice piece in a homophonic texture. Be sure to use good voice leading and in particular to avoid parallel fifths and octaves between any two voices.

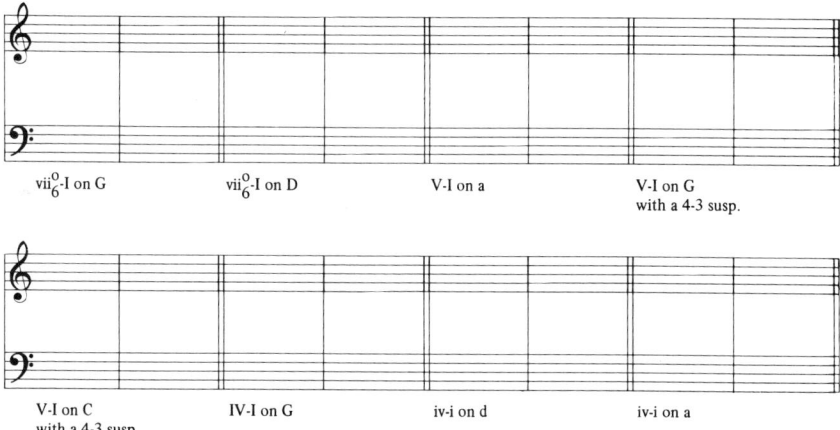

4. Write a strict two-part canon at the pitch interval of a fifth and at the time interval of one measure. Make it at least fifteen measures long. Include one internal cadence and use at least two suspensions.
5. Write the following cadences:

6. Complete the following for the given chanson (song) by Josquin.
   a. Indicate all imitative entries and compare them for development and complexity.
   b. Indicate all cadences and label them as to type.
   c. Provide an analysis of root movement.

Before Reading Chapter 8

1. Sing the plainchant *Kyrie* from the Requiem Mass, LU 1807 (page 155). Bracket each phrase and sing again.
2. Sing each line of the first "Kyrie" (measures 1–15) from the *Missa pro Defunctis* (Requiem Mass) by Palestrina (page 156).
3. Analyze the harmonic structure of the first "Kyrie" (root, quality, and inversion).
4. Identify all dissonance in the entire movement, paying close attention to suspensions.
5. Compare the chant with the polyphonic setting.

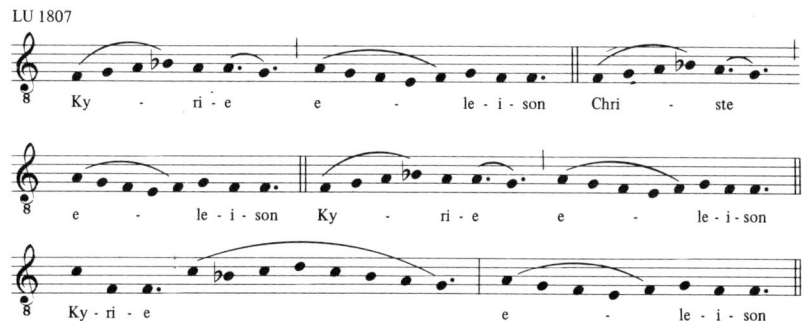

Kyrie from Missa pro Defunctis

G. F. da Palestrina

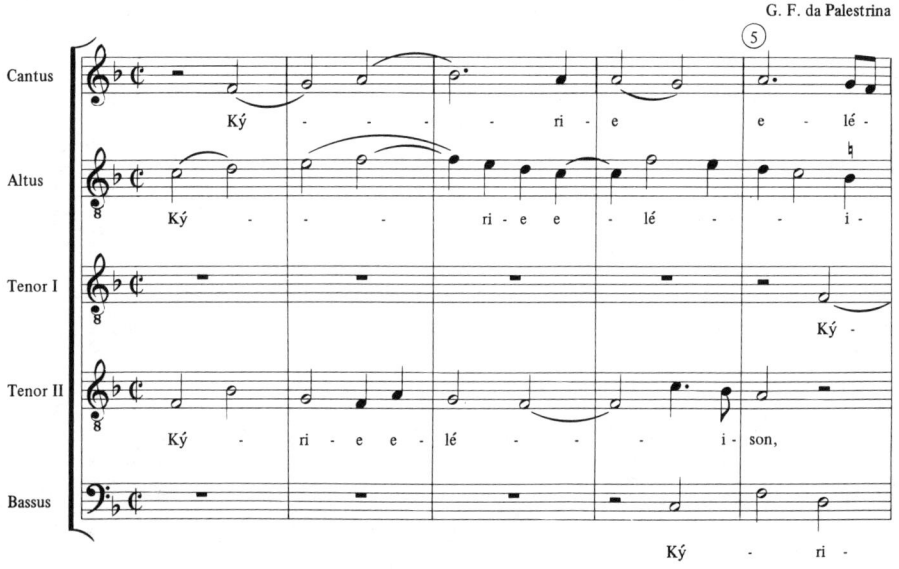

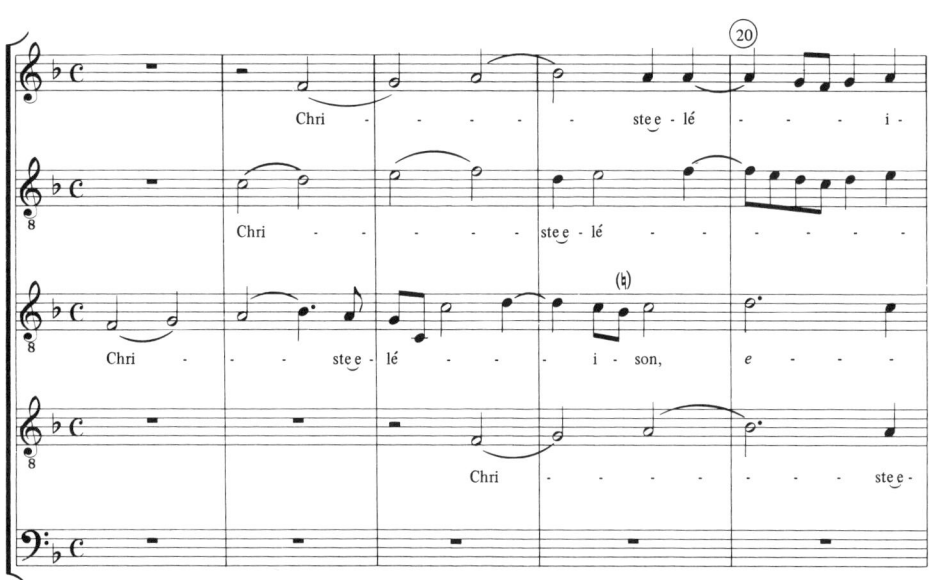

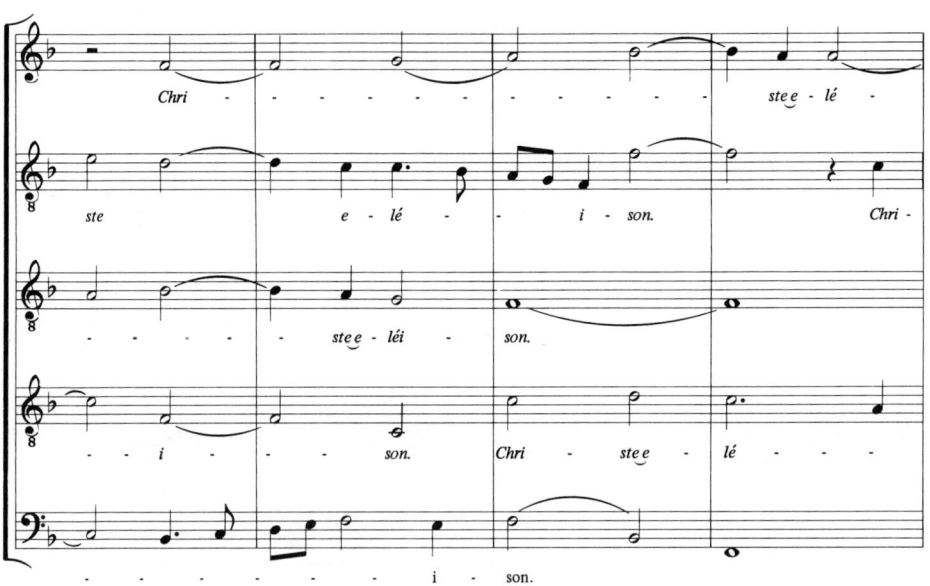

159

© Instituto Italiano per la Storia della Musica; used by permission.

8

Giovanni Pierluigi da Palestrina

Kyrie from the *Missa pro Defunctis*

Perhaps more than any other composer, Palestrina (ca. 1525–1594) has been considered the master of counterpoint. Composers in each succeeding generation have studied his work, written exercises based on his style, and learned intimately the tenets of his craft. Indeed, in most music schools today, when students enroll in a course on sixteenth-century counterpoint, they invariably concentrate on this giant of his time.

Although he employed the basic style features of his period, Palestrina was somewhat conservative, since he wrote mostly sacred music in a time when much secular music was being composed. However, for sheer craft, for an understanding of melodic control, shape, logic, and sixteenth-century techniques, he is the touchstone of the age.

One is struck first by Palestrina's fluid, controlled, and superbly directed line. The ***melodic shape*** always has a direction and logic that almost moves the line by itself; the rhythm is welded to this with an equally compelling sense of direction. At almost any given moment in a piece, the removal of rhythm will produce a line very close to chant.

ex. 8-1

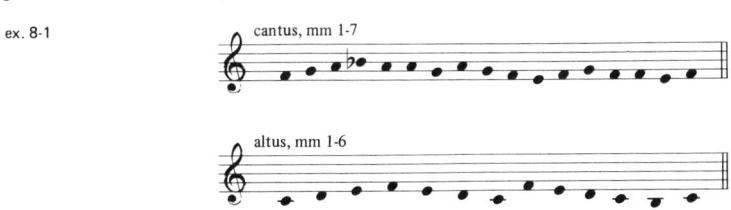

In some cases the lines are derived from chant deliberately; in others the similarity is apparently merely the result of the years of Palestrina's exposure to the liturgy of the Catholic church. The melodic structure of these lines is, like chant, restricted mostly to intervals of seconds, thirds, an occasional fourth or fifth, and rarely, a minor sixth. No major sixth or major or minor seventh is permitted, but octaves are found on occasion. The primary goal is one of fluidity and direction, without the dramatic gestures obtainable by large and frequent leaps.

The **rhythm** adds to this fluidity, following the same basic "rules" we found in Josquin. Palestrina continues to favor starting with larger note values and proceeding to smaller ones. A possible difference from Josquin is Palestrina's preference for arriving sooner at faster values.

In addition, he seems to favor a thicker texture with more voices sounding at the same time, utilizing faster note values, in a great contrapuntal interplay.

The above line is typical of Palestrina. It is a **paraphrase** of the Kyrie chant from the Requiem Mass (LU 1807); thus the pitches in the first eight measures are taken almost note-for-note from the chant. Palestrina provides the rhythm: a slow beginning, faster note values toward the end, and a cadence on a strong beat.

The suspension in measure six, with its repeated resolution, is referred to as ***portamento motion.*** In a sense, it anticipates the next note of the line, which occurs on the next strong beat. Its typical rhythm is seen in measures 3–4, with the dotted half and quarter, and in measure 6, with its dotted quarter and eighth. In this latter case, as in many others, the portamento occurs as a part of the resolution of a suspension. The description of the entire figure would be a 4–3 suspension with a portamento resolution.

ex. 8-4

Another special kind of resolution of a suspension, found increasingly in Palestrina's works, is the ***embellished resolution.*** It is simply an extended resolution, using a lower neighbor tone in conjunction with the resolution tone.

ex. 8-5

Typically, this type of motion occurs around the leading tone. These two resolutions, plus the normal suspension resolution, occur throughout Palestrina's work.

The normal dissonances encountered in Palestrina are the same as those in the earlier part of the sixteenth century—the suspension, passing tone, and neighboring tone. A special dissonance is the **nota cambiata.** The cambiata is not used extensively but is nevertheless important. It is nothing more than a special kind of escape tone. The entire three- or four-note figure is termed the *cambiata figure.*

ex. 8-6

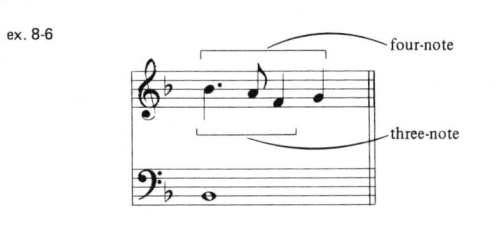

The dotted rhythm is necessary, as is the step down followed by a skip of a third down, and motion back up (by step) afterwards. The only note that is actually dissonant is the single eighth after the dotted quarter. Sometimes the cambiata is easy to spot because of its recognizable rhythmic-melodic pattern, but the only one in this piece is rather difficult to identify. It is found in the middle voice in measure 46 (see Ex. 8–5).

The cambiata can occur in longer note values as well.

ex. 8-7

This dissonance can be found in the music of various composers of the Renaissance, as far back as Josquin and occasionally even in the music of Dufay.

An important consideration in this melodic, linear style, is the firm control and projection of the harmony. With very few exceptions, all of the triads have thirds, even at important internal and final cadences. Thus, we have finally rejected the Medieval practice of ending with a perfection. The basic harmonic interval of this music is that of the third. The fifth is omitted on occasion, but the third is almost always present, even in two-part settings.

The structure of these triads is also well controlled. In almost every case they are in either root position or first inversion. The number of second-inversion triads is small, their placement is always rhythmically weak, and their duration is brief. In the present example, only root-position and first-inversion triads appear.

The root movement is similar to that in earlier music, since it is still largely based on linear and modal concepts. But there are a few changes that put the stamp of the individual on the works, as well as a few items that seem to point to future developments. In many cases there is root movement by second or third, but the exact nature of this is sometimes revealing. Frequently the root movement of a second is as follows:

ex. 8-8

ex. 8-9

Here, instead of a V–I cadence, Palestrina alters the motion to C–B♭–F, or V–IV–I. This shift at the cadence creates a typical Renaissance sound. Note that this motion precedes that of a stronger cadence, V–I, in measures 27–28. Although the piece incorporates the V–IV–I progression, the important cadences are usually V–I. This free usage of V, IV, and I, with the V–I reserved for the most important cadences, gives us a strong impression that root relationships of fourth and fifth are being stressed more and more.

Within the phrase, there is still a tendency to use root movement of a second or third. In the latter instance, an important reason for the particular root movement results from linear procedures. As in Josquin, the **5–6 motion** above the bass produces the root change of a third.

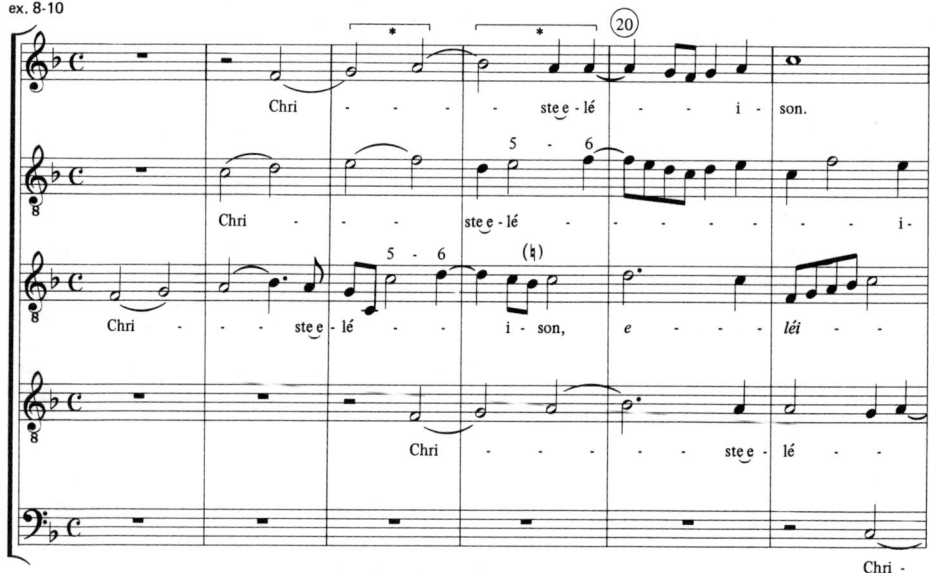

ex. 8-10

This kind of root movement helps to create the strongly modal sound of the piece. It must be remembered, however, that the strength of the cadential motion by fifth is slowly changing the emphasis. The fifth motion is being "extended backwards" at the cadence, i.e. not only is C–F motion used, but g–C–F can be seen as well.

As we have noted previously, the movement of voices at cadences is crucial. The V–I motion is characterized primarily by the root of the V chord resolving to the root of I. The leading tone (the third of the V chord) in most cases resolves to the tonic pitch; the fifth can resolve either to the root of the next chord or to its third.

ex. 8-11

As can be seen above, in a setting of four or more voices, the voices doubling the root move in two different ways—one to the root of the next chord, the other maintaining a common tone which becomes the fifth of the next chord.

Another voice-leading principle deals with the dissonance of the **tritone,** the d5 or A4. In previous centuries, this interval was prohibited. However, in the fifteenth century and to an even greater extent in the sixteenth century, it began to be used within the **diminished triad.** Usually used in first inversion with the third of the triad (the bass voice) doubled, it occurred in this way:

ex. 8-12

The inner two voices, $e^\flat$ and a, produce the tritone, in this case an augmented fourth. **Augmented intervals usually resolve outward, while diminished ones resolve inward.** This rule indicates the proper resolution of most tritones.

ex. 8-13

A4 - m6   d5 - M3

Palestrina follows this principle almost everywhere he uses a tritone. Note that here the a functions as a leading tone and resolves correctly to $b^\flat$.

ex. 8-14

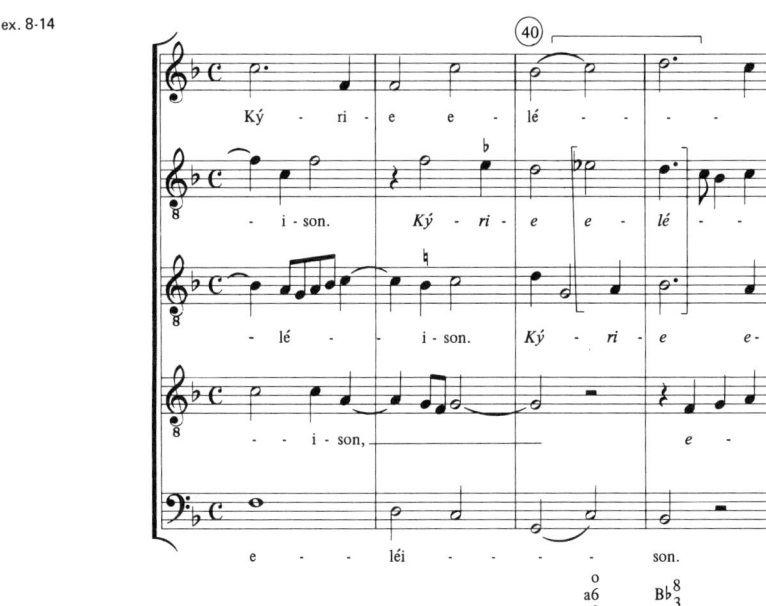

Other examples of tritone motion suggest harmonic practices which will become important in the next century. The example in measure 27 is an interesting one.

ex. 8-15

The tritone e–$b\flat$ resolves as a diminished fifth should, inward to f–a. However, instead of being part of the diminished triad e–g–$b^\flat$, the e belongs to a C major triad and the $b\flat$ is really a passing tone. It is a significant passing tone, however, since when added to the triad, it produces a seventh chord.

ex. 8-16

This chord is a major triad with a minor seventh added to it. This major-minor seventh (Mm7) is the typical sound and structure in the ***V7 (dominant seventh) chord.*** We will see an ever-increasing use of this sonority in the future. The presence of the tritone within it generally dictates the voice-leading procedure described above.

Like many polyphonic Masses of the sixteenth century, the present work borrows material from a pre-existing piece, in this case a chant from the Requiem Mass of the Roman liturgy. The technique employed is paraphrase technique. We have observed it before, but its use is much more pervasive here. The lightly paraphrased chant line can be seen throughout the movement. It appears in every vocal part, each voice imitating the opening paraphrased line.

In certain other Masses by Palestrina, the borrowed material is used in a strict form in the tenor line alone, exemplifying the so-called *cantus firmus* technique. In other works the borrowed material may be more than one line of a polyphonic piece, such as a whole section of four-voice chanson or madrigal. In this case the composer "parodies" the work by using it as his starting point and developing his own musical ideas on the basis of the earlier work. This is called *parody technique*.

In the present example the use of the chant is fairly clear throughout, not always the case in paraphrase Masses. The opening soprano line, measures 1–8, clearly outlines the opening chant phrase.

The "Christe" portion of the movement similarly follows the "Christe" portion of the chant. However, those phrases contain exactly the same notes as the "Kyrie" phrase. In order to alter the texture, the lines are more strictly in imitation, with entries occurring faster and lines piling up as a result.

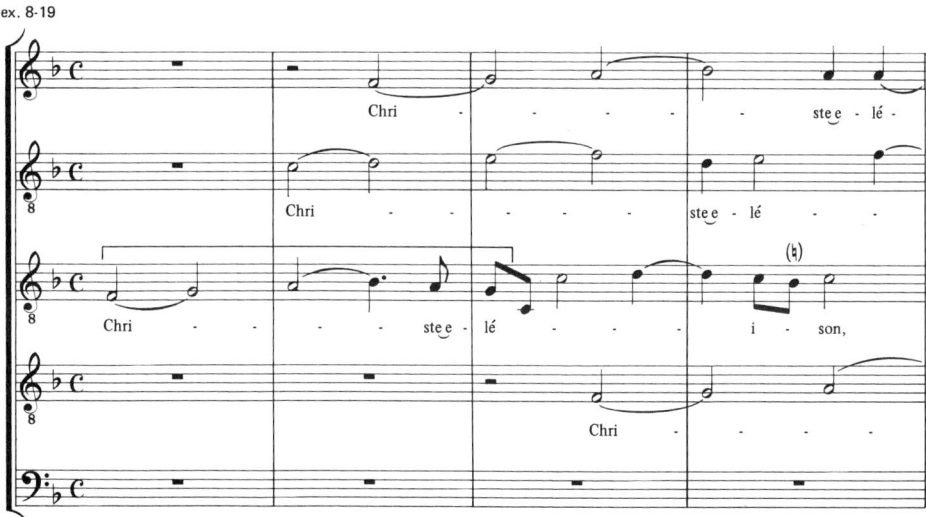

In the second "Kyrie" section, a new point of imitation occurs, with a new melodic motive. It directly relates to the second "Kyrie" of the chant, which begins with the downward leap of a perfect fifth. This chant line is paraphrased in the alto and first tenor lines, but is kept more strictly in the soprano and second tenor.

ex. 8-20

    This paraphrasing of the chant line gives the piece a tightly knit structure within which to work. Paraphrase is much used by Palestrina, though in some cases only the opening phrase of the chant is employed to any great extent; perhaps this "signature" was seen as enough to give the work a character of its own. But in this and other works, he maintained a close relationship to the entire chant, exploring its melody phrase by phrase.

STYLE CHARACTERISTICS: MID- TO LATE SIXTEENTH CENTURY
based on Palestrina's *Kyrie* from the *Missa pro Defunctis*

melody	mostly stepwise and chant-like • occasional use of fourth and fifth • rare use of minor sixth and octave • no use of seventh or major sixth • balanced in directional flow • motion up is balanced by motion down
harmony	triads with thirds used almost always, including at final cadences • use of $\frac{5}{3}$ and $\frac{6}{3}$ • rare use of $\frac{6}{4}$ • root movement of second and third • movement by fourth and fifth especially at cadences • 6–5 motion producing root movement of a third • cadences: authentic, plagal, half, and deceptive
dissonance	passing tones • neighboring tones • escape tones • suspensions (frequent, especially at cadences) • cambiatas (both three- and four-note types)
rhythm	phrases often start with longer note values, proceed to shorter ones • moderate use of syncopations such as ¢ ♩ ♩ ♩ or ¢ ♩ ♩. ♪ ♩ • directional, with an increase in rhythmic tension and release in the cadence • eighth notes in pairs, unless preceded by a dotted quarter • sixteenth notes are rare, and usually occur in pairs (two or four at a time)
techniques	paraphrase • imitation • cantus firmus • parody

Glossary

Cantus firmus technique a compositional technique in which a borrowed melody (sacred or secular) is quoted in the tenor voice of a four- or five-voice piece.

Embellished resolution (of a suspension) the extension of the resolution of a suspension by means of a lower neighboring tone below the resolution note.

Nota cambiata (cambiata figure) a fifteenth- and sixteenth-century dissonance figure with a three- or four-note construction, always employing a dotted rhythm such as ♩. ♪ ♩ ♩ or ♩. ♩ ♩ ♩ . The second note is the only actual dissonance, and the construction is always

Paraphrase technique the embellished melodic use of a chant line; in the sixteenth century it is used throughout the four- or five-voice texture because of the use of imitation.

Parody technique a compositional technique of borrowing several lines or entire sections from another polyphonic work and using them as the starting point of a new work.

Portamento resolution (of a suspension) a type of resolution of a suspension in which the suspended note anticipates the resolution note and then repeats it.

Tritone the interval of three whole tones. While the tritone can be either an A4 or d5, it is most often seen as an A4 in the sixteenth century and subsequent centuries.

V7 chord (dominant seventh chord) a major triad with the addition of a minor seventh. In the Renaissance the minor seventh is generally a passing tone.

Suggested Exercises

1. Analyze the harmonic structure and identify all dissonance in the *Kyrie* from the *Missa Aeterna Christi munera* by Palestrina (pages 175–178).
2. Compare the following *Sanctus* from the *Missa Aeterna Christi munera* (pages 178–181) to the chant upon which it is based (page 182).
3. Complete the following:

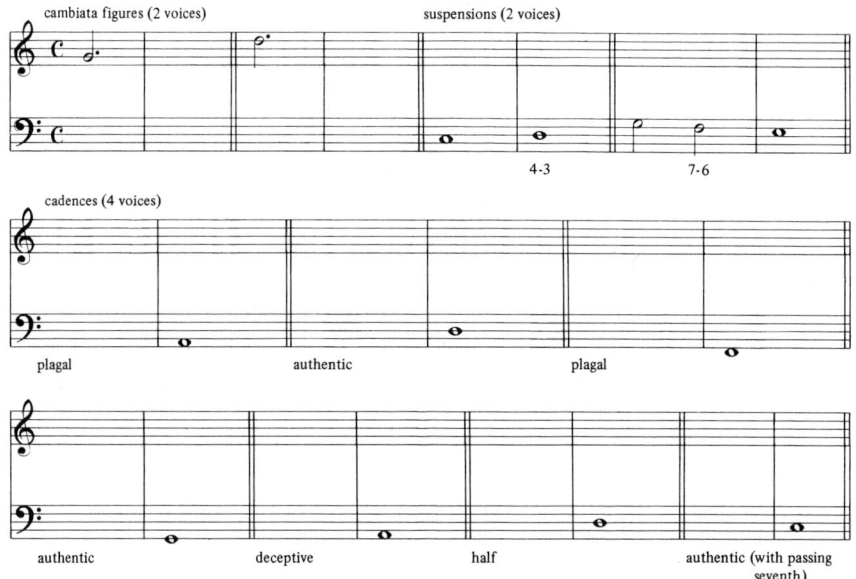

4. Resolve the following tritones, keeping in mind that augmented fourths resolve outward and diminished fifths resolve inward.

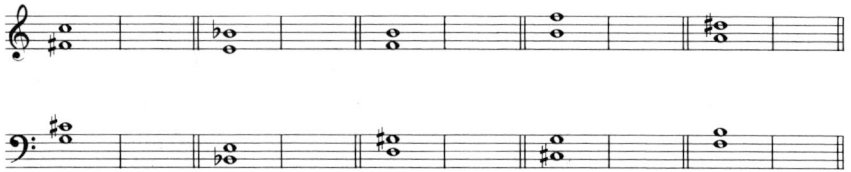

5. Compose a piece in four voices, using good voice leading, according to the following harmonic-rhythmic scheme.

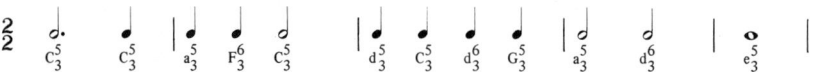

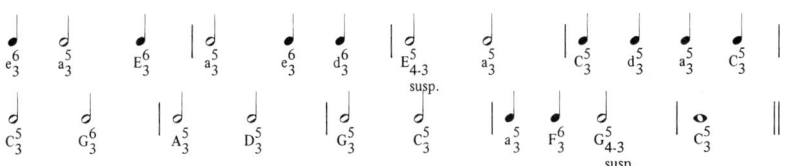

Missa Aeterna Christi munera
Kyrie

G.P. da Palestrina

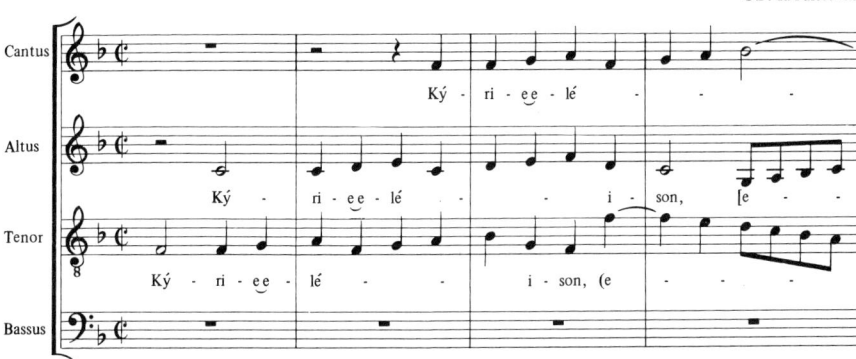

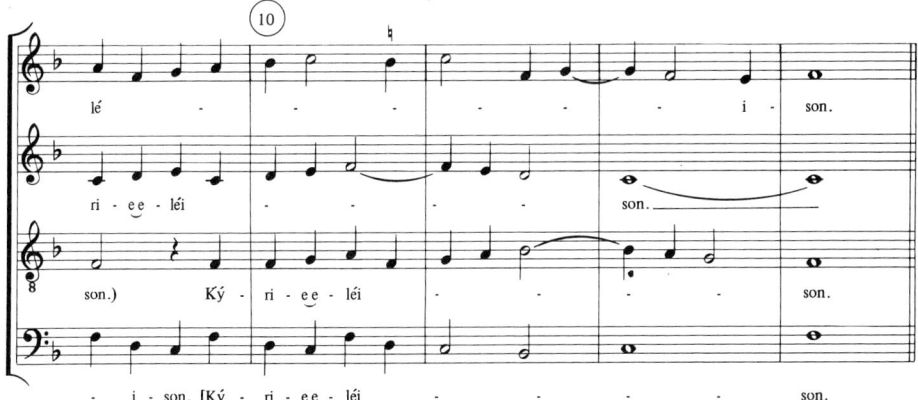

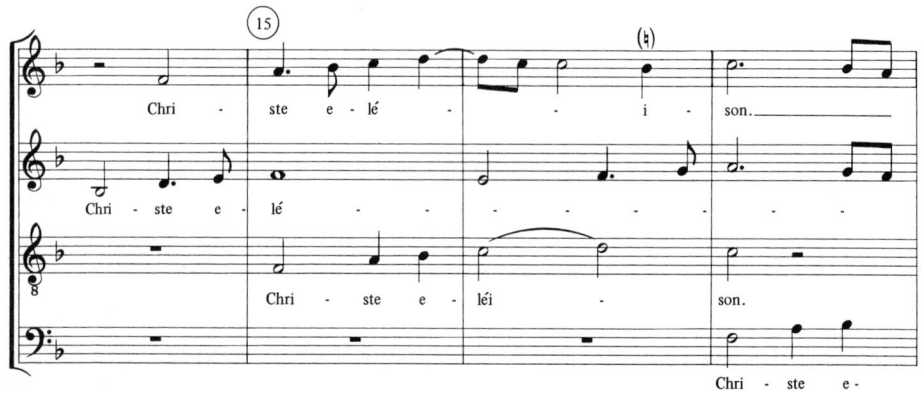
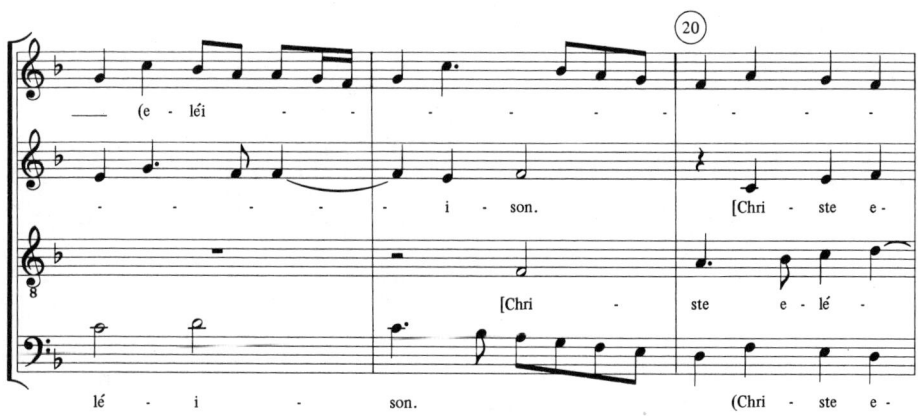
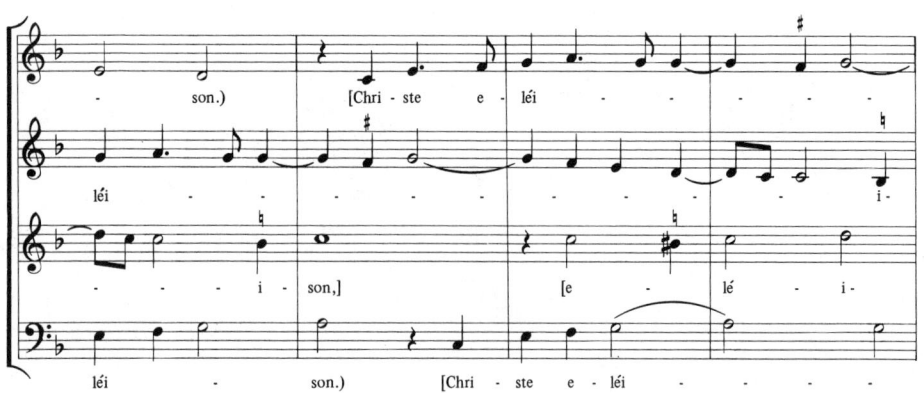

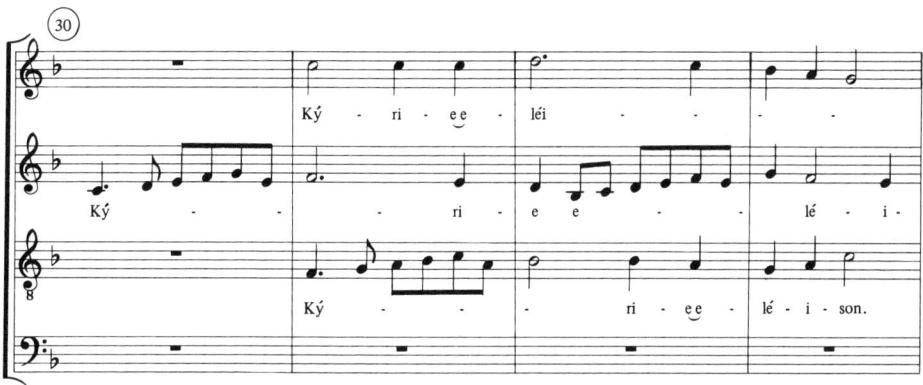
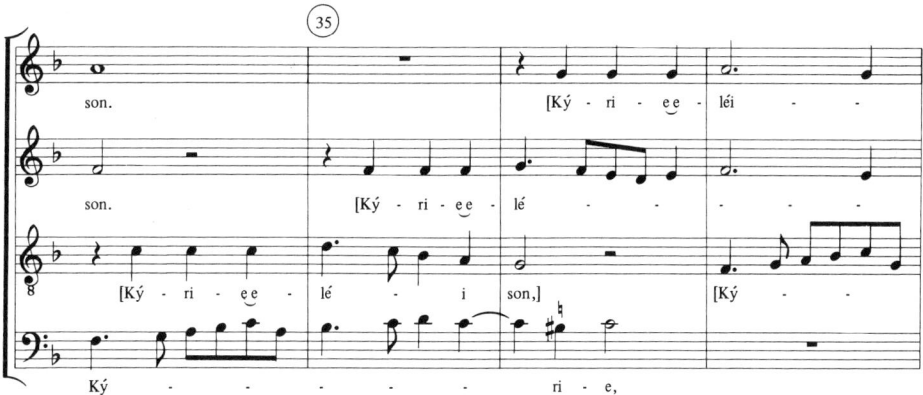

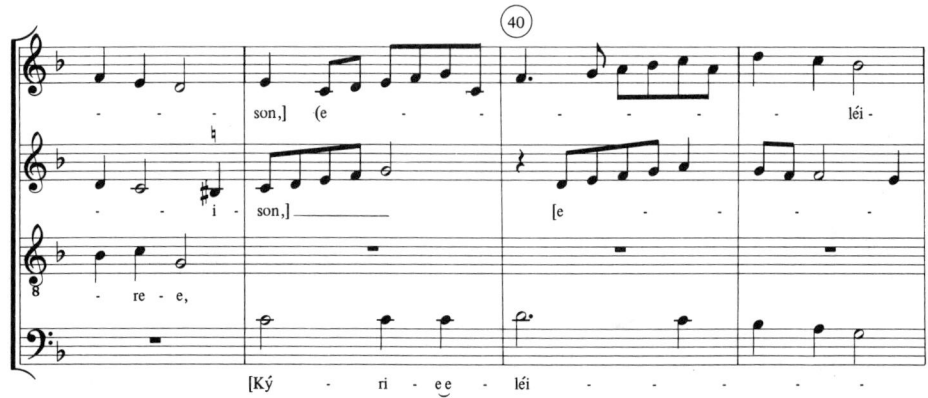

Sanctus

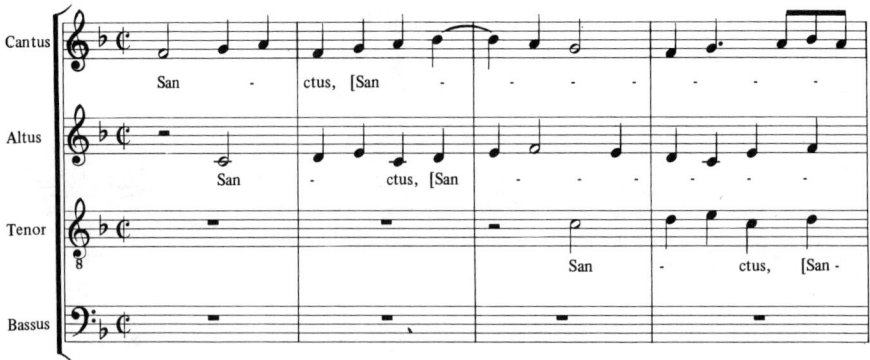

Giovanni Pierluigi da Palestrina

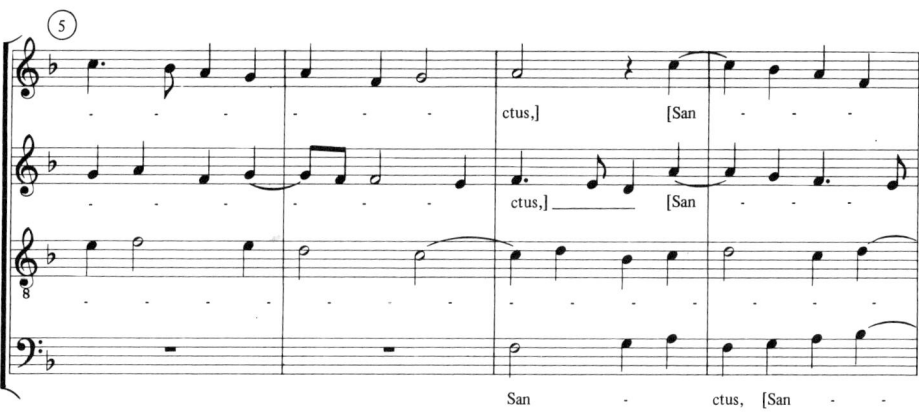

© Instituto Italiano per la Storia della Musica; used by permission.

chant:

Before Reading Chapter 9

1. Listen to the final scene of *The Coronation of Poppea* by Monteverdi.
2. Analyze harmonically (for chord root, quality, and inversion) measures 1–19 of *Pur ti miro* (pages 182–184).
3. Sing and play the two vocal lines together, then add the bass line.

Pur ti miro
from The Coronation of Poppea

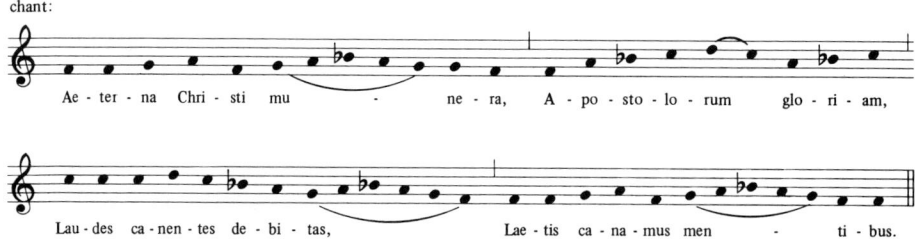

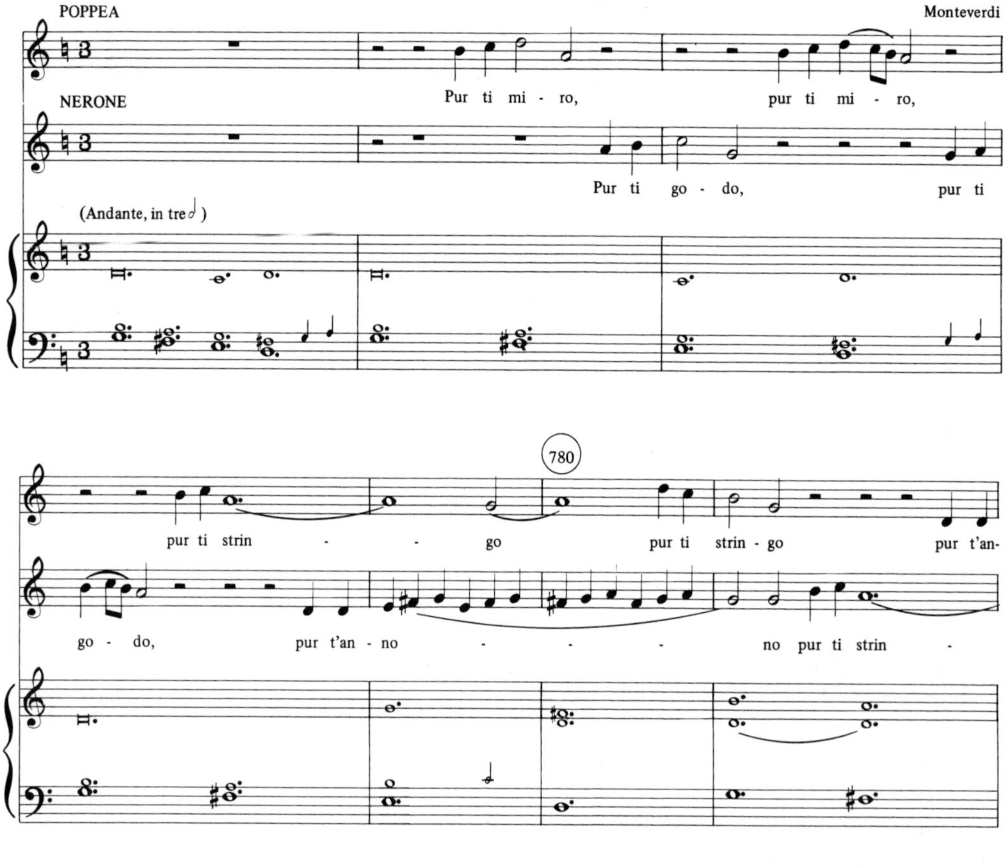

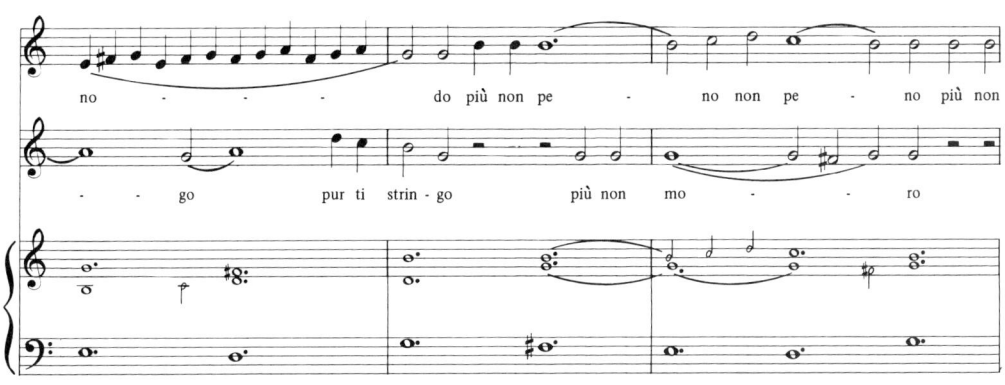
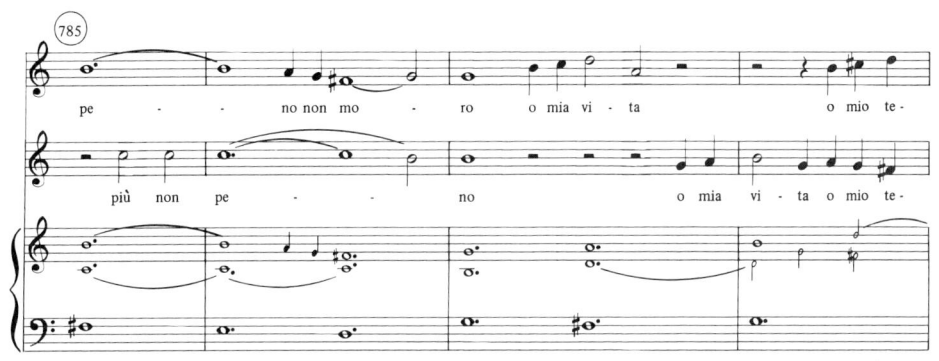

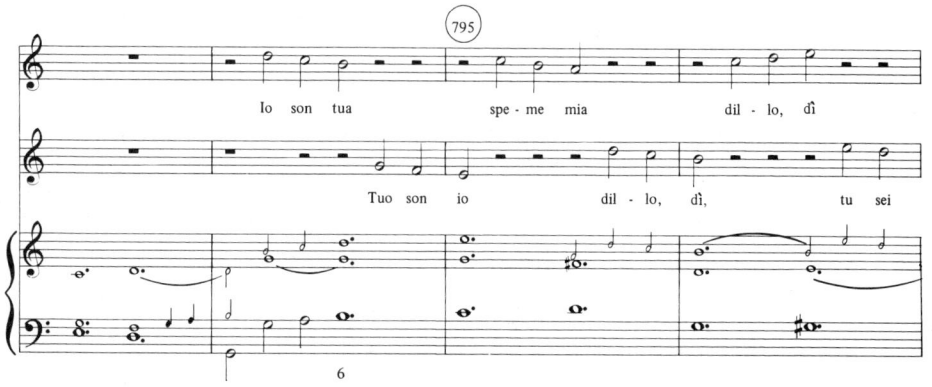
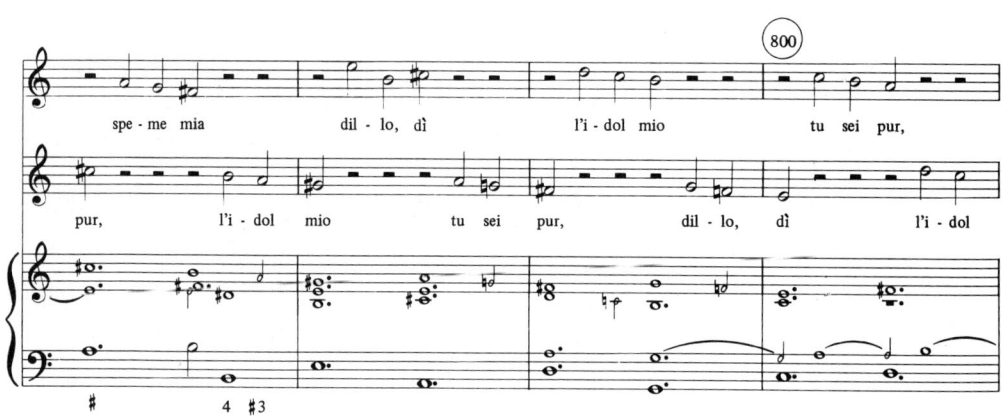

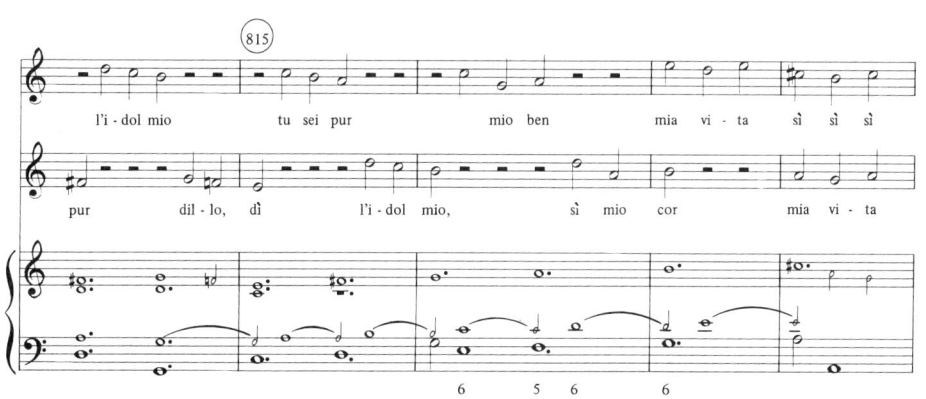

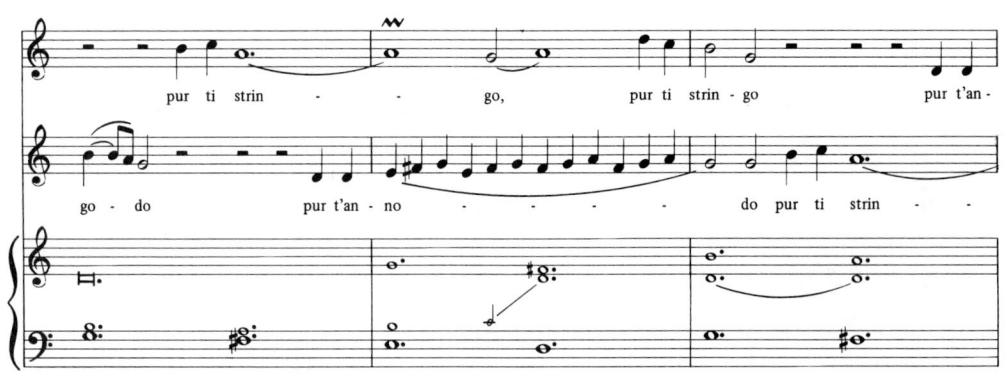

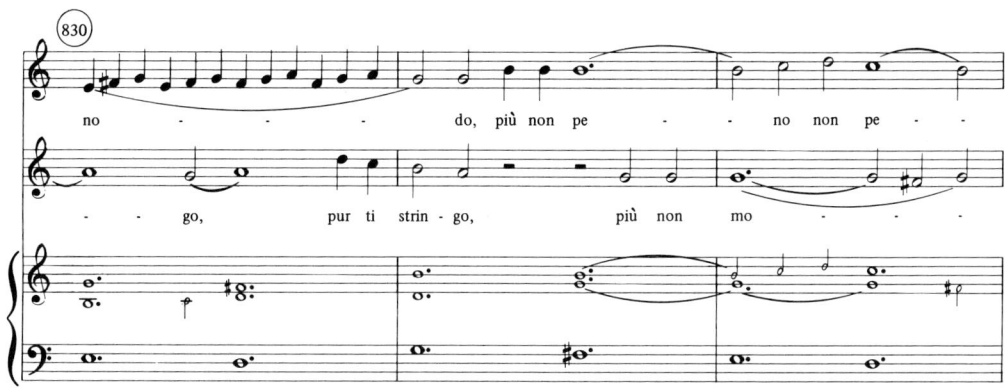

© Universal Edition; Complete Works of Claudio Monteverdi, ed. by G. Francesco Malipiero. Used by permission.

9

Claudio Monteverdi

Pur ti miro from *The Coronation of Poppea*

    Numerous changes in music occurred toward the end of the sixteenth century, for a variety of reasons. The two most significant innovations were the striking changes in texture—from highly contrapuntal to chordal—and in harmony—from a modal concept to a tonal one. Actually, composers did not suddenly forsake either modality or contrapuntal texture. Composers before the seventeenth century wrote some works, as we have seen, that were decidedly tonal in sound, basically homophonic. So the change from the Renaissance to the Baroque period was not an immediate one, nor a truly radical one, but a logical and gradual outgrowth of developments that had begun years before.

    Texture is the most immediately noticeable change. In the example on page 182, Monteverdi (1567–1643) has provided only a harpsichord accompaniment for the two vocal lines. In addition, the harmony is not completely written out for the performer. The original score includes the two vocal parts, plus the bass line (written in larger notes here) and the figures below the bass line.[1] The figures

---

[1] Monteverdi used a more sparsely notated score than did many later composers. Therefore, many of the figures are assumed and not actually written in by the composer or editor.

direct the performer to play the indicated intervals above the bass note; thus, they form a kind of shorthand system of notation. This system, which gradually became widespread, was known as ***figured bass*** or *basso continuo*.

Certain figured-bass abbreviations became standard. A note without figures was assumed to represent a $\frac{5}{3}$, or root-position chord. A note with a 6 called for a $\frac{6}{3}$, or first-inversion triad. $\frac{6}{4}$ was the designation for the second-inversion triad.

ex. 9-1
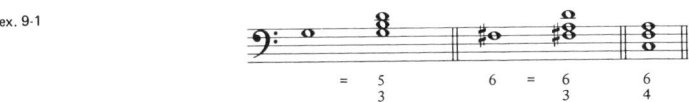

Whenever a sharp, natural, or flat appeared without a number immediately after it, it always referred to the third above the bass.

ex. 9-2
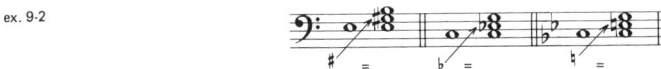

If a triad was to have a seventh added, it had to be indicated.

ex. 9-3

In every case the number given referred to an *interval above the bass*.

Figures were employed to produce not only chordal sounds, but also linear figures, such as suspensions, passing tones, and neighboring tones.

ex. 9-4

If the composer desired to alter the third above the bass, then he simply added ♯ or ♭ or ♮. But altering any other note required both the accidental and the figure: ♯5, ♭6, ♮7, and so forth. Sometimes a slash was used for the sharp sign; thus 6̸ and 5̸ are equivalent to ♯6 and ♯5.

A short example is given below with its "realization"—that is, as it might be performed.[1]

ex. 9-5

[1]Figures have been added to the original score to demonstrate these procedures.

Because of figured bass and its resultant emphasis on chordal harmony, composers began to think in terms of the chords within the scale. Each note of the major or minor scale can be the root of a triad. If the triad uses only the notes of the diatonic scale, the chords within a major scale will always produce the following qualities.

ex. 9-6

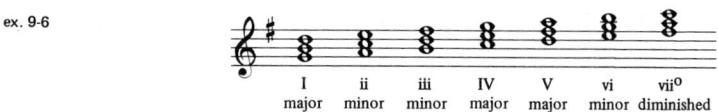

I	ii	iii	IV	V	vi	vii°
major	minor	minor	major	major	minor	diminished

Roman numerals, such as those seen above, are employed in the analysis of tonal music, and they serve to differentiate tonal harmony from that of the modal period. Note that intervals are always designated by Arabic numerals and chords by Roman numerals. Although Roman numerals were not used by composers and theorists in the seventeenth century, they have since become the norm for analysis, and for this reason we will use them here.

The chord root can now be indicated by the appropriate numeral. The quality can be shown by capital and lowercase letters—for example, V is major, ii is minor. If a chord is diminished, a circle is placed after the lowercase numeral—for instance, vii°. If it is augmented, a plus sign is placed after the capital numeral—for instance, III+.

In addition to a Roman-numeral designation, each scale degree was given a name.

I: tonic   IV: subdominant   vii°: leading tone
ii: supertonic V: dominant
iii: mediant   vi: submediant

The names supertonic and leading tone designate their relation to the tonic pitch. The reasons for the other names are a bit more obscure. The dominant is the most important pitch (and chord) after the tonic, and it lies a fifth above the tonic. The subdominant lies a fifth below the tonic, hence its name.

ex. 9-7

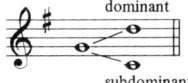

The mediant is halfway to the dominant; the submediant is halfway to the subdominant.

ex. 9-8

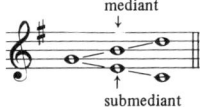

In the seventeenth century, chords begin to be used diatonically within a key, thereby giving a basic structure and sound to the key itself. We find this type of usage in some sections of the Monteverdi example, while others use chords outside of that key center.

In the opening section, the bass line moves *away* from the tonic pitch.

ex. 9-9

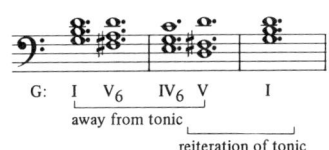

It is followed by a strong reiteration of the tonic via the V–I cadence.

This chord pattern and bass line are repeated continuously throughout this section of the piece. This is a Baroque variation technique called ***passacaglia,*** which perhaps shows some resemblance to the isorhythm of the fourteenth century. It occurs with the repeated bass line throughout and uses linear variations above. The term ***chaconne*** is also sometimes used for such pieces. A chaconne is based on the continuous repetition of the same basic chordal pattern, though not necessarily the same bass line. The ideas of passacaglia and chaconne were sometimes difficult to distinguish, as in the present example.

The harmonic pattern is simple in this opening section, and strongly centered on the tonic. Beginning in measure 794, the harmony becomes more chromatic. G major moves to C major (measures 793–794), D major moves to G major (measures 794–795). This fits into the key structure of G major, but the following chord, in measure 796, is E *major,* which is outside of G (remember, in G major the vi chord will be E *minor*). This E major chord does move to A—i.e. V–I on the level of A. We then see a B major (!) chord that moves to E—V–I on the level of E. In measure 798 the E major moves to A major which in turn moves to D major, G major, and finally C major. Only at this point does the motion stop, to center on diatonic chords in G major once again. Let us look at this sequence of chords:

```
G--C--D--G--E--A--B---E----A----D----G----C----(D--G)
V  I  V  I  V  I  V   I
               V   I
                   V   I
                       V   I
                           V   I  V  I
```

Notice that the progression is entirely based on V–I motion. As will be recalled, it is necessary that a V chord be *major* in order to contain a half-step leading tone to the next chord. All of these chords do contain the leading tone; as a result, the combination of leading-tone function and root movement by fifth downward projects the harmony forward.

This is the system of **secondary function** that we have seen as far back as Josquin. The means used for this are **secondary dominants,** or triads that function as dominants to triads other than the tonic of the key. Any degree of the scale can become a secondary tonic, if a secondary dominant is constructed to lead to that pitch.

ex. 9-10

I   ii   iii   IV   V   vi   vii°   I

V/I — I   V/ii — ii   V/iii — iii   V/IV — IV   V/V — V   V/vi — vi   V/vii — vii°

Monteverdi understands the implications of sequential V–I motion, and is able to extend it for poignant effect. He senses the instability it creates and the ultimate need for resolution and for solidification of the original tonic. This is accomplished by the final section, a quasi-repeat of the first, in which G major is emphasized throughout.

The entire middle section is given below. Note the two different analytical symbols used: V/A when the key is unstable and V/V when it is stable.

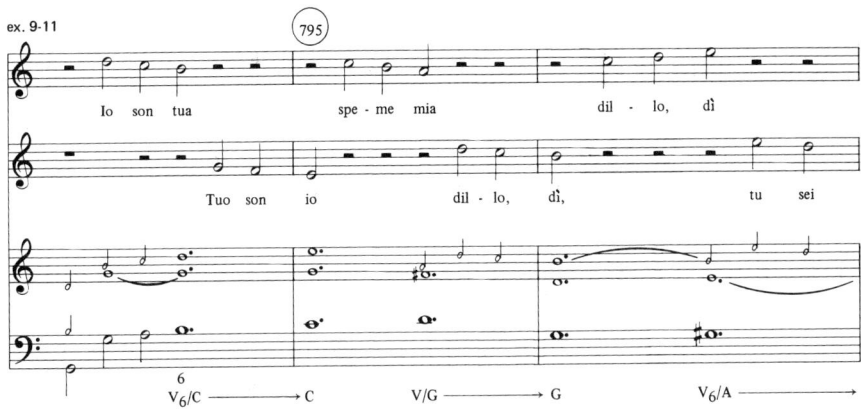

It should be pointed out that root movement by fifth and secondary function are not necessarily the same. Secondary function employs secondary dominants, which *must* be major chords, whereas sequential root movement by fifth may employ minor chords as well. This makes it necessary for secondary function to use accidentals outside the primary key.

Another important contribution of Monteverdi is his use of the seventh chord. Sevenths had always been considered as dissonant to triadic harmony, either as passing tones or neighboring tones. Beginning with Monteverdi, this practice slowly changes, and other composers soon begin to experiment with the full seventh chord.

The triad first used as a basis for the addition of the seventh was the dominant. The reason lies in the sound, structure, and function of the chord itself. In early music the tritone was avoided because of its harsh sound. In the **V7 chord,** the interval between the third and the seventh is the tritone, and it is primarily this sound that creates the character and strong resolution tendency of the chord. As we have seen, diminished fifths have a great tendency to resolve inward, just as augmented fourths tend to resolve outward.

ex. 9-12

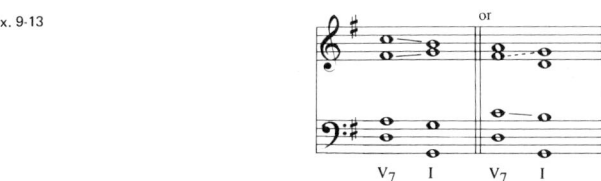

In the progression from V7 to I, the leading tone resolves to the tonic, and the fourth scale degree resolves to the third of the tonic triad. These two motions, coupled with the normal resolution of the other members of the V7 chord, produce a strong impulse toward the tonic and a satisfying resolution.

ex. 9-13

Under normal circumstances, the leading tone will resolve upward, but occasionally (as in the second progression of Ex 9–13) another note will substitute for it in the resolution and allow the leading tone to move elsewhere (usually to the fifth of the next chord).

The same is *not* true of the seventh of the chord. *Regardless of the voicing, inversion, or structure, the seventh of the V chord resolves downward by step.*

As in any chord, if the root is not in the bass, an inversion results. In the **dominant seventh chord,** three **inversions** are possible. The inversions and their standard resolutions are shown in the next example. Note that the seventh in each case resolves downward by step. These are not all of the possible resolutions, but they may serve as a general guide.

ex. 9-14

When the leading tone is in the bass (V^6_5) it should resolve properly. Likewise, when the bass note is the seventh of the chord (V^4_2) it should resolve downward by step, resulting in a I_6 chord.

Another term for the dominant seventh is "major-minor seventh"—that is, a major triad with a minor seventh added to it. Since it is a unique intervallic construction, it usually functions as a V7 chord and resolves to a chord whose root is a fifth lower than its own.

In the Monteverdi example, again starting in measure 797, it is seen that all of these V chords (secondary dominants) have sevenths attached, thereby increasing the impetus to the next chord. Notice that accidentals are sometimes needed to produce the minor seventh above the bass, as well as to produce the major third which functions as the leading tone. Also notice that the seventh always resolves downward by step, both in the keyboard realization and in the voice.

Two other small points should be mentioned regarding the present example. The ending cadence of the second section, measures 807–808, introduces two very important tonal considerations: the **cadential I_4^6** and the **anticipation**.

In measure 808 the progression is, in G major, I_4^6–V (with a g and b added after the V chord has sounded)–I.

ex. 9-15

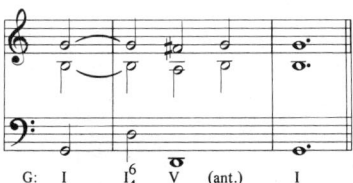

G: I I_4^6 V (ant.) I

The sound is distinctly that of a double suspension on the downbeat. Because it also seems to constitute a chord, it is referred to as a cadential I_4^6 chord. There are two important ways that the $_4^6$ chord is used: 1) as a cadential I_4^6, used on the strong beat at the cadence and resolving to a V chord; and 2) as a passing chord. The second category will not be discussed until later, since it represents a less important usage. The cadential I_4^6 is, however, a very important chord and is used frequently in cadential progressions.

The notes before the tonic chord in root position are usually referred to as anticipations because they are part of the next chord (the I) rather than of the present V chord. In other words, they anticipate the new harmony. This example is a little unusual in that there are two anticipations happening at once.

The design of the piece, then, depends on two different ways of using harmony—the purely diatonic harmonies in the first and last sections, and the chromatic alteration which creates secondary dominants in the extended middle section. The middle section produces a certain kind of instability and tension that is resolved and released by the final section, a repeat of the first section. This gives the piece an overall sectional balance of **ABBA.**

STYLE CHARACTERISTICS OF THE EARLY SEVENTEENTH CENTURY
based on *Pur ti miro* from Monteverdi's *The Coronation of Poppea*

melody   smooth • leaps of a sixth and seventh occasionally used • more closely related to chord structures—melody derived from the harmony • more fragmented rhythmically and motivically, less fluid than in previous centuries

harmony	use of all diatonic triads within a key • secondary dominants are used extensively • seventh chords, particularly the V7 chord, are used • first-inversion and root-position triads prominent, but second inversion can also be used, especially for the cadential I_4^6 • cadences: authentic, plagal, deceptive, and I_4^6–V–I
dissonance	passing tones • neighboring tones • suspensions • anticipations • escape tones (rarely)
rhythm	relatively smooth, with no great shifts rhythmically • syncopation is used sparingly • much alternation of motion between parts • simple rhythmic patterns used in the keyboard realization
texture	homophonic • chordal
techniques	passacaglia and chaconne • sequence • figured bass

Glossary

Anticipation a rhythmically weak dissonance approached by step and repeated. Although dissonant on the weak beat, the harmony moves to make the pitch consonant on the strong beat.

Cadential I_4^6 a tonic $_4^6$ chord used at the cadence; it occurs on a strong beat and resolves to the V chord.

Chaconne a Baroque variation technique based on the continued repetition of a short chordal pattern throughout the piece. (Not consistently distinguished from passacaglia.)

Figured bass (basso continuo) a notational process of indicating the bass note and intervals above that note; used in the seventeenth and eighteenth centuries.

Passacaglia a Baroque variation technique based on the continued repetition of a short bass line (ground bass) throughout the piece. (Not consistently distinguished from chaconne.)

Primary function diatonic root movement emphasizing the fifth.

Roman-numeral analysis used for designating chords built on each scale degree of a major or minor scale. The quality of the triad can be designated by the way the Roman numeral is written: I = major; i = minor; I+ = augmented; i° = diminished.

Secondary dominant a dominant chord (always major) of a key other than the tonic.

Secondary function V–I movement on a level other than the primary tonic level.

Suggested Exercises

1. Write and resolve the following seventh chords:

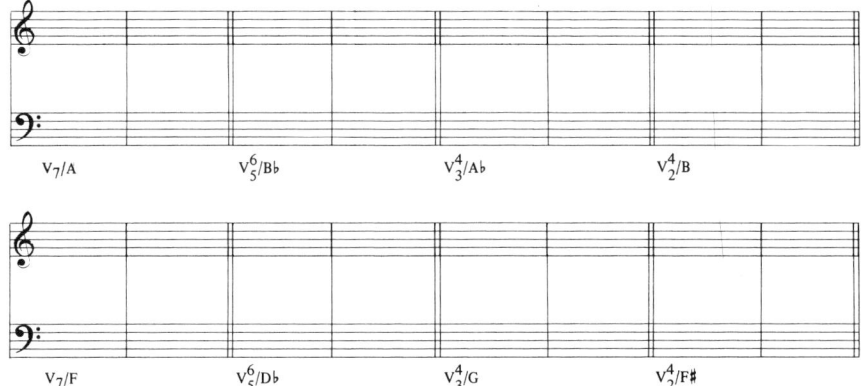

2. Complete the following figured-bass example in keyboard texture, and write a melodic line for violin or flute above.

3. Complete the following progressions in four-voice texture.
   a. G: I V6 I IV V I
   b. F: I V7 I V/ii ii V I
   c. C: I IV I$_4^6$ V I V7/V V I
   d. A: I ii V I V/vi V/ii V/V I$_4^6$ V7 I

Before Reading Chapter 10

1. Sing each line of *Veni creator Spiritus* by Johann Schein (page 200).
2. Compare the chant version (page 199) to the polyphonic hymn.
3. Analyze the harmonic structure carefully, especially the cadences.
4. Play and sing all four parts together.

10

Johann Hermann Schein

Veni creator Spiritus

In the late sixteenth century, composers began to produce simple harmonic settings of hymn tunes in a four-voice texture. These settings were in direct response to a need for liturgical music for the newly established Lutheran church. The melodies, in many cases, already existed. And, like chant in the Catholic church, they were borrowed and used in a variety of different settings, one of the earliest being that of **homophonic hymns.**

These hymns took on a decidedly tonal sound, as did other genres of the same time. The next example demonstrates the use of harmony in this early Baroque period, and is a convenient piece with which to study voice leading and harmonization procedures. The composer, Johann Hermann Schein (1586–1630), based his hymn on the *Veni creator Spiritus* hymn chant. Both the chant version and the chordal setting are given below for comparison.

ex. 10-1

ex. 10-2

Schein

As in any **paraphrased melody,** certain melodic notes are left out and others are altered. The line is essentially the same, however, and is easily recognized as being derived from the chant. The most significant changes are the inclusion of certain accidentals. In every case they function as leading tones. So, instead of the strict Mixolydian mode of the chant, the hymn is in G major due to the sharping of the *f*. The further inflection of *c* to *c*♯ sometimes produces the effect of D major.

The melody has been "plotted" by the composer both for harmonic possibilities (the melodic notes have to be part of the harmony) as well as cadence possibilities. Notice that each cadence is chosen for its relationship to the home key: C (IV) and D (V) and G (I). There are, therefore, both variety and unity in the cadential motion. Like most hymns, *Veni creator Spiritus* remains in its tonic key throughout, with no true modulation.

ex. 10-3

Most of the hymn utilizes only the chords of G major. Secondary dominants are occasionally used, and each moves to its proper secondary tonic. Keys other than the tonic are suggested at several points, though. For example, there is a strong suggestion of I–V–I in C major at the end of the first phrase. The closing progression of the next phrase seems to be ii$_6$–V–I in the key of D major. The next phrase has two such "pockets" of alternative tonality: V–I in C for the opening two chords and IV–vii$^{\circ}_6$–I in D major for the final three.

The strength of these chords to the various tonics is probably a direct result of their relationship both to the tonic key and to the inflected key. The possibilities of being in two key areas at once is reserved for only a few chords—they must be diatonic in two different keys at the same time. However, their use is important in a *pivotal* sense. They can help pivot from one key area to another using means that are diatonic to each area. This is the smoothest possible motion, creating the least possible shock. The process of shifting keys is called **modulation** and in this case, because the means used are diatonic, it is referred to as **diatonic modulation.** Diatonic modulation usually occurs via a **pivot chord:** a chord that appears diatonically in both the original and the new key, and which serves as a bridge between the two.

It must be emphasized that the real difference between a strong modulation and an inflection to a given area has to do with length. A modulation occurs when the key changes for an extended period of time. Thus, the present examples are not modulations. Instead, they merely represent inflections, very brief motions to other degrees of the scale.

In either case, one must recognize the use of the raised leading tone and of V–I on another degree of the scale. This secondary V–I motion produces only an inflection unless the new key area is prolonged, in which case it becomes a modulation.

The analysis of the third phrase of the hymn demonstrates the V chord and the vii° chord, both of which tend to move to I. This is true not only within the key but also in any secondary position. Therefore, the vii$^{o}_{6}$–I cadence on D in the third phrase functions also as a vii$^{o}_{6}$/V–V in the key of G. Both V and vii° can function in this way because of the strength of the leading tone contained in both.

The relationships of the individual chords within the phrase are not left to chance. The cadences are well established by means of the fifth movement of the chord roots. Within the phrase, numerous uses of chords can be seen, but they usually fall into a few basic patterns:

$$\begin{array}{ll} \text{IV–V–I} & \text{ii–V–I} \\ \text{vi–IV–I} & \text{IV–vii°–I} \end{array}$$

The common feature here is that of the position of each chord in relation to the tonic. A IV or ii chord usually precedes a V chord. A vii° or V chord almost always precedes a I chord (the exception being the plagal motion of IV–I). And vi almost always precedes a IV or a ii chord, occasionally a V chord. This relationship of chords, progressing by fifths toward the tonic, is referred to as **tonal function.** A general pattern that can be used to describe a great number of progressions in tonal compositions is:

$$\text{iii} \quad \text{vi} \quad \text{ii} \quad \text{V} \quad \text{I}$$

All the root movement in the progression is by fifth. This progression leaves out two important chords, IV and vii°. The chart can be modified to include them in the position in which they are commonly found.

$$\begin{array}{ccccc} \text{iii} & \text{vi} & \text{ii} & \text{V} & \text{I} \\ & & \text{or} & \text{or} & \\ & & \text{IV} & \text{vii°} & \end{array}$$

With this in mind, look at the chorale again. Every progression follows this pattern, with only two exceptions. First, there is the deceptive motion V–vi (D–e) in measure 2 (labelled deceptive because it deceives the expectation that V will proceed to I). Second, there are a few instances when IV moves to I, apparently skipping the dominant. Such elisions of steps within the basic progression are sometimes seen (it is rare, however, to see the elision of two steps at once). It should be pointed out that the tonic chord may move anywhere.

This chart should not be regarded as strict dogma to be followed by every piece, all of the time. But it is remarkable how much tonal music does in fact follow similar progressional patterns. Functional harmony is defined by this general pattern of diatonic root movement by fifths downward (or fourths upward).

Although not appearing in the present example, there is another cadence type that was used in the early seventeenth century, as well as occasionally in the sixteenth century. This cadence ends on the V chord, indicating not a modulation to the dominant area, but rather an incomplete harmonic motion. This is called a **half cadence,** and obviously can never be used as a final cadence.

ex. 10-4

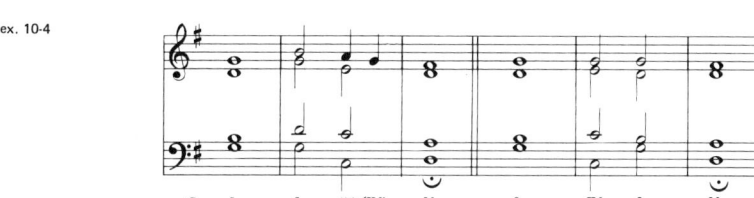

The approach to the V chord of the half cadence is variable, normally I or ii or IV or vi. If V is approached diatonically, without the use of a secondary dominant, this will tend to produce the incomplete effect of the half cadence.

Guidelines for Voice Leading

1. General smoothness in every line should be emphasized. Avoid leaps of more than a third or fourth. Only occasionally use a leap of an octave; reserve these for the soprano or bass voices.
2. A *general* guide for doubling procedure is as follows:
    root position: double the root
    first inversion: double the soprano
    second inversion: double the bass (fifth of the triad)
   Only use second-inversion triads in passing and in cadences. Rarely double the third of a triad. (An exception to this is given below in Ex. 10-5.) But never omit the third of a triad.
3. Be very careful of the resolution of tritones. The d5 will resolve inward and the A4 will resolve outward.

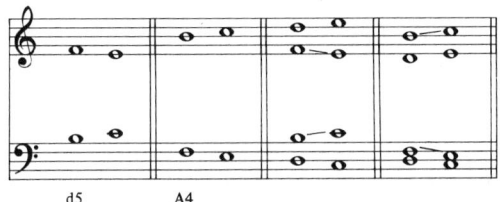

ex. 10-5

Because each tone must be resolved, neither of these pitches should be doubled. Thus in a diminished triad (vii°) never double the root or fifth; always try to double the third.

4. In V chords, resolve the leading tone to the tonic. There is one exception to this:

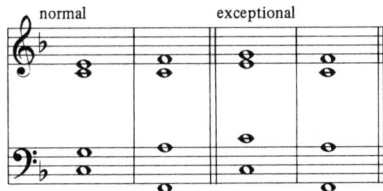

ex. 10-6

In the second case, the soprano takes over the resolution to the *f,* freeing the alto to move to *c,* the fifth of the chord. *Avoid doubling the leading tone.* If two leading tones resolve to the tonic, the result is parallel octaves.

5. In the V7 chord, the leading tone resolves to the tonic, the seventh resolves down by step, and the fifth and root have variable resolutions depending on the context.

ex. 10-7

6. Linear motion is important. Not only smoothness of line, but strong motion to the cadence is necessary.

Guidelines for Harmonization of a Melody

The most important aspect of the process of harmonizing a melody is linear motion. A good linear conception can help to project the harmonic motion of the piece in a convincing way. This general principle of linear control should always be considered when harmonizing a chorale melody.

1. Analyze the cadences for possible harmonic and modulatory motion and for the general tonal motion within the piece.
2. Determine the chordal possibilities of each note of the melody. A melodic note can be the root, third, or fifth of a given triad. (Keep in mind that it could be a dissonance as well.)
3. Determine a chord progression by choosing chordal possibilities that form a strong, functional pattern. These progressions should produce a general movement toward the cadence.
4. Write a bass line that follows the best chordal progression. This should be a rather simple line, using root position extensively.
5. Modify the bass line to make it more melodically interesting and to establish a good relationship with the soprano line. Contrary motion should be used as much as possible. Harmonies should be mainly in root position and first inversion, though the bass may also use passing tones and other controlled dissonances.
6. Add inner voices which employ a smooth, linear motion. Attention should be given to the avoidance of parallel fifths and octaves and to the production of a singable line in general.

An example is given below, in a step-by-step arrangement.

STEPS ONE AND TWO: Chord possibilities, based on melodic notes.

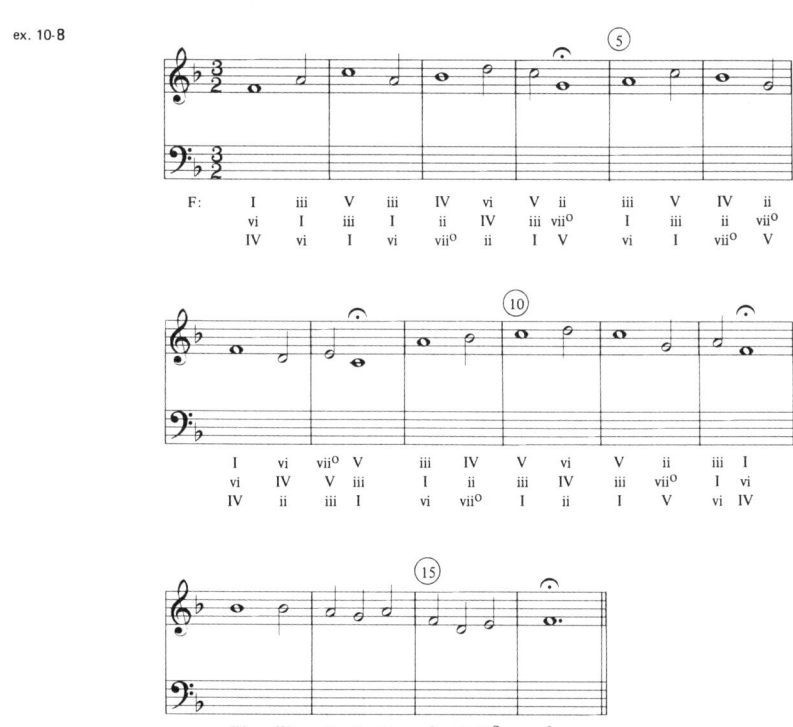

ex. 10-8

Note that in a few cases the composer does not follow normal procedures: in measure 10, V–ii, then V–I; in measures 13–14, ii–vi, then vi–V–I. This is called *retrogression,* or proceeding backwards, functionally speaking. It is used mostly in the body of the phrase, but should be de-emphasized because it retards strong functional progression.

STEPS THREE AND FOUR: Bass line sketched in, using *root position* only.

Note two problem areas: in measures 9–10 and 14 occur parallel fifths and octaves. These must be removed before the final draft.

STEP FIVE: Bass line changed producing several inversions; cadences slightly altered.

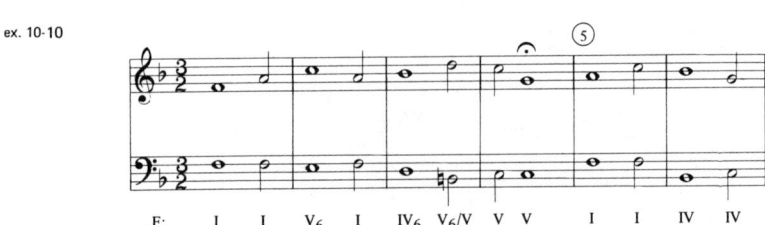

Parallel fifths and octaves may be eliminated by altering the bass line, creating inverted triads. Root-position chords by themselves produce a choppy bass line. Secondary function can enhance the harmonic motion at times. Use it with care, but do not avoid the possibilities it offers.

STEP SIX: Filled-in inner parts.

Quem pastores laudavere

ex. 10-11

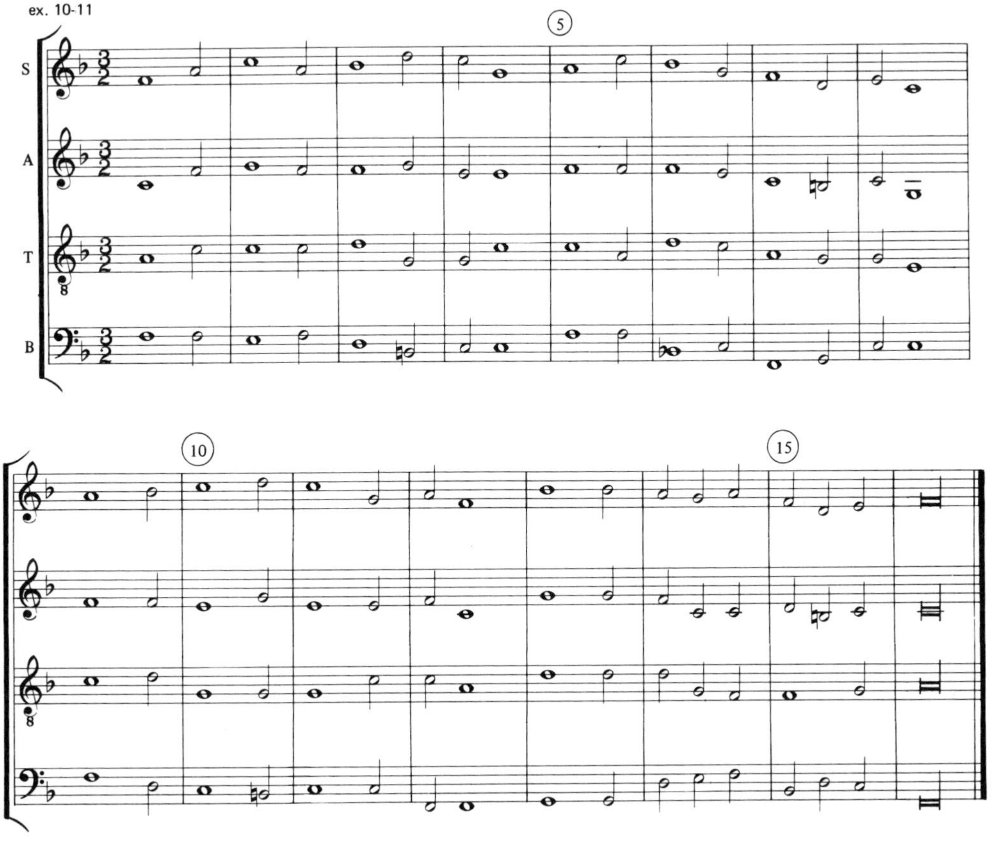

Style characteristics of the literature in chapter 10 are reviewed in the preceding Guidelines.

Glossary

Diatonic modulation modulation to a key whose tonic pitch is present in the original scale.
Homophony chordal texture in which the voices move rhythmically together.
Modulation the process by which a composer moves from one tonic area to another.
Pivot chord a chord which appears naturally (that is, diatonically) as part of two different keys, and thus can be used to move smoothly from one key to another.
Retrogression a chordal progression that moves contrary to the precepts of tonal function. Instead of moving toward the tonic, $IV-V-I$, it moves away from it, $V-IV$.

Suggested Exercises

1. Provide a harmonic analysis of the following chorales. Note the cadences used, and the linear approach to each. Be careful of secondary dominants and possible modulations.

Verzage nicht, o frommer Christ

J. H. Schein

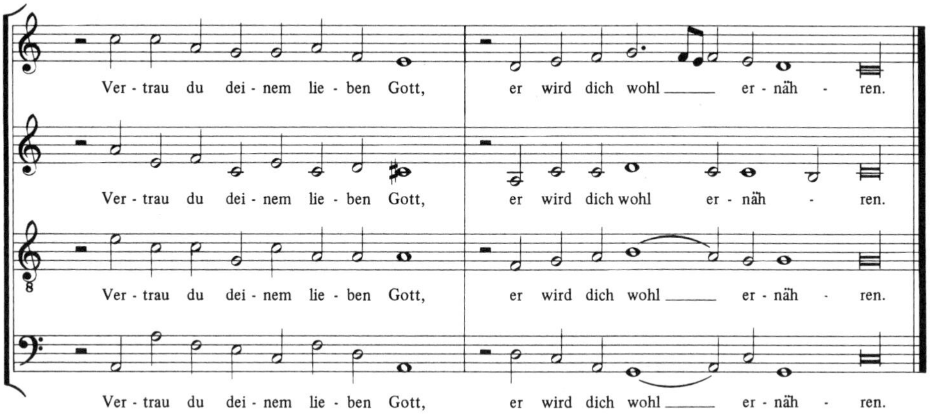
Ver - trau du dei - nem lie - ben Gott, er wird dich wohl ___ er - näh - ren.
Ver - trau du dei - nem lie - ben Gott, er wird dich wohl er - näh - ren.
Ver - trau du dei - nem lie - ben Gott, er wird dich wohl ___ er - näh - ren.
Ver - trau du dei - nem lie - ben Gott, er wird dich wohl ___ er - näh - ren.

Fröhlich wollen wir Alleluja singen

Johann Agricola

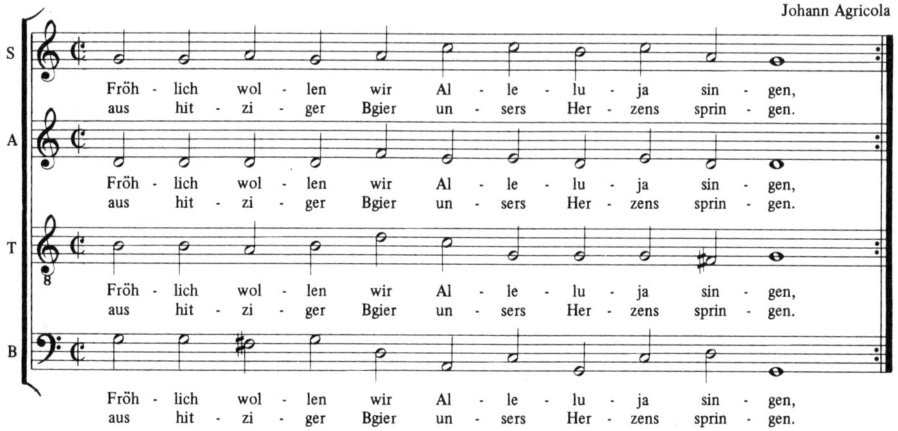
S
Fröh - lich wol - len wir Al - le - lu - ja sin - gen,
aus hit - zi - ger Bgier un - sers Her - zens sprin - gen.
A
Fröh - lich wol - len wir Al - le - lu - ja sin - gen,
aus hit - zi - ger Bgier un - sers Her - zens sprin - gen.
T
Fröh - lich wol - len wir Al - le - lu - ja sin - gen,
aus hit - zi - ger Bgier un - sers Her - zens sprin - gen.
B
Fröh - lich wol - len wir Al - le - lu - ja sin - gen,
aus hit - zi - ger Bgier un - sers Her - zens sprin - gen.

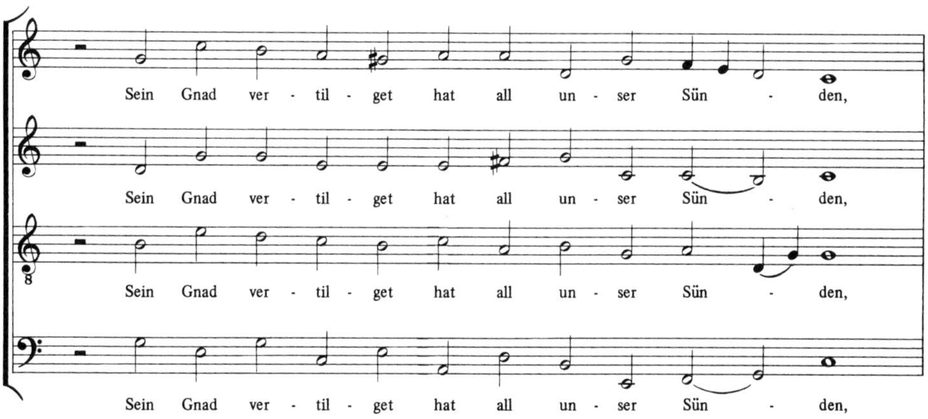
Sein Gnad ver - til - get hat all un - ser Sün - den,
Sein Gnad ver - til - get hat all un - ser Sün - den,
Sein Gnad ver - til - get hat all un - ser Sün - den,
Sein Gnad ver - til - get hat all un - ser Sün - den,

2. Complete the following figured-bass example in four parts, chordal style. Provide a harmonic analysis, being careful to indicate all secondary dominants and any pivot-chord modulations.

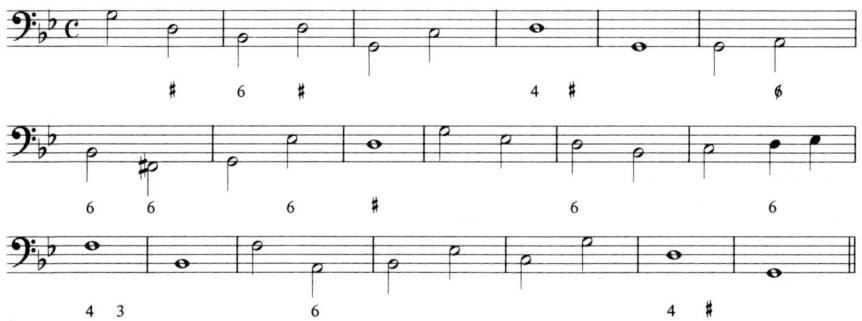

3. Harmonize the following melodic lines in homophonic style. Follow the step-by-step procedures (see pages 204–207). In each case try to use at least one secondary dominant (usually at the cadence); be sure to indicate any such secondary functional activity.

Freut euch, ihr lieben Christen

Before Reading Chapter 11

1. Listen to "Dido's Lament" from Purcell's *Dido and Aeneas*.
2. Bracket the repetition of the bass line throughout.
3. Bracket the phrase structure in the vocal part.
4. Compare harmonically measures 1–10 and 55–64.

20
laid in earth, may my wrongs cre - ate No trou - ble, no trou-ble in thy

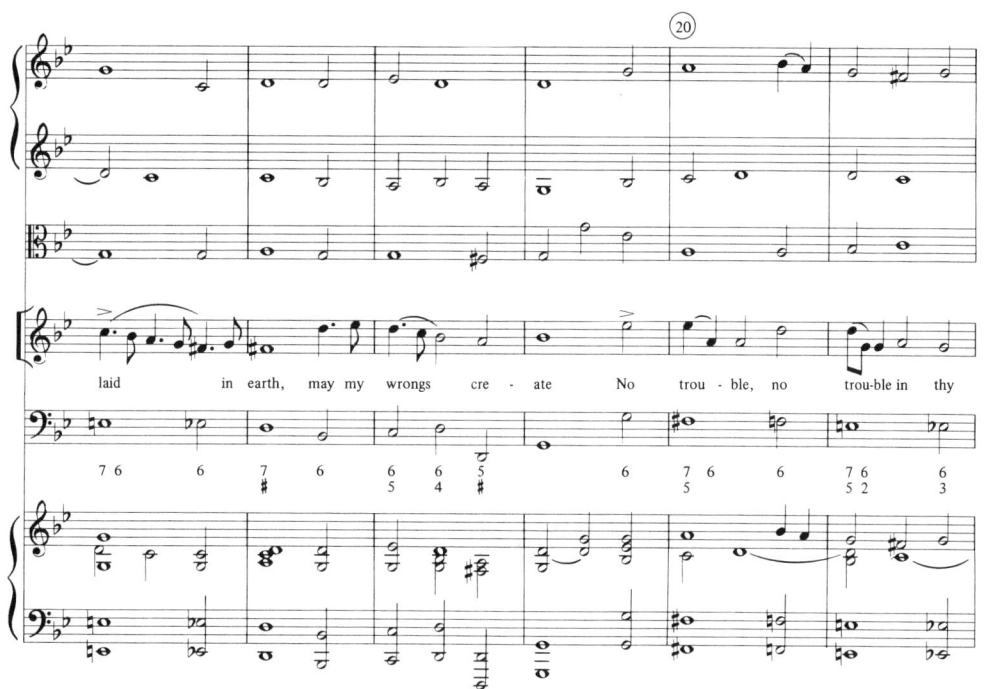

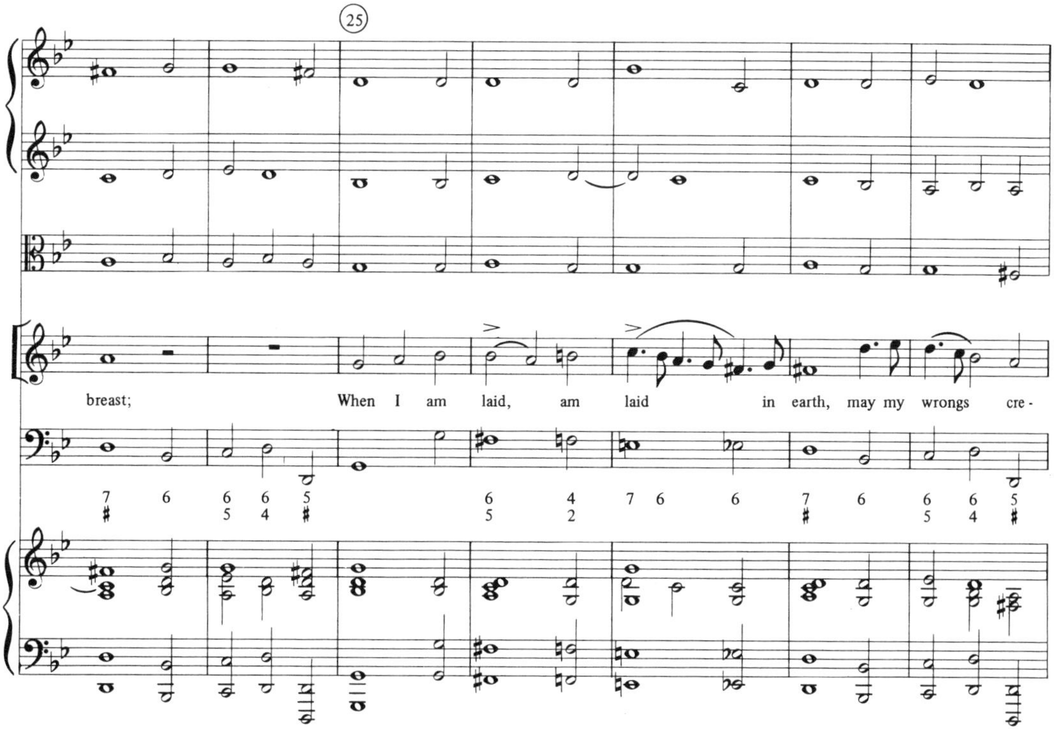
25
breast; When I am laid, am laid in earth, may my wrongs cre -

11

Henry Purcell

"*Dido's Lament*" from *Dido and Aeneas*

Although opera was one of the greatest musical genres of the Baroque period, England produced almost no great opera composers during the Baroque period. The only exception was Henry Purcell (1659–1695), who wrote many stage works, including one true opera, *Dido and Aeneas.* The preceding excerpt is the final aria from the work.

Purcell is noted for, among other things, his extensive use of the technique of *passacaglia.* His examples of this variation technique are somewhat longer and more complex than the short example by Monteverdi, but they employ the same basic pattern of a repeated bass line with variations above. As is normal in a passacaglia, the meter is always a slow triple.

"Dido's Lament" is based on a repeated thematic idea in the bass, usually called a **ground bass.** This bass line is typical in that its motion is from the tonic down to the dominant.

ex. 11-1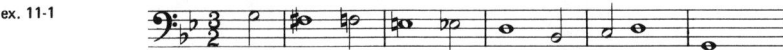

The chromatic pattern helps create tension both melodically and harmonically; the dramatic qualities of this motion, and their relationship to the opera, are of special significance. At this moment in the opera, Dido has just been left by her lover Aeneas, and she is about to die by her own hand. The idea of death is portrayed musically, as well as dramatically, by the chromatic descent of the ground bass. The use of the minor mode, the chromaticism, and the large amount of dissonance add to the pathos.

The harmonic motion of the piece is well established in the beginning. The ground bass limits the possible harmonic progressions in much the same way that isorhythm affected the harmonic motion in the motets of the fourteenth century. The chromatic motion temporarily weakens the feeling of key, but the tonality is strengthened at the end of every presentation by a strong V–I cadence.

Before tackling this aria in detail, we should consider the ***melodic/harmonic use of the minor scale*** and the construction of diminished and half-diminished seventh chords. It should be noted that this particular ground bass includes all of the notes found in the upper tetrachord (the final four notes) of the melodic minor scale:

ex. 11-2

A most important feature of the minor scales is that they contain great melodic and ***harmonic possibilities.*** The inclusion of so many chromatic notes in its normal scale formations produces a vast array of chordal possibilities.

ex. 11-3

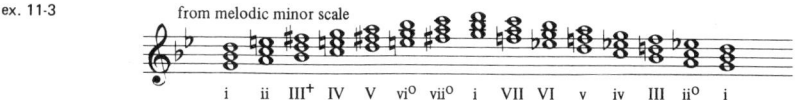

The possibilities of a minor *and* a major subdominant and dominant chord is of special interest, since Purcell mixes these frequently. Note that the minor v chord is normally used when moving *away* from the tonic harmony (measure 15) and the major V chord is used to push *toward* the tonic (measure 18).

An important feature of the minor mode is the use of both the ***half-diminished and fully diminished seventh.*** The former occurs on the second scale degree in minor (ii$^{\o}_7$) and the latter occurs on the seventh scale degree.

ex. 11-4

The intervallic construction of the vii°₇ is diminished/diminished: a diminished triad with a diminished seventh added to it. The resolution is usually as follows:

ex. 11-5

The voice-leading procedure is quite simple: resolve the tritones. In a fully diminished seventh chord there are two tritones; in root position, both are diminished fifths, so each should resolve inward.

ex. 11-6

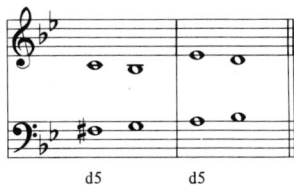

The same procedure may be followed for the inversions. Once again, augmented fourths should be resolved outward; diminished fifths, inward.

ex. 11-7

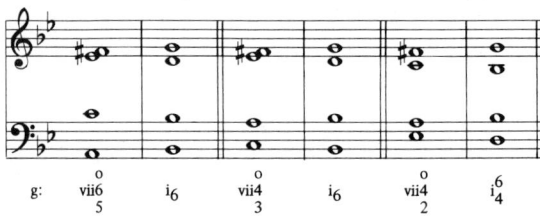

It is possible to use a slightly modified version of the above resolution. For purposes of sonority in the chord of resolution, it is sometimes preferred to double the root. This can be accomplished by resolving one of the tritones differently.

ex. 11-8

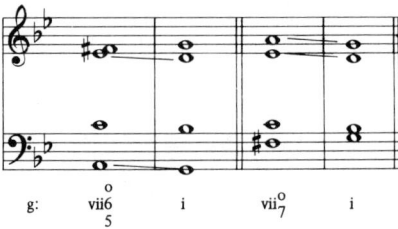

Any chord that has a strong tendency to move to the tonic chord may be used in a secondary function. Thus, since vii$°_7$ has a strong pull toward the tonic, vii$°_7$/iv will have a strong pull toward the fourth scale degree. In every case, the ***secondary diminished-seventh chord*** is built a half step below the chord of resolution. In g minor, *c* is the fourth scale degree; therefore the root of vii$°_7$/iv is *b*, a half step below *c*.

ex. 11-9

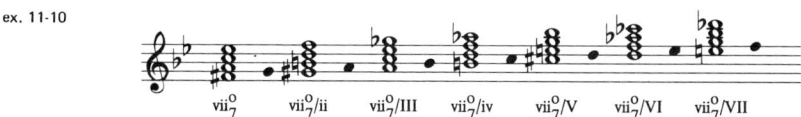

The same procedure may be followed for all of the scale degrees.

ex. 11-10

vii$°_7$ vii$°_7$/ii   vii$°_7$/III   vii$°_7$/iv   vii$°_7$/V   vii$°_7$/VI   vii$°_7$/VII

The resolution of each is to a chord whose root is a half step above the root of the diminished seventh.

The half-diminished-seventh chord normally appears on the second scale degree in minor, and on the seventh degree in major. Its resolution tendency is not quite as strong as that of the fully diminished chord because of its construction: a diminished triad with a *minor* seventh. The minor seventh has a tendency to diffuse some of the intensity of the fully diminished seventh.

ex. 11-11

g: ii$ø_7$ B♭: vii$ø_7$

The actual function of the ii and vii triads remains the same as before: ii$ø_7$ will still resolve to V and vii$ø_7$ will move to I.

ex. 11-12

g: ii$ø_7$ V$_7$ B♭: vii$ø_7$ I

Below is given a brief analysis of the first 11 measures of the aria, beginning with the vocal entry. Notice the juxtapositions of the major and minor versions of the IV chord, the use of the ii$ø_7$, and a secondary usage of the half-diminished seventh. In all cases the chordal function and progression follow the norm.

ex. 11-13

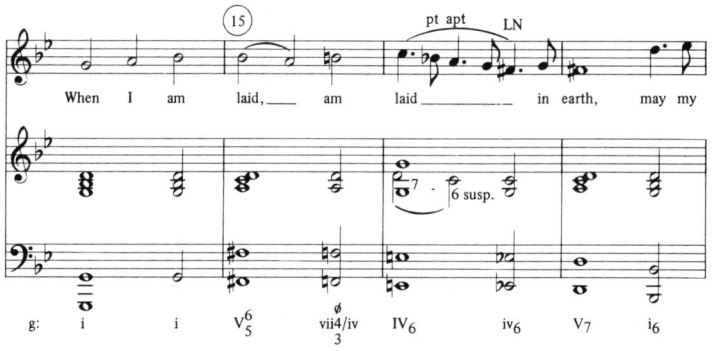

In addition to the strongly functional chord progression, there is much emphasis on dissonances, which contribute to the overall tension and forward motion of the piece. A characteristic area is in the last two measures of the above excerpt. Note both the intimation of a vocal suspension ($e^\flat$–d) as well as the passing tone/suspension/upper neighbor idea in measures 20–21.

The chords tend to follow progressional patterns that have become well established in the period. The V and vii° chords normally move to the tonic, as we know; progressions to the dominant are more varied, however. The ii° chord tends to move to V, as does the iv chord; VI occasionally moves to V or vii°. The tonic has the ability to move in any direction and to any chord. The primary patterns, then, are:

a. ii°   V   i   (see measures 28–29)
   (iiø₇ V   i)
b. iv   V   i   (see measures 23–24)
   (IV   V   i)
c. VI   viiø₇   (then to V₆) (see measures 29–30)

220

Secondary patterns (which are still functional in nature) are:

a. V/iv–iv
b. vii°/V–V
   etc.

The first pattern displays the stability of root movement by fifth: ii V i. By extending this back from the ii chord we can produce **tonal function** which was discussed in the last chapter, only this time in the minor key:

III VI ii° V i

The other chords in the key may be substituted as in the following:

III VI ii° V i
         or   or
         iv   vii°

The quality of these chords is determined primarily by the harmonic minor scale, rather than the melodic. However, it is always possible that the melodic scale will influence chord quality. The minor mode, as we have seen, is quite versatile in this respect.

One might inquire of the quality of the III chord in a harmonic minor scale. Theoretically, it should be augmented. However, if one analyzes a large body of music from this and succeeding periods, it will be found that the III+ chord is rarely used. Therefore, we will use the major III chord that is actually used by the composers.

An important point to remember is that in order to function as a dominant chord (that is, to resolve to the tonic chord) the V chord must be a major chord. Likewise, the vii° chord must be built on the raised leading tone.

ex. 11-14

If the seventh degree is not raised, the function of these chords is altered, and they will not generally resolve to the tonic. The use of a minor v chord is possible, but it usually moves *away* from the tonic harmony rather than toward it.

ex. 11-15

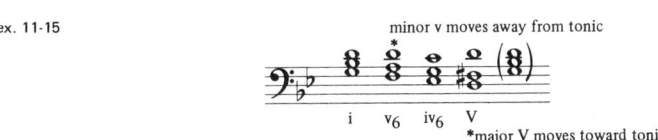

minor v moves away from tonic

i v6 iv6 V
*major V moves toward tonic

As in all previous periods, composers extend the use of harmony in the seventeenth century. Not only are the various functional patterns employed, but the use of seventh chords is extended beyond the V7, ii⌀7, and vii°7 to include all the scale degrees of the key. The addition of the seventh does not normally change the functional use of the chord; only the color is altered. The **seventh chords,** with an analysis of both triad quality and seventh quality, are given below for the minor key.

ex. 11-16

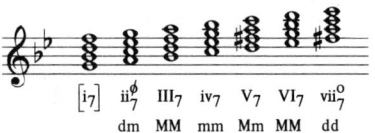

$[i_7]$ ii⌀$_7$ III$_7$ iv$_7$ V$_7$ VI$_7$ vii°$_7$
      dm   MM   mm   Mm   MM   dd

It should be noted that the tonic chord, if used as tonic and not as V/IV, does not use a seventh. The stability of the tonic is generally maintained through the simpler, and more stable, triad.

The major key likewise begins to utilize sevenths, with the following qualities:

ex. 11-17

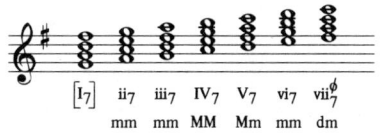

$[I_7]$ ii$_7$ iii$_7$ IV$_7$ V$_7$ vi$_7$ vii⌀$_7$
       mm   mm   MM   Mm   mm   dm

Note that the strength of the IV$_7$ results in part from its highly dissonant major seventh above the major triad. Partly as a result of this strong dissonance, it is used sparingly.

Generally, the tones of the seventh chords resolve like those of the V$_7$: the third moves upward and the seventh moves downward. In the V$_7$ this motion is extremely important; in the other seventh chords it is usual, but more variable. If the voice leading from chord to chord is smooth, there are numerous possible resolutions. Again, *the seventh does not alter the function of the chord;* only the sound, or color, is affected.

A much-used seventh chord, especially in cadences, is the **ii$_7$** (in major) or **ii⌀$_7$** (in minor). Much of the time you will find this chord used in the first inversion, and it normally will be followed by the V chord.

a. ii$^6_5$–V–I   (major)

b. ii⌀$^6_5$–V–i   (minor)

In certain progressions it has a sound similar to the IV chord. The subtle change in color is of crucial importance, as the following examples will attest.

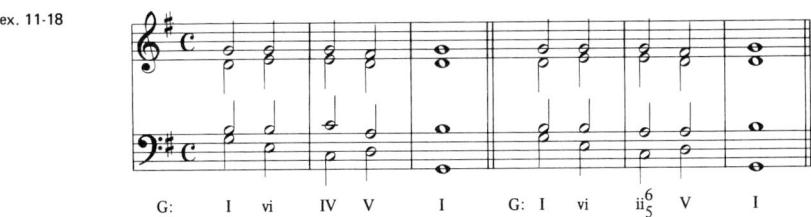

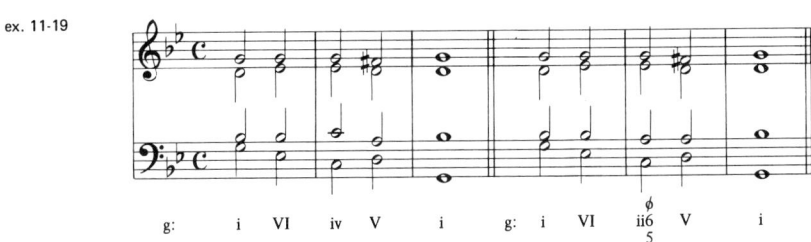

The ii_7 and $ii^{\varnothing}_7$ chords contain the IV and iv chords, respectively, in their upper three notes, thereby producing an ambiguous effect.

This cadence is similar to the Phrygian cadence found in the modal period, but the resolution is slightly different and its function is considerably changed.

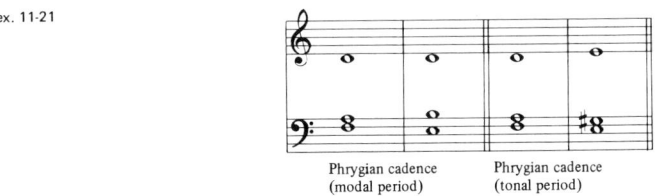

Note the change in function. In the modal period, the final chord is the tonic of the Phrygian mode; in the tonal period, the final chord is the dominant of the key.

The Phrygian cadence was used frequently in the Baroque. It was gradually modified by using a ***chromatic passing tone.***

ex. 11-22

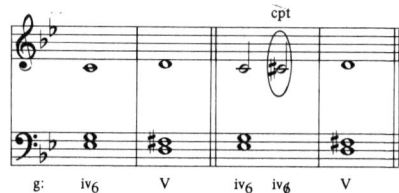

This chromatic passing tone came to be incorporated into the cadential chord.

ex. 11-23

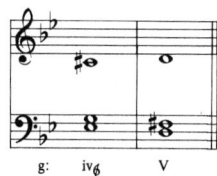

This is an example of the ***augmented-sixth chord,*** so named because of the interval of the augmented sixth between the outer voices. The augmented-sixth interval resolves outward, as augmented intervals normally do. By adding the augmented sixth to the chord, the Phrygian cadence has been intensified. This is referred to as an altered chord, not being either a secondary dominant or a secondary diminished-seventh chord.

This example is a type of iv chord: iv$_6$ with the sixth sharpened, thus iv$_{\cancel{6}}$. It is usually called the ***Italian sixth chord.*** Note that the essential function of this iv chord has not changed, since it moves directly to V.

The other augmented-sixth chords are the **German sixth,** iv$^{\cancel{6}}_5$, and the **French sixth,** ii$^{\cancel{6}}_3$. Both contain the Italian sixth chord, with the addition of one note.

ex. 11-24

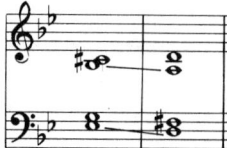

Although all three chords eventually resolve to the V chord, the German sixth usually moves to V via the i$^6_4$ chord. The reason for this can be seen in the voice leading. If it were to resolve directly to V, parallel fifths would ensue; by moving first to a i$^6_4$, these can be avoided.

ex. 11-25

Though the augmented-sixth chord is employed in the Baroque period, it is not used frequently until the Classic period.

The linear motion within this piece is remarkable. The lines seem to grow out of the harmonic patterns, but also push against them in a never-ending pattern of tension/release and dissonance/resolution. The most striking dissonance is the suspension, including both tied suspensions and rearticulated suspensions.[1] Example 11-26 provides a harmonic analysis of the Purcell recitative, followed by the beginning of the aria. Note the extensive use of dissonance (especially suspensions) in both sections.

[1] A rearticulated suspension is one in which the suspended note is not tied.

Numerous examples of ***rearticulated*** suspensions can be found in the example. (Although they are sometimes referred to as appoggiaturas, this will not be followed here.) The most prominent and wrenching examples of this occur toward the end of the aria, from measure 55 onward; the amount of dissonance from this point to the end of the example is extraordinary. The multiple suspensions, escape tones, passing tones, and chromatic resolutions create a constant tension and a forceful downward thrust through the entire section. Although the harmonic aspect is generally well controlled and functional, it must be seen through melodic eyes, for the tension is melodically conceived and controlled.

ex. 11-27

STYLE CHARACTERISTICS: LATE SEVENTEENTH CENTURY
based on "Dido's Lament" from Purcell's *Dido and Aeneas*

melody	combination of smooth and angular • skips are an important style feature, but generally the motion is quite conjunct
harmony	chromatic inflections in minor keys, but progressions remain highly functional • use of V7, secondary V7, vii°, and secondary vii° • occasional use of augmented-sixth chord • cadences: authentic, plagal, half, Phrygian, deceptive
dissonance	much use of suspension figures • passing tones, neighboring tones, escape tones, anticipations, chromatic passing tones • greater emphasis on dissonance than in the early seventeenth century
rhythm	generally smooth, with little syncopation • occasional use of "snap" rhythm: ♬.
techniques	passacaglia • figured bass

Glossary

Augmented-sixth chords   chords containing an augmented-sixth interval.

    ITALIAN SIXTH: iv_6
    GERMAN SIXTH: iv^6_5
    FRENCH SIXTH: $ii^{6}_{4\ 3}$

Cadences: authentic   V–I (V–i)
  Plagal   IV–I (iv–i)
  Deceptive   V–vi (V–VI)
  Half   ending on V.
  Phrygian iv_6–V (in a minor key)

Chaconne   a Baroque variation technique based on the continued repetition of a short chordal pattern throughout the piece.

Diminished-seventh chord   a chord which contains a diminished triad and a diminished seventh. It functions as a leading-tone chord, resolving up a half step from its root to the tonic.

Ground bass   the repetitive bass line in a passacaglia.

Half-diminished-seventh chord   a chord which contains a diminished triad and a minor seventh. It is found naturally on the second scale degree of a minor key ($ii^{\varnothing}_7$) and on the seventh scale degree of a major key ($vii^{\varnothing}_7$).

Passacaglia   a Baroque variation technique based on the continued repetition of a short bass line (ground bass) throughout the piece.

Secondary diminished-seventh chord   a chord which is a vii°_7 to a scale degree other than the tonic. It is always an altered chord.

Secondary dominant   a V chord (or V_7) which functions on a level other than the tonic. It is always major and usually contains an altered pitch.

Secondary function   the tonal emphasis of pitch levels other than the primary one of the piece. This is usually accomplished through the use of secondary dominants or secondary diminished-seventh chords.

Suggested Exercises

1. Write and resolve the following:

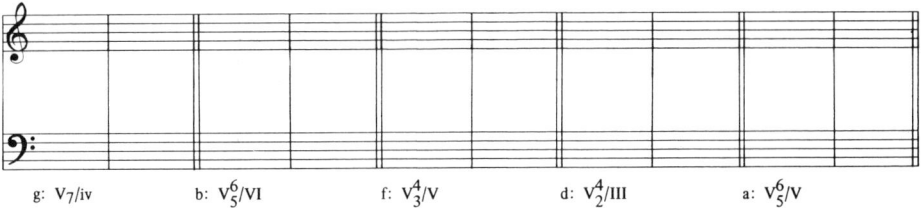

g: V_7/iv b: V^6_5/VI f: V^6_3/V d: V^4_2/III a: V^6_5/V

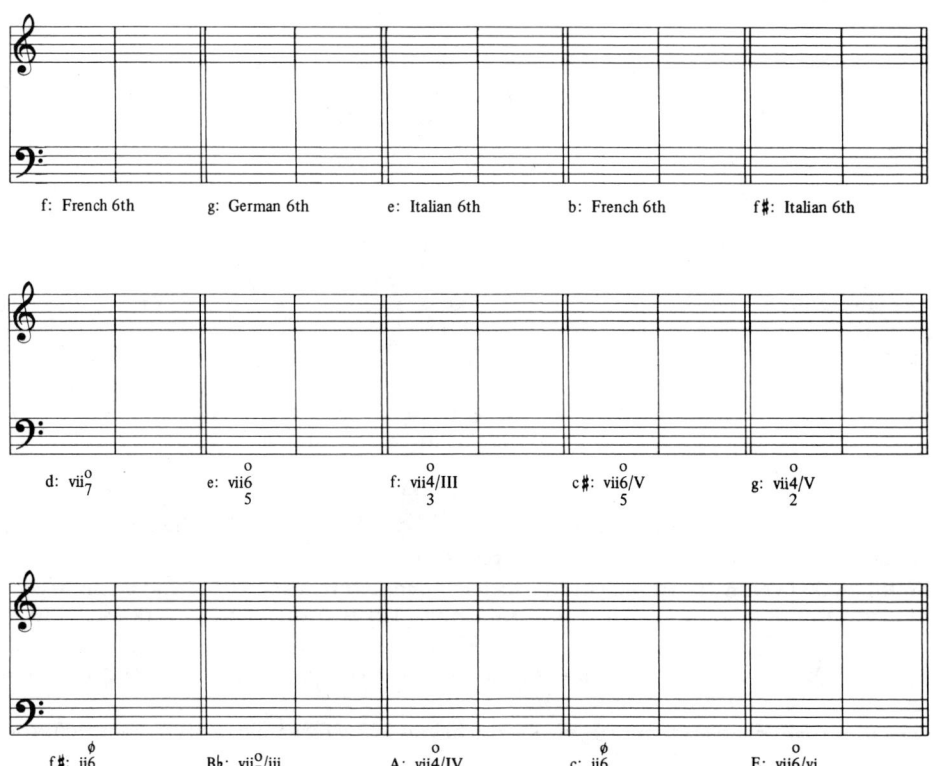

2. Realize, in four voices, the following figured-bass patterns. Eighth notes need not use separate harmonies.

3. With the following bass line, construct a 20-measure passacaglia in four voices.

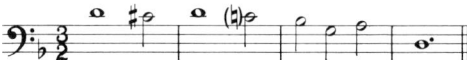

4. Complete the following progressions in a four-voice texture.

a. g: i | VI ii$^{ø6}_{5}$ | V | i V$^{6}_{5}$/V | i$^{6}_{4}$ V | i ‖

b. d: i | VI ii$^{ø6}_{5}$ | V | i iv$^{6}_{5}$ | i$^{6}_{4}$ V | i ‖

c. D: I | V$^{6}_{5}$/vi vi | IV V$^{6}_{5}$/V | I$^{6}_{4}$ V | I ‖

Before Reading Chapter 12

1. Listen to the entire Sonata for Violin and Continuo, Op. 5, No. 7, by Corelli.
2. Realize the figured bass for the *Sarabanda* movement.
3. Bracket key areas (however brief) in the *Sarabanda*.

Henry Purcell

Arcangelo Corelli

Sonata for violin and continuo, Op. 5, No. 7

    Throughout the Baroque period there are numerous examples of solo sonatas written for one instrument and ***continuo***. The most favored instrument for these sonatas, especially in the middle to late Baroque, was the violin. The continuo was usually notated in figured-bass fashion—that is, as a bass line with figures below. It was performed on the harpsichord or other keyboard instrument, and the bass line was reinforced by a sustaining instrument, such as the cello or bassoon. Thus, a group of three instruments was required for the actual performance.

    Corelli (1653–1713) was a well-known violinist and composer. His entire output was for strings, and comprised solo sonatas, trio sonatas, and concerti grossi. The present example is from the set of twelve sonatas for violin and continuo.

    This sonata has four movements: Preludio, Corrente, Sarabanda, and Giga. The individual movements are similar in form; all are in two sections of approximately the same length, with similar material in each. In addition there seems to be a consistent motion to the dominant (either as a secondary tonic or simply as the goal of a half cadence) at the end of the first section, with motion back to the tonic by the end of the second section. This tonal/formal scheme can be outlined as follows:

```
         ‖:A        :‖:B        A:‖
major key:  I--------V    V--------I
minor key:  i--------III  III--------i
       or i--------v      v--------i
```

It is a binary (that is, two-part) form, and is usually referred to as **Baroque binary** because of the frequency of its use in this period. Dance movements such as these invariably display this general outline.

The *Sarabanda* is perhaps the easiest to approach because of its slow, readily identifiable harmonic rhythm, its relative simplicity, and its brevity. A detailed analysis will reveal Corelli's harmonic and melodic style.

The general key motion is typical.

```
                              (modulation)
       d minor:   i ---------- V    V ---------- i
```

The phrases are consistently two or four measures long throughout, with a suggestion of a cadence at the end of each four-measure segment. Again, this is quite typical.

The harmonic content of the first section is quite straightforward. Functional usage of chords is standard. The final four measures contains a progression and a bass line which is typical in a minor key.

ex. 12-1

$$\text{6♭} \quad \text{7-6} \quad \text{7-6} \quad \sharp$$

The bass moves away from the tonic and toward the dominant, down the melodic minor scale. The harmonic motion follows the bass, with parallel $^6_3$ chords that move from VI$_6$ to v$_6$ (note that the v chord is minor—a leading tone would demand resolution to the tonic) to iv$_6$ and finally to V. The final two chords of this progression produce a Phrygian cadence.

The second half of the binary form explores new key areas, after the tonic has been well established in the first half. The first chord in measure 9, V/iv, resolves to a major IV chord. The raised third of this chord implies that it is itself a dominant. It does in fact function in this way, moving to C major, or V/III, which in turn resolves to III. This harmony moves to a first-inversion tonic chord and the final cadence confirms d minor. The overall motion in measures 9–12 is thus:

```
V/g --------V/C -----------V/F-----------F
V/iv--------IV[V/VII]----VII[V/III]---III
```

The progression moves entirely by fifths, and the first three chords are dominant in function. The temporary goal of F major is logical; since F is the relative major of d minor, the return to d minor from this point is harmonically simple.

This is the logical section in which to explore new harmonic/key areas. After the establishment of the primary key, the ear expects further tonal development and finally a return of d minor.

Notice the use of sequence in measures 9–12. As discussed earlier, **sequence** can be either *tonal* or *real*. In this case it is real, both in the violin and the bass line.

Sequence is an important feature in tonal music, especially as it serves two functions: to emphasize and solidify the key of the piece, especially through tonal sequence, and to help change the key center, through real sequence.

An extension of the melodic form is **harmonic sequence.** Invariably combined with melodic sequence, it helps to produce the modulation found in the second section of the Sarabanda.

After the return to d minor in measure 13 there is an unusual chord, seemingly not functioning in either F major (the former key) or d minor. It is an E♭-major chord in first inversion, an altered chord with a striking sound—partly like a iv chord, partly like a ii chord, but with a flavor different from either. It moves directly to the V chord in the next measure. It always has a root of the lowered second scale degree, is usually found in the minor key in the first inversion, and is always a major chord. Its traditional name is the **Neapolitan 6th chord.**

ex. 12-2

The Roman-numeral designation is ♭II$_6$. As in the other altered chords we have seen (the augmented-sixth chords) the actual function of the II chord has not changed at all, since the ii chord, like the ♭II, usually moves to V. The root movement is E♭–A, a tritone, which perhaps accounts for the unusually pungent quality of the progression.

Be careful of the resolution. The motion is mostly by step and the root (e♭) usually "circles" the tonic pitch with an upper and lower leading-tone motion (e♭–c♯–d). An alternative resolution, equally effective, moves stepwise to a i$_4^6$ chord before proceeding to V. Both are shown below.

ex. 12-3

The remaining progression, measures 14–16, is easily analyzed.

ex. 12-4

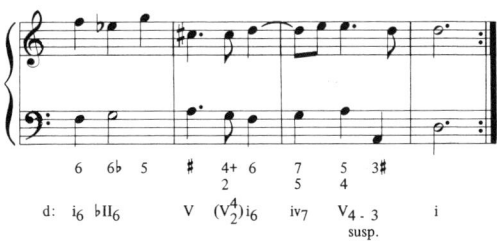

The other movements should be carefully examined, for they reveal many of the same harmonic features as this small movement. For example, the second movement generally follows the same harmonic outline.

Corrente:

‖: i---(III--VII--i)----v :‖: V-----(i--VII--III--iv)-----i :‖

The various dissonances used by Corelli and other composers in this period can be seen in the *Sarabanda*. Immediately noticeable are the suspensions in measures 6, 7, 10, 12, and 15. The 7–6 and 4–3 suspension are used frequently, with the latter used especially at cadence points. In the other movements can be seen frequent 9–8, 2–1, and 2–3 suspensions as well.

In addition to suspensions, there is the normal usage of passing tones (none in the *Sarabanda*), neighboring tones, and escape tones. A typical dissonance of the Baroque is used most strikingly by Corelli: the **anticipation.** As discussed in chapter 9, the anticipation is rhythmically weak and is approached by step; it anticipates a pitch of the next harmony, and is therefore dissonant with the first.

ex. 12-5

It is also referred to occasionally (especially at cadences, as in measure 15) as the "**Corelli clash.**" The clash is created by the leading tone and tonic sounding together. Corelli and other composers employed it frequently.

ex. 12-6

Finally, we may examine one interesting feature of the rhythm in this short movement. In certain pieces of music there exists a vacillation of metric grouping, as if shifting from a two-beat meter to a three-beat meter, or vice versa. This metrical shift is a displacement of accents and is usually referred to as **hemiola.** Normally it occurs in a piece in triple meter, in which case the meter seems to shift from the three-beat grouping to a two-beat grouping.

ex. 12-7

Frequently this shift into a two-beat arrangement will occur at the cadence. This is typical in the Baroque period, and is found at the cadence in this piece.

ex. 12-8

Hemiola can add a strong rhythmic flavor, and can be quite effective in moving a phrase toward a strong cadence.

STYLE CHARACTERISTICS: EARLY EIGHTEENTH CENTURY
based on Corelli's Sonata VII for violin and continuo, Op. 5, No. 7

melody	angular much of the time • instrumentally oriented • chordally derived, at least on the surface
harmony	functional, based on fifth progression • altered chords, especially N_6, can be used • modulation, usually diatonic, to ii, IV, or V in major, or III in minor • harmonic sequence is used for modulatory purposes
rhythm	in fast movements: "motor" rhythm, steady eighth-note motion • in slow movements subtle shifting of accents, hemiola especially in triple meter and at the cadence • phrases are usually two or four measures long • often irregular phrase-lengths in slow pieces
texture	for sonatas: usually harpsichord with cello (or bassoon) reinforcing the bass line plus one to three upper parts
dissonance	passing tones • neighboring tones • occasional escape tones • great use of suspensions of all types • anticipation is used, especially at the cadence

(creates the Corelli clash when the tonic anticipation and leading tone occur together)

techniques   figured bass • Baroque binary form • sequence (tonal and real)

Glossary

Anticipation   a rhythmically weak dissonance approached by step and repeated. Although dissonant on the weak beat, the harmony moves to make the pitch consonant on the strong beat.

Baroque binary   a binary form with a hint of repetition of A at the end: ‖: A :‖: B A :‖
It is used in most movements of dance suites.   I   V   V   I

Continuo   a designation for the bass line and figures in a piece using figured bass; it requires two performers, a keyboard instrument (usually harpsichord) and an instrument doubling the bass line (usually cello).

Harmonic sequence   repetition of a chordal progression on different scale degrees. It can be modulatory (real) or diatonic (tonal).

Neapolitan sixth chord   a chord, usually in a minor key, whose root is the lowered second scale degree: ♭II$_6$. It is always a major chord.

Phrygian cadence   a cadence related to the Medieval cadence of the same name; in tonal music it is a type of half cadence iv$_6$–V in a minor key. The characteristic sound, contributing to its name, is the half-step motion in the bass voice.

Suggested Exercises

1. Complete a harmonic analysis of one of the other movements of the Sonata.
2. Make a keyboard realization of the figured bass in the first movement.
3. Analyze all the dissonances in the *Corrente*.
4. Write a violin line above the figured bass below. Use suspensions and anticipations in the new solo line. Pitches marked should not be harmonized; they are passing tones.

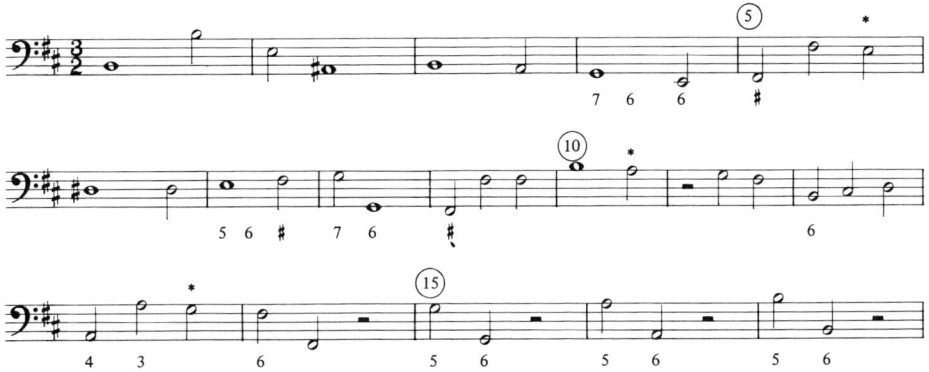

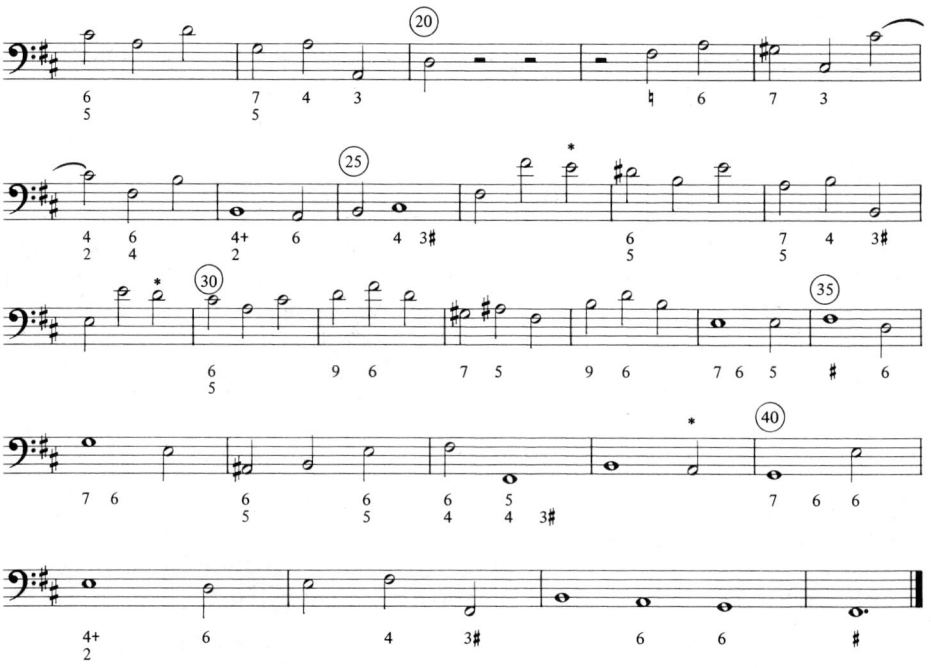

5. Write and resolve the following:

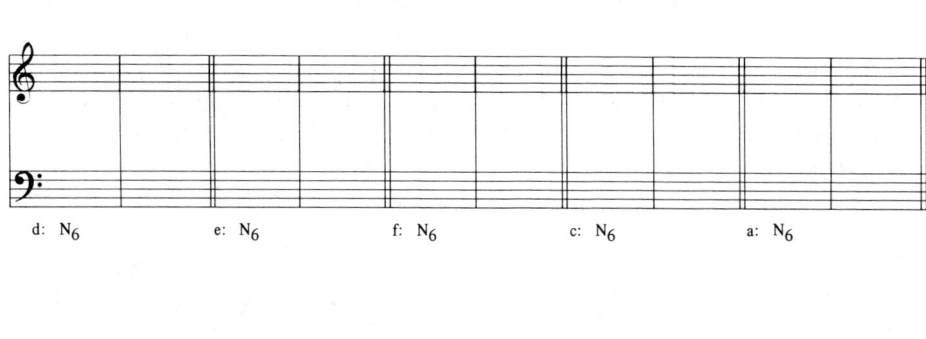

d: N_6 e: N_6 f: N_6 c: N_6 a: N_6

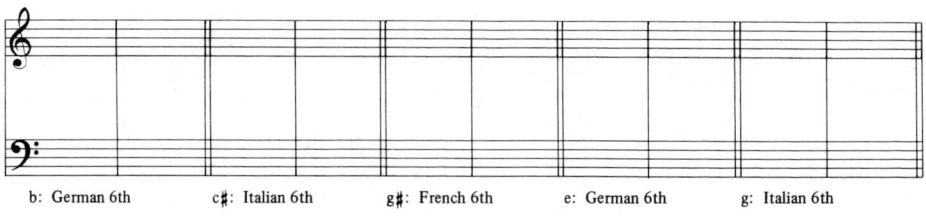

b: German 6th   c♯: Italian 6th   g♯: French 6th   e: German 6th   g: Italian 6th

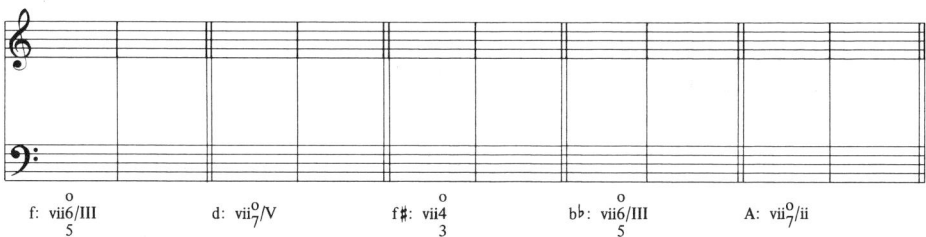

f: vii6/III₅   d: vii°₇/V   f♯: vii°4/3   b♭: vii°6/III₅   A: vii°₇/ii

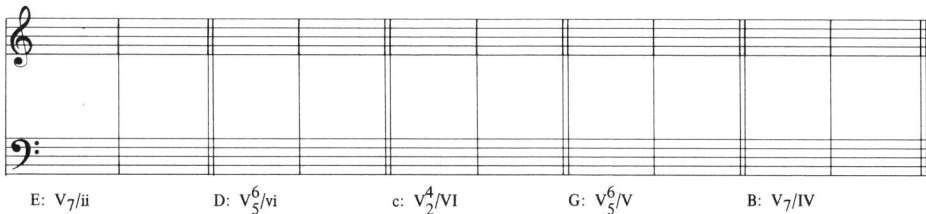

E: V₇/ii   D: V⁶₅/vi   c: V⁴₂/VI   G: V⁶₅/V   B: V₇/IV

Before Reading Chapter 13

1. Sing through the chorales on pges 247 and 249.
2. Note their cadence structure and general chordal usage.
3. Listen to the Prelude and Fugue in g minor from the *Well-Tempered Clavier*, Book I, by J. S. Bach.
4. Analyze the key structure of both the Prelude and the Fugue.
5. Listen to the *Sarabande* from Bach's *French Suite* in b minor.
6. Analyze the tonal structure of the *Sarabande*.

13

Johann Sebastian Bach

The chorales

Prelude and Fugue in g minor
Well-Tempered Clavier, Book I

Sarabande from the *French Suite in b minor*

One of the most famous and revered composers in music history is J. S. Bach (1685–1750). His sensitive musicality, technique, and sheer fecundity of output all point to a genius of the first order. His music, covering all genres of the early eighteenth century, has been used for every possible musical purpose, including pedagogical ones, since its rediscovery in the early nineteenth century. His works both sum up the Baroque period and establish many of the basic technical and musical premises of tonal music in general.

Of the numerous genres in which Bach worked, the one most often employed for teaching purposes is the chorale. The reason is clear: these works present the essence of his harmonic style in simple, well-controlled, homophonic settings. His principles of line, key relations, and harmony are all found in these miniatures.

The purpose for the **chorales** was liturgical. In connection with his church duties, Bach wrote numerous cantatas and other functional pieces. The chorales were used as parts of the cantatas (each cantata was usually based on a chorale melody and ended with the chorale itself) but more often were sung by themselves.

Bach did not compose the melodies of these chorales; his contribution was in their harmonization. In many cases we have two, three, or more of Bach's harmonizations of the same melody. Below is a relatively simple setting of a chorale. Later, we will see the same melody treated differently.

Ermuntre dich, mein schwacher Geist

The setting is highly homophonic; the voices almost always move together throughout the piece. As we have seen before (in Chapter 10, with the Johann Schein example), the treble and bass lines are the important factors in establishing the harmonic progression. This "polarity of the outer voices" is especially important to establish linear progression. The key is well established, with only minimal motion away from the primary tonic area, especially in the opening section.

The second section modulates more freely, to two other degrees of the G-major scale: a (ii) in measure 12, and e (vi) in measure 16. The primary key returns for the final section.

Notice that the **cadences** determine the modulatory motion of the piece. Bach surely planned from the outset to move toward D in measure 4, G in measure 8, a in measure 12, e in measure 16, D in measure 19, and G in measure 22. Notice also that each cadence is different from the previous. This creates heightened interest and contrast within the piece and allows Bach to explore various modulatory areas.

The harmonic progressions and voice-leading procedures are not unusual, but are extremely well handled. Diatonic modulation is expertly accomplished; the use of pivot chords is both simple and effective.

The second chorale is based on the same melody as the first, but this chorale is quite different in general character and mood.

Ermuntre dich, mein schwacher Geist

ex. 13-4

The meter has been shifted from 3/4 to 4/4, and in the process the melody has had to be slightly altered. The cadential structure is the same (the cadences fall on d, G, a, e, d, and G) but the expanded harmonic usage and the increase in eighth-note motion is quite evident. Compare the first phrases of each:

ex. 13-5

The increase in eighth-note activity is the most obvious change, but the added chromatic inflections also produce a subtle increase in harmonic motion. The basic chord progression is actually much the same. The second section, however, produces a much more individual sound.

ex. 13-6

Measures 5 and 6 of the second chorale change but little. The changes in measure 7 are most significant, adding chromatic inflections on e, a, and b and eventually (measure 8) cadencing on e.

The phrase ending is similar to that in the previous chorale setting, but the eighth-note additions create tension through suspensions and passing and neighboring motion. The actual progression is much the same as in the first chorale. Compare:

ex. 13-7

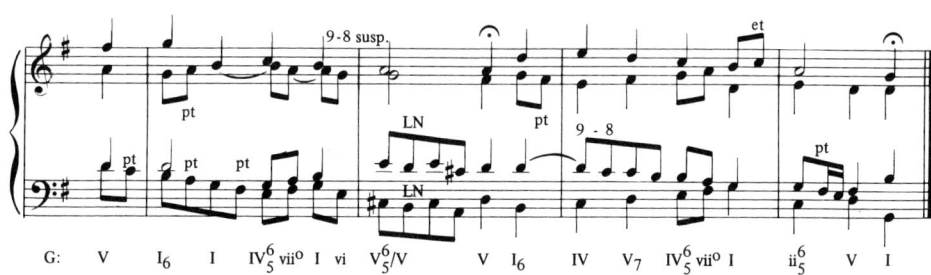

These two chorales show both the processes of Bach's musical thought as well as the basic stylistic features of the period. Particularly in the second example we see the increased use of dissonances, especially chromatic passing tones and suspensions. Chromatic inflection can be viewed as both linear and chordal. The overall function of each chord is generally not changed by the addition of chromatic tones. The chromaticism enhances the progressions and increases the impetus of forward motion, often by creating secondary function.

The larger structure of these two chorales can be used as a touchstone for much of Bach's structural design (as well as for other composers of this period). The surface design is **A A B,** or a traditional ***German bar form,*** a form first seen in the monophonic songs of the twelfth century.

This, however, does not tell the full story. The tonal design is actually very much like that seen in the Corelli suite:

1. establishment of the key, with motion to the dominant;
2. motion to more distant tonal areas, with development of various keys through diatonic modulation;
3. return of the tonic key to balance the motion away from the tonic.

This basic tripartite design—stability, instability, and return to stability—was used by Bach and numerous other composers. It will be seen in the other pieces in this chapter, and the student is encouraged to look for it in other periods of music as well.

Prelude XVI

Fugue XVI

Johann Sebastian Bach

The preceding piece is a Prelude and Fugue from Bach's *Well-Tempered Clavier,* Book I. Designed as a pedagogical work for the keyboard (there is no specific designation which keyboard instrument is to be used), this collection contains two preludes and fugues in each of the 24 keys. Generally speaking a prelude is based on a more harmonic setting than the more rigorously contrapuntal setting of the fugue. As can be seen in the present example, Bach elicits a great deal of contrapuntal activity from this basically chordal Prelude, but the Fugue is definitely more linear in its total conception.

The G minor **Prelude** opens with a prominent tonic pedal through the first two measures. This tonic harmony is confirmed in the V–I motion in measure 5.

If Bach follows the tonal design we have found in the chorales, the next large section should be an exploration of various diatonic keys. This is indeed what happens. Immediately after the V–I motion in measure 5, there is motion away from the tonic, to F major briefly and then to B♭ major.

ex. 13-10

Measure 8 introduces a shift to c minor:

ex. 13-11

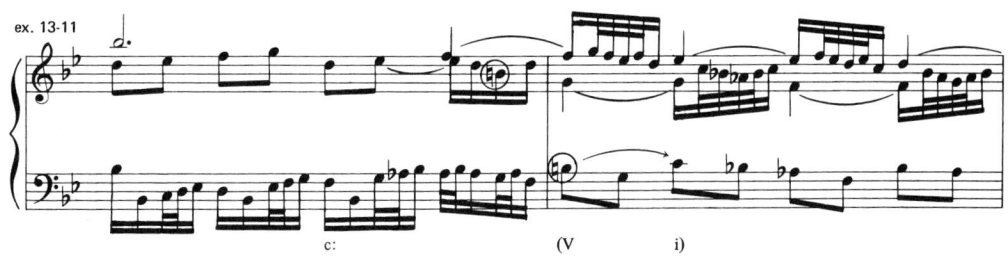

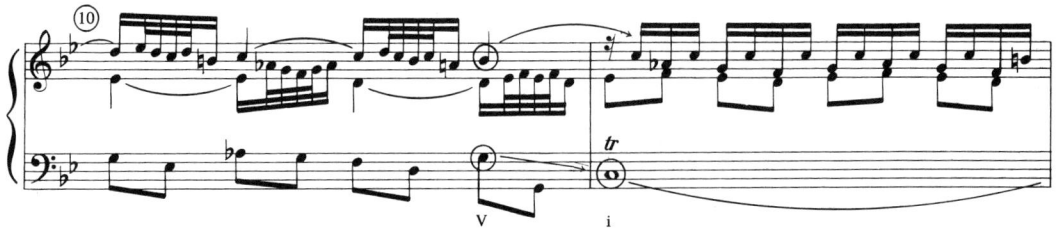

From the modulation in measure 12 to the end, the piece remains in g minor. Although there are chromatic inflections which produce secondary dominants and altered chords, there is no true modulatory activity.

The harmonic motion in a polyphonic piece such as this is sometimes difficult to extract. For example, because of linear motion and the use of pedal points, measures 13–16 are slightly obscure. By reducing this passage to its essentials, we can examine the harmonic structure more easily.

ex. 13-12

This kind of "translation" is often valuable for an understanding of chordal motion and overall direction. Although Bach's version is infinitely more interesting, the reduction helps us to see its harmonic underpinning.

The student should analyze the phrase structure and trace the use and development of motives in the Prelude. Along with the harmonic aspects of the piece, these areas are of significance to overall understanding.

Fugue is a favorite technique of Baroque composers. It is based on immediate imitation of the opening ***fugue subject,*** but unlike earlier pieces using points of imitation, the eighteenth-century fugue is *monothematic.* The basic sections in a "classical" fugue are the **statement section** (sometimes called the exposition), where all voices are brought in one by one, each stating the subject; the **working-out section;** and the **restatement** or **stretto section** at the end. In actual practice this is a fairly loose format and, with the exception of the original statement section, can be altered and rearranged and changed radically depending on musical circumstances.

The G minor Fugue generally follows this rather standard format. The opening statement section brings in the four independent voices one at a time. As is normal, the first is in the tonic, the second in the dominant. The second entry, which is slightly altered intervallically, is generally referred to as the ***answer*** to the subject. There are two types of fugal answers, real and tonal. As in the sequence, the real answer is exactly the same as the subject but in the dominant; the tonal answer is also on the dominant level, but is slightly altered, usually because of the tonal dictates of the opening subject. As a general rule, the tonal answer is used if the original subject begins on the dominant pitch.

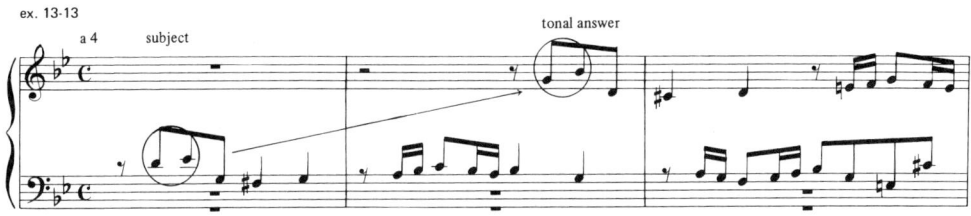

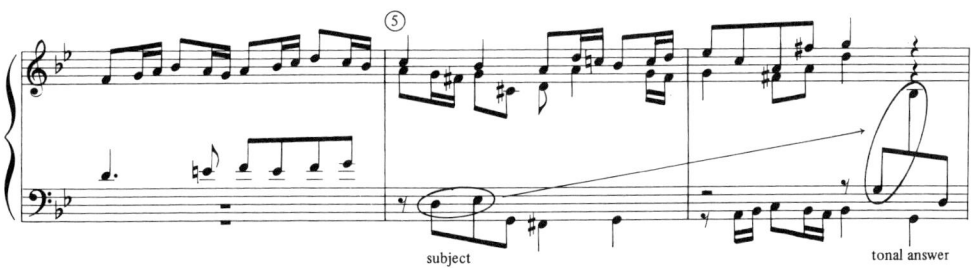

After the second entry, the tonic–dominant sequence is variable. In this case, case, however, the bass and tenor entries are identical to the alto and soprano respectively. The order of entries in this section is

soprano
answer (V) ---------

alto
subject (I) ----------

tenor
answer (V) ---------

bass
subject (I) ----------

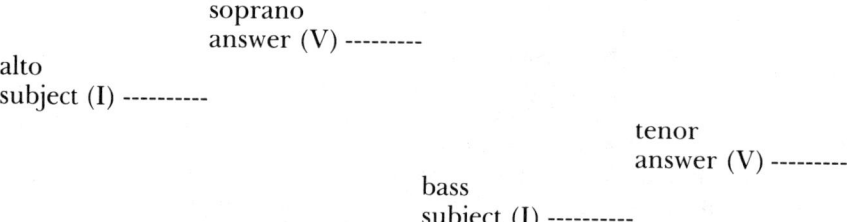

In this fugue, and in many others as well, the counterpoint to the answering voice is repeated with every subject entry. This second voice, or continuation of the subject, is called the ***countersubject*** when it remains the same for each entry.

ex. 13-14

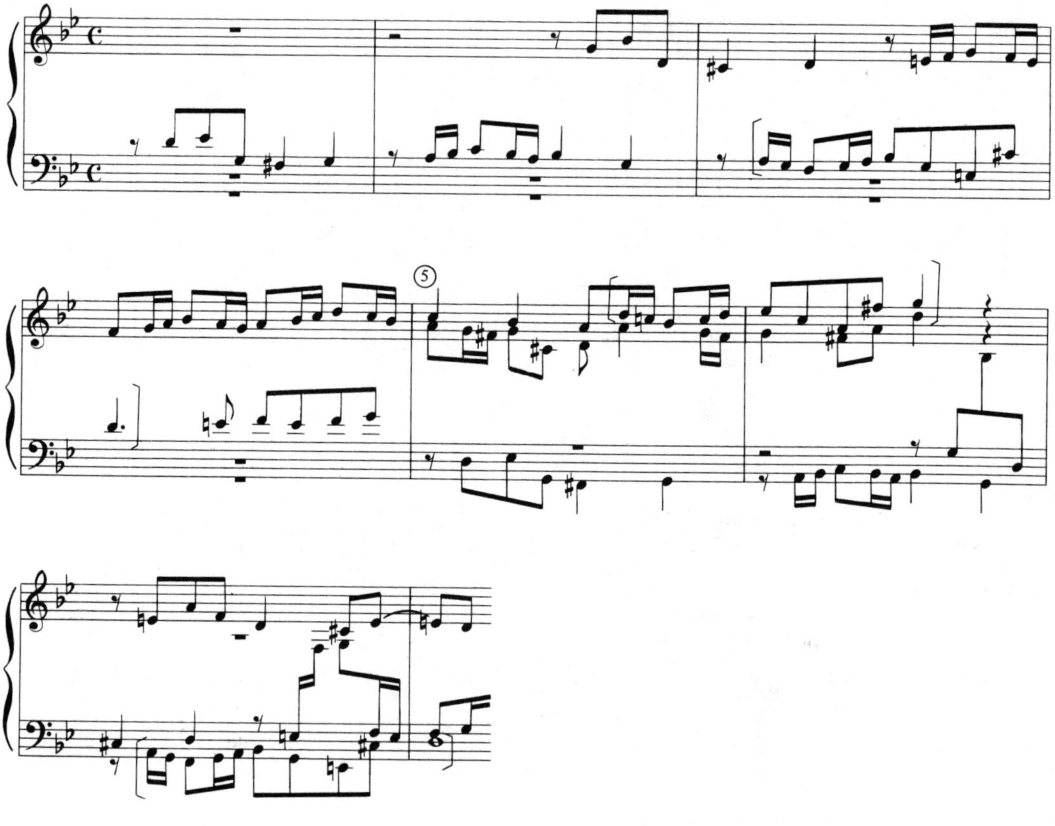

In some fugues the counterpoint is different for each entry and therefore does not constitute a true countersubject.

The ***working-out section,*** starting in measure 12, is preceded by a four-measure extension of the statement section. Part of the purpose of this extension is to move from g minor to the relative major, B♭; this is accomplished in the strong cadence in measure 12.

Beginning in measure 12, the content and use of the material looks exactly like another statement section, only this time in the key of B♭. As at the beginning, the key remains stable, there are four entries (I, V, V, I), and the countersubject remains intact throughout.

ex. 13-15

From this point the complexity increases. With the introduction of $a♭$ in measure 17 the harmonic flow moves toward E♭ major, then briefly to f minor, and finally to c minor. Harmonically, melodically, and contrapuntally this is the high point of the piece.

ex. 13-16

The next brief section leads us back to the original tonic through a series of sequences.

The use of suspensions within this complicated structure adds to the tension, as does the gradual shifting from B♭ to E♭ to c and finally to g. G minor emerges in measure 27, but the strong impetus to this key is provided by the cadence in measures 27–28. The sound resembles a Phrygian cadence, but the *c♯* chromatic passing tone adds a further push. The whole complex is found to be an **augmented-sixth chord (Italian 6th)**.

ex. 13-18

This strong cadence to the dominant of g ushers in the final section of the piece, the ***stretto.*** A stretto consists of a piling-up of voices using the fugue subject: a second presentation of the subject begins before the first has been completed, another begins before that is completed, and so on. Measures 28–29 contain a good example.

ex. 13-19

The final four measures are basically cadential, but Bach nonetheless includes a final presentation of the subject in the alto, followed by another in the tenor voice.

This fugue, then, is thoroughly based on the subject. There are only two short passages that use a fragmented portion of the subject—the end of the statement section (measures 8–11) and the end of the working-out (measures 25–27). Both of these are based on the second measure of the subject. Otherwise the entire subject is used in nearly every measure of the piece. This is not the case in some fugues, particularly in larger, more complicated works. In these, there are generally long passages that do not employ the subject in its entirety (although they may use fragments from it). These sections without the subject are referred to as *episodes.* There are thus two different types of fugue, those using episodic sections and those retaining complete statements of the subject throughout.

Bach's large output of keyboard music includes three sets of *dance suites:* the English Suites, the French Suites, and the Partitas. These, like earlier suites, are collections of dances from various countries. By Bach's time, the order of dances in the suite was fairly standard:

Prelude or Overture
Allemande (German)
Courante (French)
Sarabande (Spanish)
Optional: various dances could be used here—Minuet, Bourrée, Gavotte, and others
Gigue (English)

The standard form of the dance movements–Baroque binary–was established by the time of Corelli, and in every case this form is used by Bach as well. Linear and harmonic complexity, however, distinguish Bach's suites from those of other composers. The Sarabande from the b minor *French Suite* is a good example of this.

The *Sarabande*'s tonal structure is normal for pieces in the minor mode.

‖: A   :‖: B   A :‖
b: i   III III (v VII)   i

The tonal design, like that of the chorales and the Prelude and Fugue, includes the establishment of the tonic, followed by modulation to the relative major (in major keys, the dominant), exploration of various key centers (usually diatonic), and a close in the home key.

The proportions of each tonal area are also important for our consideration.

‖: A   :‖: B   A :‖
   4 +   4   12 +   4
   b   D   D (4) f♯ e (f♯) b

As can be seen from the above, emphasis is placed on the exploratory section of the movement.

The **_harmonic progression_** in the first four measures is quite simple and straightforward, as can be seen if we extract the harmony from the surface complexities.

ex. 13-21

It is the "additions" that are the interesting feature here. Not only the arpeggiation, but especially the use of accented passing tones and numerous suspensions add to the intensity of the opening measures. This is extended and increased in the next four measures, and is even greater in the B section of the piece.

ex. 13-22

An additional dissonant figure begins to be used in the early eighteenth century—*changing tones,* a double dissonance. In the changing-tone pattern, two dissonant tones occur in succession, one above and one below the following consonant note.

ex. 13-23

The *Sarabande* contains a few examples of changing tones, which are among the most strongly dissonant pitches in the piece.

ex. 13-24

**STYLE CHARACTERISTICS: LATE BAROQUE
(EARLY TO MIDDLE EIGHTEENTH CENTURY)
based on Bach's chorales, preludes and fugues, and suites**

melody	predominantly harmonically generated • various types, depending on genre: chorales will be generally smooth, with few leaps larger than a fifth or sixth • instrumental pieces will be more angular, with greater leaps and more arpeggiation
harmony	V7 • secondary V7 • vii°$_7$ • secondary vii°$_7$ • Neapolitan sixth • augmented sixth (not used extensively) • modulation is generally to closely related keys—rarely more than one or two sharps or flats away from the tonic • cadences: authentic, plagal, deceptive, half, Phrygian
dissonance	passing tones • neighboring tones • escape tones • suspensions • anticipations • changing tones
rhythm	all types, but generally of one basic rhythmic unit throughout any given piece
texture	all possible types • various keyboard pieces (harpsichord, organ, clavichord) • various instrumental combinations • chorus and orchestra, vocal solos, etc.
techniques	figured bass • fugue • Baroque binary • sequence • passacaglia • chaconne

Glossary

Answer   in the statement section of a fugue, the second statement of the subject usually on the dominant level.
Bar form   a binary form in which the first part is repeated: A A B. Chorales often use this form.
Baroque binary   a binary form with a hint of repetition of A at the end:
  ‖: A   :‖: B   A :‖   It is used in each of the movements of a dance suite.
         I   V   V   I
or: I   III III   I
Countersubject   the counterpoint to the answer in a fugue. This is only called a countersubject if it appears with the subject and answer throughout the fugue.
Episode   a section of the working-out section of a fugue that does not contain a complete statement of the subject, but rather develops fragments derived from the subject or from new material.
Fugue   a Baroque technique based on imitative entries all using the same basic subject throughout the piece. Typically it has a statement section, working-out section, and restatement section.
Monothematic   having one theme only. Typically describes a fugue which uses only one subject in the course of the piece.
Prelude   often a companion piece to a fugue, it tends to be more homophonically conceived, as a contrast to the contrapuntal fugue.
Statement section   the first section of a fugue, in which all voices enter with either the subject or answer. Also called *exposition*.
Stretto   a piling-up of voices, in which one voice begins the subject and the other voices enter with the subject before the first has completed its statement.
Subject   the opening melodic idea of a fugue, usually containing one or more motivic ideas used for development later in the piece.
Suite   typically, a series of Baroque dances, usually arranged in the order Allemande–Courante–Sarabande–Gigue. Various other dances may appear between the Sarabande and the Gigue.
Working-out section   the middle section of a fugue in which the material of the subject is developed.

Suggested Exercises

1. Study the following two chorales for chordal motion, paying close attention to voice leading as well. Analyze the modulatory motion carefully.

a.

2. Several chorale melodies are given below. Harmonize each one in the style of Bach, using the basic structure of the preceding examples, and including secondary dominants and secondary seventh chords for modulatory purposes. When you have completed your harmonization, compare it with Bach's version.

Brumquell aller Güter

Mach's mit mir, Gott, nach deiner Güt'

Vater unser im Himmelreich

3. Analyze the following preludes and fugues for thematic content and development as well as harmonic content.

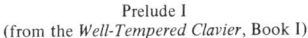

Prelude I
(from the *Well-Tempered Clavier*, Book I)

Johann Sebastian Bach **273**

Fugue I

Johann Sebastian Bach

Prelude II
(from the *Well-Tempered Clavier*, Book II)

Fugue II

4. Analyze the following suite movements harmonically, labelling all dissonant pitches specifically. Be careful to indicate all modulations and pivot chords.

Sarabande
from English Suite in E♭ major

J. S. Bach

Courante
from French Suite in E minor

J. S. Bach

Johann Sebastian Bach

Index

Accidental, 14, 35
Accidentals (in figured bass), 189
Acoustics, 23–27
Adieu mes amours (Josquin), 152
Agricola, Johann, 209
Altered chords, 251
Ambitus, 28, 29, 32, 33, 34, **42**
Amplitude (loudness), 23
Anapestic, 41
Answer (in a fugue), 259, 260, **269**
Anticipation, 196, **197**, 228, 241, 242, **243**
Apel, 27, 36
Ars Nova, 76, **85**
Attack, 24
Aucun/Lonc Tans/Annuntiantes (Petrus de Cruce), 55, 59
Augmentation, **89**, 119, **123**
Augmented fourth, 167, 195
Augmented intervals, 17, 167
Augmented sixth, 82
Augmented sixth chord, 82, 224, 225, 228, **229**, 263, 268
Augmented triad, 17, 18
Authentic cadence (V-I), 142, 143, 144, 146, **150**, 166, 173, 228, 229

Authentic modes, 28, 29, 32
Ave Maria (Josquin des Prez), 127, 138, 142, 144, 147, 148, 150, 151
Ave maris stella (Dufay), 102, 112, 113, 114, 123
Ave maris stella (Dunstable), 89, 91

Bach, Johann Sebastian, 245, 246, 247, 248, 251, 256, 264, 268
Bamberg Codex, 68
Barbour, 27
Bar form, 251, **269**
Bar lines, 9
Baroque binary form, 239, **242**, 264, 268, **269**
Baroque Period, 82, 199
Basic theory, 13
Bass, 91
Bass clef, 3, 7
Basso continuo, 189
Bass suspension, 144
Beams, 8, 9, 10
Binary form, **42**
Bone Pastor (Machaut), 1, 69, 76

Cadence, 66
    in Bach, 268

Cadence (*Cont.*)
    13th century, 66
    14th century, 85
    15th century, 95, 98 (early), 123 (middle)
    16th century, 150 (early), 173 (late)
    17th century, 196–97 (early), 228 (late)
    18th century, 242–43 (early), 268 (late)
    to write, 102, 151
Cadential $\frac{6}{4}$, 196, **197**
Cambiata (nota cambiata), 164, **173**
Canon, 147, 148, 149, **150**
    to write, 151
Cantus firmus technique, 118, **123**, 138, **173**
C clef, 2, 8
Cell, 37, **42**
Cento, 35
Centonization, 35, 38, **42**
Chaconne, 191, **197**, 268
Changing tones, 268
Chant, 42
Chorale
    Bach, 245, 246
    to analyze, 269
    to harmonize, 270f
Chordal doubling, 116, 142, 148, **150**, 203
Chordal function, **197**, 202
Chordal inversion, 189
Chord function (minor key), 220, 221
Chord Quality (in diatonic scale), 190
Chromatic inflection, 250, 257
Chromatic passing tone, 223, 224, 228, 251
Church modes, 13, 14, 28ff
Circle of fifths, 26
Clausula, 52, **52**, 59, **67**
Clef, 2
Color, 65, **67**, 77, 78, **85**
Composite organum, 47, **52**
Compound meter, 7
Conjunct, 34
Consonance, 62, 63
Continuo, 238, **243**
Contra, 119
Contra-bassus, 119
Contra-octave, 5
Contrary motion, 48, **52**, 81, 114
Contra-tenor, 118
Corelli, Arcangelo, 231, 238, 239, 241, 242
Corelli clash, 241, 243
Coronation of Poppea (Monteverdi), 182, 188, 196
Countersubject, 260, 261, **269**
Crossing voices, 117
Cycles per second, 23

Dactylic, 41
Dance suite (movements listed), 264
Decay, 24
Deceptive cadence, 143, 148, 150, 173, 203
Decibels (dB), 23

Deo confitemini/Domino (motet), 54. 59
Diatonic modulation, 202, **208**, 248
Diatonic scales, 35, 190
Dido and Aeneas (Purcell), 211, 212, 228
Dido's Lament, 211, 212, 216, 228
Diminished fifth, 167, 168, 195
Diminished intervals, 17, 167
Diminished seventh chord, 217, 218, 219, 228, **229**
Diminished triad, 17, 149, 167, 168
Diminished triad (use in cadence), 96, 97
Diminution, 77, 80, 83, 84, **85**, 120
Discantus, 62
Dissonance, 60, 62, 63, 64, 66, **67**, 85, 93, 143, 164, 197
    13th century, 66
    14th century, 85
    15th century, 98 (early), 123 (middle)
    16th century, 150 (early), 173 (late)
    17th century, 196–97 (early), 228 (late)
    18th century, 242–43 (early), 268 (middle)
Dominant, **42**
Dominant chord, 190, 191
Dominant seventh chord, 168, **173**, 194, 196, 204
    resolution of, 195
Dominant (tenor), 28, 30, 31, 32, 33, 34, 35
Dorian mode, 29, 31, 32, 34, 61
Dots (use of), 9
Double canon, 148, **150**
Double-leading-tone cadence, 65, 66, **67**, 82, **85**, 98
    to write, 86, 95, 102, 122, 126
Double suspension, 94, **98**, 123
Double under third, **123**
Doubling procedure (of triads), 116, 142, 148, 203
Dufay, Guillaume, 102, 103, 112, 114, 117, 119, 120, 121, 122, 123, 124, 139, 140
Dunstable, John, 89, 91, 92, 93, 94, 95, 96, 98, 114, 121
Duplum, 60, 61, 64, **67**, 78, 81
Dynamic markings, 10

Ecclesiastical modes, 28ff
Echappee, 93
Eleventh century, 2
Elision, 203
Embellished resolution (suspension), 163, **173**
Embellishing tones, 93
English discant, 121
English Suite in E♭ major (Bach), 277
Envelope, 24
Episode (in a fugue), 264
Equal temperament, 26
Er muntre dich, mein schwacher Geist (Bach), 247, 249
Escape tone, 93, 96, **98**, 115, 122, 123, 173, 197, 227, 228
    to write, 102, 126
Exposition (of a fugue), 259

Fauxbourdon, 121, **123**
  to write, 126
F clef, 2, 3
Fifth (of a triad), 18
Figured bass, 189, 190, **197**, 210, 243, 268
Final (finalis), 28, 29, 31, 32, 33, 34, 35
Fins cuers doulz (Machaut), 86
First inversion (of a triad), 18, 63, 81, 116, 203
Five-line staff, 2
Five-six-five motion (16th century), 166
Flat, 15
Four-line staff, 2
Free organum, **52**, 47, 48, 52
French sixth chord, 224, 230, 244
French Suite in b minor (Bach), 245, 246, 264, 265
French Suite in e minor (Bach), 278
Frequency, 23
Fugue, 259, **269**
Fugue subject, 259, 260, 264, **269**
Functional chord (of a minor scale), 217, 220, 221
Function (harmonic), **197**, 202, 203, 239, 242
Fundamental pitch, 24, 25

G clef, 2, 3
German bar form, 251
German sixth chord, 224, 230, 244
Graduale, 61
Grand staff, 4
Great octave, 5
Gregorian chant, 28
Ground bass, 216, 217, **229**

Haec dies, 61
Half cadence, 173, 203, 228, 229
Half diminished seventh chord, 217, 218, 219, 228, **229**
Half tone, 14
Harmonic content (organum), 52
  13th century, 66
  14th century, 85
  15th century, 96, 123
  16th century, 142, 150 (early), 17 (middle)
  17th century, 197 (early), 228 (late)
  18th century, 242–43 (early), 268 (middle)
Harmonic minor, 15, 16
Harmonic progression, 266
Harmonic rhythm, **123**, 150
Harmonic sequence, 240, 242, **243**
Harmonization (of a melody), 204ff
  exercise, 210
Harmony (of minor scale), 217
Haydn, Joseph, 13
Hemiola, 242
Hocket, 84, **85**
Hodie Nobis (LU 376), 35ff
Homophonic, 92, 93, **98**, 139, 147, 247
Homophonic hymns, 199
Homophony, 199, **208**

Hypodorian mode, 29, 31, 34
Hypolydian mode, 30
Hypomixolydian mode, 29, 39

Iambic, 41
Iio7 chord, 222, 223
III chord (in minor key), 221
Imitation, 138, 146, 147, 148, **150**, 169, 171, 259
Imperfect consonances, 59, 65, **67**
Inflection, 200, 201, 202
Intervals, 16
Inversion (of a triad), 18, 63, 81, 116, 203
Inversions of V7, 195
Irregular meter, 7
Isorhythm, 60, 66, **67**, 77, 78, 79, 80, 84, **85**, 91, 98, 119, 123, 191
Italian sixth chord, 224, 230, 244, 263

Josquin des Prez, 127, 136, 138, 139, 140, 141, 148, 149, 150, 152, 166
Just temperament, 26

Key signature, 15
Kyrie (Mass IX), 33

Landini, Francesco, 76
Las Huelgas Codex, 59
Lauda Sion, 77
Leading tone, 40, 82, 83, 92, 96, 118, 167, 192, 195, 196, 200, 202, 204
Leading tone chord, 190, 191
Leap-frog technique, 148
Liber Usualis (LU), 29
Linear 6-5 motion, 142
Loudness (amplitude), 23
Lower leading tone, 82, 240
Lydian mode, 30, 32

Machaut, Guillaume de, 69, 76, 77, 82, 83, 84, 88, 91, 114, 119, 140
Major intervals, 16, 17
Major–minor seventh chord (dominant seventh chord), 194, 195, 196
Major scale, 13, 14, 15, 16, 41
Major triad, 17
Mean-tone temperament, 26
Mediant chord, 190, 191
Melismatic chant, 33, **42**
Melismatic organum, 48, 49, 51, **52**
Melodic minor, 15, 16
Melodic sequence, 37, **42**, 139
Melody (chant), 42
  organum, 52
  13th century, 66
  14th century, 85
  15th century, 98 (early), 123 (middle)
  16th century, 150 (early), 173 (late)
  17th century, 196–97 (early), 228 (late)
  18th century, 242–43 (early), 268 (middle)

Meter, 6, 7
Middle c, 4
Minnesingers, 41
Minor intervals, 17
Minor scale, 13, 14, 15, 16, 41
Minor scale (harmonic use of), 217
Minor triad, 17
Missa Aeterna Christi munera (Palestrina), 174, 175
Missa L'homme arme (Dufay), 102, 103, 114, 118, 119, 123
Missa pro Defunctis (Palestrina), 155, 156, 173
Mixolydian mode, 29, 32
Modal system, 28ff, **42**
Modes, rhythmic, 41
Modulation, 202, **208**
Modulation (in Bach), 248
Modulation, of modes, 33, **42**
Monophonic, 40, **42**, 47
Monophony (secular), 40
Monothematic, 259, **269**
Monteverdi, 182, 188, 191, 192, 196, 216
Motet, 52, 59, 61, 65, **67**, 76, 77, 83
Motive (chant), 33, 34, 36, **42**
Musica ficta, 84, **85**, 92, 118, 149

Natural minor, 15
Neapolitan sixth chord, 240, 242, **243**, 244, 268
Neighbor tones, 60, 63, 64, **67**, 85, 93, 95, 98, 115, 123, 144, 173, 197, 220, 228, 241, 242, 250, 251
  in figured bass, 189
Neumatic chant 33, **42**
Nonperiodic sound (noise), 24
Nota cambiata, 164
Notation, 1, 5, 8
Notre Dame organum, 50, **52**
Numerological basis, 66

Oblique motion, 48, **52**
Octave, 14
Octave identification, 4, 5
Octave-leap cadence, 117, **123**
  to write, 126
One-line octave, 4
Ordo (ordines), 51, **52**
Organal voice, 46, 47
Organum, 46ff
Overtone series, 24, 25

Pairing of voices (Josquin), 147
Palestrina, Giovanni Pierluigi da, 156, 161, 166, 167, 168, 172, 173, 174, 175
Panisorhythm, 79, **85**, 98
Parallel $\frac{6}{3}$ chords, 96, 121
Parallel fifths, 116, 142, 207
Parallel motion, 46, 48, **53**, 114, 122
Parallel octave, 116, 117, 142, 204, 207
Parallel organum, 46, 47, 52, **53**

Paraphrased melody, 200
Paraphrase technique, 92, 98, **99**, 122, 123, 162, 168, 169, 171, 172, **173**
Parody technique, 169, **173**
Partials (in overtone series), 24, 25
Passacaglia, 191, **197**, 216, 228, **229**, 268
Passing tones, 60, 62, 63, 64, 66, **67**, 85, 93, 95, 98, 115, 123, 144, 168, 173, 189, 197, 220, 227, 228, 241, 242, 250, 251
  accented, 266
Perfect consonances, 59, 65, 114
Perfect intervals, 16, 17
Period (of a sound wave), 23
Petrus de Cruce, 54, 55, 59, 61
Phrygian cadence, **84**, 142, **151**, 223, 228, 229, 239, **243**, 263
  to write, 86, 102, 126
Phrygian mode, 30, 32, 82, 143
Pierre de la Croix, 61
Pitch identification, 4, 5
Pivot chord, 202, **208**, 248
Plagal cadence, 143, 150, **151**, 173, 228, 229
Plagal modes, 28, 29
Plainchant, 28ff
Points of imitation, 138, **146**, **151**
Polyphonic, 48
Polyphonic hymn, 89, 91
Polyphony, 46, **53**
Portamento resolution (of a suspension), 163, **173**
Prelude (Bach), 256, **269**
Prelude and Fugue in C major
  WTC Book I, 271ff
  WTC Book II, 275ff
Prelude and Fugue in G minor (WTC Book I), 245, 246, 256, 252ff
Preparation (of a suspension), 94
Primary function, **197**
Psalms, 31
Pulse, 6, 7
Purcell, Henry, 211, 212, 216, 225, 228
Pur ti miro (Monteverdi), 182, 188, 196
Pythagoras, 25, 26
Pythagorean comma, 26
Pythagorean tuning, 26

Quam pulcra es (Dunstable), 99
Quem pastores laudavere (Schein), 207

Range (ambitus), 28, 29, 32, 33, 34
Real answer (in a fugue), 259
Realization (of a figured bass), 189, 196, 197
Real sequence, 139, **151**, 240
Reciting tone (dominant), 28, 30, 31
Recordans de my signora (Josquin des Prez), 136, 138, 148, 150
Relative minor scale, 16
Requiem Mass (Palestrina), 155, 161, 162, 173
Resolution, 94

Retrograde, 120, **123**
Retrogression, 206, **208**
Rhythm (notation), 5, 6
    13th century, 66
    14th century, 85
    15th century, 98 (early), 123 (middle)
    16th century, 140, 141, 150 (early), 173 (late)
    17th century, 197 (early), 228 (late)
    18th century, 242–43 (early), 268 (middle)
Rhythmic modes, 5, 41, **42**, 50, 51, 52, 66
Roman numerals, 190
Roman numeral analysis, **197**
Root (of a triad), 18
Root movement, 64, **67**, 98, 117, 142, 148, 149, 150, 202, 203
    14th century, 85
    16th century, 165, 173
Root position (of a triad), 18, 116, 203

Sarabanda (Corelli), 231, 238, 239, 240, 241
Sarabande (Bach), 245, 246, 264, 268
Scale degrees, 14
Schein, Johann Hermann, 198, 199, 208
School of Notre Dame, 50, 52
Score, 7
Secondary diminished seventh chord, 219, **229**, 268
Secondary dominants, 192, 194, 196, **197**, 201, 202, 208, **229**, 257, 268
Secondary function, 192, 194, **197**, 201, 207
    with viio7 chord, 219
Secondary tonics, 144, 148, 149
Second inversion (of a triad), 18, 116, 203
Secular monophony, 40
Se la face ay pale (Dufay), 124
Sequence (harmonic), 240, 242, **243**
    melodic, 37, 40, 240, 242, 262
    tonal, real, 139, **151**
Seventh chord, 189, 222, 228
Sharp, 14
Similar motion, 48, **53**, 81
Simple meter, 7
Sine wave, 23
Single leading tone cadence, 95, 96, **98**, 142
    to write, 102, 126
Six-five motion, 173
Slurs, 9, 10
Small octave, 5
Sonata for violin, op. 5, no. 7 (Corelli), 231, 235, 238, 242
Sound wave, 23
Spondaic, 41
Statement section, 259, 260, 261, 264, **269**
Stems, 1, 8
Stretto, 259, **269**
Style characteristics (chant), 42
    organum, 52
    13th century, 66
    14th century, 85

Style characteristics (chant) (*Cont.*)
    15th century, 98 (early), 123 (middle)
    16th century, 150 (early), 173 (late)
    17th century, 196–97 (early), 228 (late)
    18th century, 242–43 (early), 268 (middle)
Sub-contra octave, 5
Subdivisions (of a beat), 6
Subdominant chord, 190, 191
Subfinal, **42**
Subject (fugue), 259, 260, 264, **269**
Submediant chord, 190, 191
Successive counterpoint, 61, 62, 66, **67**, 81
Suite (dance), **269**
Supertonic chord, 190, 191
Suspension, 93, 94, 95, 96, 98, **99**, 115, **123**, 144, 173, 197, 220, 225, 227, 228, 241, 242, 250, 251, 266, 268
    2–3, 144
    7–6, 144
    embellished resolution, 163
    in figured bass, 189
    with portamento resolution, 163
    rearticulated, 227
    to write, 101, 126, 151
Syllabic chant, 33, **42**
Syncopation, 66, 85, 97, 98, **99**, 118, 123, 139, 140, 197
    16th century, 173

Talea, 65, **67**, 77, 78, **84**
Techniques (in chant), 42
    organum, 52
    13th century, 66
    14th century, 85
    15th century, 98 (early), 123 (middle)
    16th century, 150 (early), 173 (late)
    17th century, 197 (early), 228 (late)
    18th century, 243 (early), 268 (middle)
Temperaments, 25
Tenor, **67**
Tenor clef, 3
Tetrachord, 217
Third (of a triad), 18
Through-imitation, 138
Ties, 9, 10
Timbre, 25
Time signature, 6
Tonal, 41
Tonal answer (in a fugue), 259, 260
Tonal cadence (V–I), 95, 97, 98, **99**, 116, 117, 123, 142
    to write, 102, 126
Tonal function, 203, 202, 221
Tonal sequence, 139, **151**, 240
Tonic chord, 190, 191
Treble clef, 3, 7
Treble-dominated style, 118
Triadic structure, **67**

Triadic use:
    13th century, 66
    14th century, 81, 85
    15th century, 98 (early), 123 (middle)
    16th century, 141, 150 (early), 173 (late)
    17th century, 197 (early), 228 (late)
    18th century, 242 (early), 268 (middle)
Triads, 17
Tribrachic, 41
Triplum, 62, **67**
Tritone, 35, 194, 203
    16th century use, 167, 168, **173**
Trochaic, 41
Troubadours, 41
Trouveres, 41
Two-line octave, 5

Under third, 116, 117, 122, **123**
    to write, 126
Upper leading tone, 82, 240
Use of melodic intervals (16th century), 162

Veni creator Spiritus (Schein), 198, 199
vii–I cadence, 202
V7 chord (dominant seventh chord), 194, 195, 196, 268
V–I cadence, 192, 202, 256
Vitry, Philippe de, 76
Vocal doubling (16th century), 167
Vogelweide, Walter von der, 39, 40
Voice leading, 64, 199
    guidelines, 203f
    16th century, 142, 167
Vox organalis (organal voice), 46, **53**
Vox principalis (principal voice), 47, 48, **53**

Was wunders (Walter von Volgelweide), 39
Well-Tempered Clavier (Bach), 256
Whole tone, 14
Working-out section (in a fugue), 259, 260, 264, **269**